CW00556999

PAUL FENTON-SMITH

TAROT MASTERCLASS

Dedicated to Alexander whose company improves my journey immensely. And with thanks to Cathy Jonas for encouragement and her editing skills.

First published in 2007

Inspired Living, and imprint of
Allen & Unwin
83 Alexander Street
Crows Nest NSW 2065
Australia
Phone: (61 2) 8425 0100
Fax: (61 2) 9906 2218
Email: info@allenandunwin.com
Web: www.allenandunwin.com

The Cataloguing-in-Publication entry is available from the National Library of Australia

ISBN 978 1 74175 127 7

Colour charts by Andrew Zagdanski
Back cover photo by Lisa Hogben
Text design by Kirby Stalgis
Set in 10.5/14 pt Birka by Bookhouse, Sydney
Printed and bound in Australia by Griffin Press

10 9 8 7 6 5 4 3 2 1

PAUL FENTON-SMITH

TAROT MASTERCLASS

inspired LIVING

ALLEN&UNWIN

CONTENTS

LIST OF COLOUR CHARTS IN THE BOOK:

INTRODUCTION

The tarot is a book of symbols which can be a valuable guide to your life's journey. It illuminates the underlying lessons in your daily struggles and highlights the approach of spring in your darkest winter. The tarot can enable you to prepare for greater joys, challenges and ascents up life's mountains. This ancient book of symbols offers insight, knowledge and wisdom to those who know how to interpret it, in order to unlock its arcane wisdom.

Tarot Masterclass offers unique colour charts for easy access to card meanings. It also includes detailed health and financial meanings for each card, along with the meaning of each card when reversed, which helps to improve accuracy.

This book details how to approach a reading in person and on the telephone, to help you to streamline your readings, making them more effective. It also demonstrates how to read cards in combination, which can be a challenge for tarot students.

Tarot Masterclass highlights the importance of the tarot as a tool for self-development including examples from actual readings and tarot courses that I have taught over the past 22 years.

How to establish and run your own tarot business and how to best approach individual clients are also covered in depth, along with effective techniques for psychic cleansing and protection. Psychic cleansing and protection are an essential part of any successful tarot practice. Intuitive development techniques are also included.

As you begin to master this ancient pack of cards, you can also focus on your spiritual growth. The tarot helps you to shorten the steps in the pursuit of your goals, highlighting the pitfalls and the opportunities. More than divination, the tarot can be effectively harnessed to clarify life circumstances so that you may avoid situations which are likely to result in disappointment.

Receiving a 'no' answer to all of your questions about a subject might simply mean that you're not asking the right question. The tarot gives clear insights when you ask precise, simply worded questions. This book offers simple, practical ways to clarify your issues, distilling them into one or two clear questions. Knowing the best question to ask the cards can mean the difference between confusion and clarity.

The questions menu included in the colour charts offers over 50 clearly worded questions, to assist you in finding the most suitable question to ask the cards. *Tarot Masterclass* offers a tarot course in a book, complete with colour charts for simple short-cuts, to help you to master the tarot, a book of life. While the tarot offers you a map for your life, *Tarot Masterclass* offers a guide to understainding that map, and your life's journey. Bon voyage.

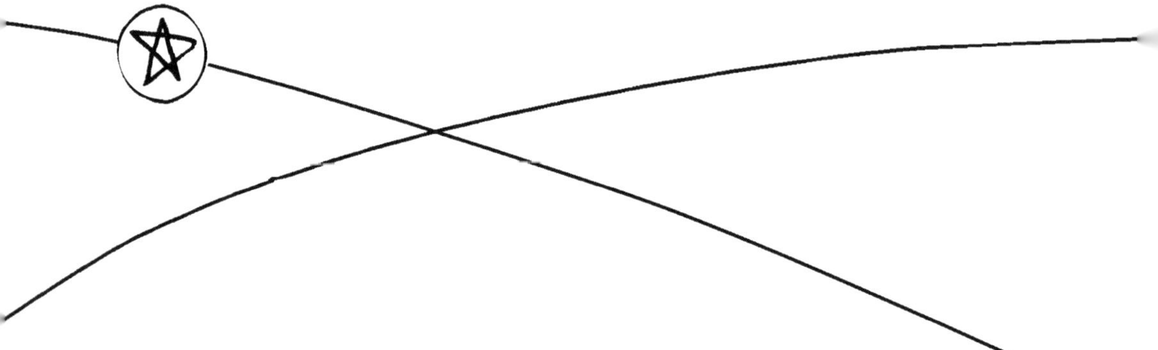

PART I

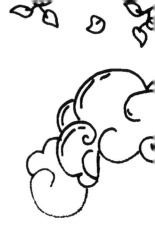

The power of the tarot

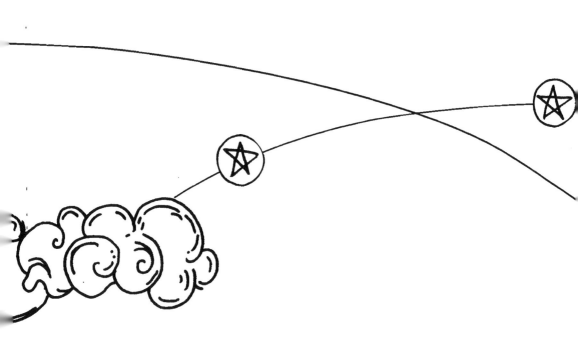

Chapter 1

WHY USE THE TAROT?

People have diverse views on what a tarot reading can offer. Some expect to be told the name and date of birth of the people they will marry, while others are not satisfied until they have the licence plate of their soul mate's car. Experienced clients treat a tarot reading as they do consulting any other specialist. They bring a list of questions, listen to what is said and then make up their own minds. Clients realise that they have the free will to accept what has been predicted or to change their destiny through their decisions and actions.

Benefits of a tarot reading

On the best days an accurate, clearly presented tarot reading can

- inspire you to fulfil your dreams,
- clarify your immediate challenges and obstacles,
- motivate you to overcome life's setbacks,
- crystallise your short-term purpose,
- illuminate your longer term purpose in life, and
- spotlight those obstacles you are currently avoiding.

In a recent reading, one client, Benita, complained of a long-term tug-of-war with her mother. As the reading unfolded it appeared that Benita derived more satisfaction from attempting to triumph over her mother than other goals in her life. A brittle, austere woman, Benita's mother controlled her daughter through a business they shared. Although they each owned 50 per cent of the business, Benita's mother controlled all the financial decisions.

Benita was exhausted with the ongoing power struggle. It was suggested she consider signing the business over to her mother and walking away to gain her personal freedom. Benita was surprised by the suggestion until it was pointed out that a painful short-term sacrifice might just be worth it to gain longer term rewards.

At this point Benita launched into a tirade about her mother, blaming her for a litany of mistakes and oversights. The following conversation revealed that Benita was more attached to winning her mother's approval than the business.

What had begun as a question about a business turned out to be a question about how Benita might secure love from her mother. The power struggle in the business masked a deeper need. The underlying issue was how Benita might find another source of love if she relinquished the business to her mother.

Some limitations of the tarot

A tarot reading cannot give you an absolute future. Anything predicted in a reading is only likely at the time of the prediction. Sometimes, even with the best intentions, readings are inaccurate. A common reason for inaccuracy is that the reading takes place when the client is in the eye of a storm. After six accurate readings over a five-year period, Erica phoned in a panic one morning for an urgent reading.

The reading revealed that Erica was in the centre of an emotional crisis at work. Her immediate supervisor wanted her out of the company and Erica had nowhere else to go. During the reading Erica was told that the company was about to be acquired by a larger corporation and that she would be promoted before her supervisor had the chance to squeeze her out.

Five weeks later Erica phoned to ask why those predictions had not occurred. She was unemployed, having been retrenched two weeks before the company was acquired. I was not surprised at hearing this.

The time clients most want a tarot reading is immediately after bad news, a shock or when they are in chaos. This is usually the worst time to have a reading because emotions cloud the underlying issues and distort the reading. When the client selects cards their intense desire for a particular outcome overrides the natural selection process, skewing the reading in favour of the desired result. Sometimes the client only receives what they desperately want to hear. If a client phones for an urgent reading while in crisis suggest a time a week or at least a few days later. If they insist on having a reading immediately and you can fit them in, treat the reading as a counselling session if you are a counsellor. Occasionally a client simply wants to be heard, to be able to cry or tell someone else what is happening. This may be as beneficial as a reading without anything more than a simple general reading being given to the client.

The inaccuracy of Erica's reading was due to her receiving the reading when she was in the eye of a storm. As she was a regular client I offered Erica a complementary reading, asking her to wait a few days if she was experiencing emotional upheaval. Eight months after the complementary reading she phoned to confirm the accuracy of that session with me.

The tarot and personal development

Occasionally students attend introductory tarot courses without any intention of reading for others. For these people the tarot offers a personal journey. This spiritual journey might consist of selecting a card each day and meditating on its meaning. Some tarot students benefit from keeping a tarot journal to record how each card is significant or how it relates personally to them. When you are more familiar with the tarot, you might ask, 'What is my lesson in this situation?' while selecting one card from the pack. By reflecting on this card for the day, you can then write up your experience of this card in your journal.

While this is often a powerful personal journey, becoming familiar with card meanings occurs more slowly than when you read for strangers. While you have the luxury of taking a whole day to reflect upon a card when taking a personal tarot journey, reading for clients forces you to make immediate sense of circumstances, tie loose ends together and complete an entire reading in a limited time. It is possible to take both approaches simultaneously—keeping a personal tarot journal while building up a private practice.

When you can apply the knowledge and understanding you have gained from tarot reading to your own life and when you recognise which suit represents your life path and how to make the most of the opportunities within this suit, you can derive practical benefits from the tarot. It also offers the chance to glimpse repetitive behaviour patterns.

Occasionally, sit quietly and ask the cards what you most need to learn right now. Shuffle the pack, reversing some cards. Close your eyes. Spread the cards across a table, select one card and turn it over sideways, to prevent it being reversed (inverted). Examine this card closely. Leave it out when you put the pack away or write it down in your diary for future reference. Look up the meaning of this card. Ask yourself how this card applies to your life.

When Dirk was struggling with his love relationship he sat for awhile and tried this exercise. Adel and he had been debating whether to separate or to re-commit themselves and move to a new home. After a week without a full night's sleep and constantly steeped in the agony of possibilities, Dirk cleared his mind and asked what he most needed to learn right now. The card selected was the Page of Wands upright, and Dirk contemplated its meanings.

- Commencing something new.
- Feeling young as you approach life in a new way.
- Planning your path to future goals.
- A child.
- An enthusiastic, sporty young person.
- Taking a trip.

Dirk reflected upon these meanings for a few days, deciding that the Page was telling him to move forward to a new home together.

Tarot dependence

When people first discover the tarot they can be tempted to consult the cards for every decision they make. In doing so they risk surrendering free will for one-card cuts based on hastily worded questions. The fact that you have survived this far into your life without the tarot suggests that you have at least reasonable decision-making skills. The tarot is not designed to replace your decision-making ability, but to enhance it.

If you carefully research an important issue, examine the choices and narrow these choices down to those most suitable for you, then the tarot can be a valuable tool to assist you in your final choice. If, however, you consult the cards before you have done any research into your options, you may find yourself asking the wrong questions.

Preparation before a reading can clarify your issues and questions. The more informed you are when receiving a reading the more value you will derive from it. New clients can waste their first reading discovering how the process works, making them keen to have another reading soon after the first one. Sometimes clients discover the tarot and are unable to sleep at night, pondering all the questions they might ask. More questions do not necessarily lead to a greater understanding.

Sometimes when clients experience decision paralysis, they seek several tarot readings in a row. Rarely does a series of readings clarify an issue. In most cases this only confuses the client or heightens their addiction.

Often readers are the worst offenders when it comes to tarot addiction. Aside from the lack of objectivity when reading for yourself, readers tend to consult the cards immediately when emotional issues surface. Clients usually have to wait a week or two for an appointment when this happens. This waiting period often allows the client to sift through possible alternatives, and explore their feelings so that sometimes they reach their own conclusions before they consult their tarot reader. In these cases the tarot reading is simply to confirm that their chosen path is the most suitable one for them at the time.

As you become more attracted to the tarot or even addicted to asking the cards questions, you will find the standard of your questions drops. The tarot is a carefully constructed system devised to help people discover their place in the universe. Becoming addicted to the tarot is often the result of becoming self-absorbed so, when clients want to continually consult you, encourage them to seek interests which refocus them.

This is not to suggest that you don't ever read for yourself if you are a tarot reader. Consulting the tarot when making practical decisions can be an effective way to make the right choice. However, if you have pressing emotional issues, it is far more important that you seek the advice of the tarot through an objective reader.

When students commence introductory or advanced courses they are issued with tarot logs and told that each reading logged has to be for someone other than themselves. I usually insist that clients do not have a reading within three months of a previous one. This allows for some of the current predictions to eventuate while encouraging clients to be self-reliant. When clients request a reading within a week of a previous one, they are told about the three-month rule and I suggest that they replay their recording of the recent reading. The exception to this rule occurs when a consultation is about practical matters such as business investments.

Chapter 2

LEARNING THE TAROT

The tarot is a powerful tool for answering clear, well-formed questions. An experienced tarot reader can help clients to find the best alternatives from infinite possible options.

As a student I worked beside my tarot teacher through ten-hour days for months at a time. We worked together in a small shop offering readings. I was the resident evening palmist while he was the tarot card reader. Throughout that long, cold winter I sat listening to Carlos give tarot readings behind the curtain. I started guessing which cards had been laid out on the table. After a while I bet Carlos a piece of baklava that I would be able to correctly identify one set of cards that the client had selected without glimpsing them. Not a man given to refusing sweets, he quickly agreed to my bargain. In a typical layout of seven cards, I averaged three at best. In the first month I was a regular customer at the baklava shop. Throughout the following months I learned the meanings of the cards and how Carlos described each card. Sometimes I was confused, especially when Carlos interpreted a pair or trio of cards in combination. With an almost infinite number of possible combinations I realised that it was going to take me much longer than the seven months we shared, to master even a portion of them.

Some students learn best by reading a book; others need to see a reading in action. Some need to colour in the card illustrations in the book to comprehend the less obvious detail in each card. When you discover the method which works best for you, practise it until you are familiar with the cards as well as the reading process. Use this book as a guide as you progress from novice to experienced reader on your tarot journey.

An overview of the tarot

The tarot consists of 78 cards made up of:

- 22 Major Arcana cards—revealing the underlying spiritual lessons in everyday events
- 56 Minor Arcana cards made up of four suits of 14 cards—detailing everyday events
- Each suit contains a king, queen, knight, page and ten numbered cards
- The four suits are Wands, Cups, Swords and Pentacles.

Understanding how tarot works

Tarot cards are laid out into a pattern or 'spread' and interpreted according to the position of each card.

- Cards are read upright or reversed as they face the reader. A reversed card suggests returning to the previous card in that suit.
- The reader decides on a meaning for each card from all their possible meanings.
- The tarot can confirm past events, clarify present circumstances and reveal the most likely outcome of actions.
- Accuracy in tarot reading is determined by
  - the reader's knowledge of the card meanings
  - the clarity of the questions
  - whether the client was focused when selecting the cards
  - the reader determining the correct meaning for each card in combination with surrounding cards.
- The tarot does not replace free will. It offers likely outcomes for choices.

- Intuition is not required when reading because the tarot as a system has been carefully designed to offer clarity to anyone who understands the cards' meanings.

An easy start

If you are unfamiliar with tarot reading, there is a simple method that can help you to master the tarot without becoming overwhelmed. By taking the cards in one suit at a time and only reading with cards you have learned, you can build your tarot knowledge step by step.

In the first week, use only the Wands and Cups suits. Using only these 28 cards allows beginners to become familiar without being overwhelmed. After two weeks read using the 56 cards of the Minor Arcana. Reading with less than a full pack has its limitations, but it is surprising how much information is still available to you. It is better to become familiar with the Minor Arcana before moving on to the Major Arcana.

The benefit of charts

Sometimes a colour chart can give you the essence of a group of cards, helping you to grasp their meanings more easily. I have resisted producing charts previously for fear of oversimplification but feedback from tarot students is that the charts found throughout the book help with the learning process.

Distilling a clear meaning from the tarot

Each group of cards within the tarot reveals aspects of the client's life, the issues being faced and the underlying spiritual lessons encountered. What is happening, who is it happening to, when it will occur and why are explained by sets of cards within the pack. As a reader, it is your task to assemble this information into a form which makes sense to the client. To do this effectively, it pays to remember that

- The 40 ace to ten cards of the Minor Arcana reveal what is happening in the client's life.
- The court cards reveal who is involved. These cards can also highlight the client's approach to life at this time.
- The Major Arcana cards reveal why events are occurring, highlighting the underlying spiritual lessons or life patterns.
- When the Minor and Major Arcana are read together they can explain to the client what has occurred or is about to occur, why it is happening and who can offer the client assistance or support at this time.
- The Minor Arcana explains what is occurring in a client's life. Students traditionally learn this pack first as it is easier to give a client a basic reading. The Major Arcana explains why events are happening, and should a student start with this part of the pack, they would be trying to explain events about which they have no details as these details are found in the Minor Arcana.

Simple steps to learning

- Read about the 14 Wands cards.
- Give several practice readings using only the Wands suit.
- Read about the Cups suit.
- Give some practice readings using only the Wands and Cups cards.
- Read about the Swords suit.
- Give some practice readings using only the Wands, Cups and Swords cards.
- Read about the Pentacles suit.
- Give some practice readings using only the Minor Arcana cards.
- Read about the Major Arcana cards from 0 to 11 (the Fool to Justice).
- Give some practice readings using only those cards you have studied.
- Read about the rest of the Major Arcana.
- Give some practice readings using the whole pack, including the blank card.

How to retain the information found in this book

- Highlight the important points.
- Colour in the card illustrations, using the tarot pack as your guide.

- Re-read one suit of cards (for example, the Ace of Wands to the King of Wands) each week to familiarise yourself with the meanings.
- When giving practice readings, do not refer to this book until you have completed the reading so that you remember what you have learned. This will prevent you becoming dependent on this book.

Chapter 3

THE READER'S QUEST

The ideal reader's quest with the tarot commences with curiosity and concludes, hopefully, with wisdom. As a beginner you are likely to be fascinated by the tarot and its possibilities. You may seek a thousand answers to as many questions, some pointless, others profound. As the novice reader, you delve into the possibilities of the tarot, beginning another, deeper journey. This is the journey of self-discovery.

If you regularly read for others you cannot help but discover characteristics in those around you which you admire or despise. In reading for others you have the opportunity to discover other world viewpoints. You can see how others cope with the same challenges you too have faced in the past. The longer you continue reading for strangers the more you are exposed to the variations on the human theme. We are all humans yet our beliefs, our circumstances and our goals reflect myriad differences, like a tray of diamonds with each one glinting uniquely in the sunlight.

Just when you feel confident that you know how to best live your life, you are likely to be faced with a client who surprises and challenges you. It is as though life has sent someone who will prevent you from settling comfortably into an unexamined belief. As you read for such clients you may feel shocked, judgemental, fearful or inspired, and the journey continues. It pays to remember that your brief glimpse into the lives of clients is not sufficient to see exactly what made them the way they are when they consulted you. You may be faced with similar dilemmas of your own, and may require astounding courage to address *your* issues.

The longer you read for others, the more you may be confronted with the question, 'Is it fair to judge someone on one wrong deed or poor decision in a lifetime, or is it necessary to balance the good with the bad, no matter how bad that single deed was?' This has been highlighted to me many times, most recently by a client who wanted to contact two deceased friends.

Mandy wanted to contact two friends who had died in a car accident two weeks after completing high school. Four students set off home after a party and Nikki, the driver, lost control of the vehicle, driving into a tree on a country road. The two boys died instantly and my client Mandy was inconsolable with grief. I felt the deepest compassion for the driver, Nikki, especially when I glimpsed her guilt and the results of this guilt.

Clairvoyantly I glimpsed 17-year-old Nikki's life until the age of 50 years. It was tragic. The guilt of surviving the accident seemed likely to lead Nikki to take drugs and develop an expensive drug habit. This in turn was liable to lead her into prostitution to feed her habit. After 25 years of living life on the edge, she was likely to collapse and end up in a psychiatric institution. The turnaround was likely to occur when she sought help for her habits, her attitudes and her self-loathing and guilt. She was to begin ongoing counselling with a psychologist and her efforts were likely to be rewarded as her life returned to normal.

After five years of hard work on herself I saw Nikki returning to study, attending university and becoming a psychologist. Her journey comes full circle when as a woman in her fifties, she specialises in teenage runaways and drug addicts. I explained to her friend (my client) that in the end, Nikki will save many more lives than she took.

Denied the opportunity to have her own children or even a long-term love relationship throughout her twenties and thirties, I glimpsed Nikki stumbling through life wondering why she didn't die in the accident instead of the boys. At the end of her life Nikki may know why she survived. She may realise that she was instrumental in saving the lives of many young people through her dedicated efforts and, to some degree, due to her own history. Her own addictions may make it easier for Nikki to relate to the teenagers she will be working with, and to prove to them through her own story, that positive change is possible.

As a book of life, the tarot offers us a window into the timeless concerns of the human race. We discover that 'the more things change, the more they remain the same'. Hundreds of years after the tarot was introduced, we still face the same challenges, seek love and to understand why we are here in the first place.

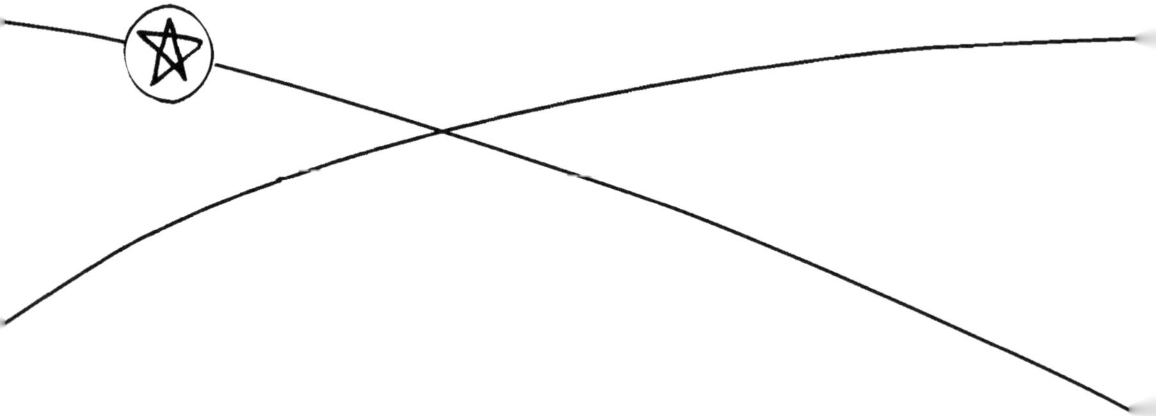

PART II

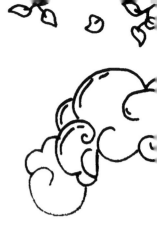

The Minor Arcana and the meaning of events

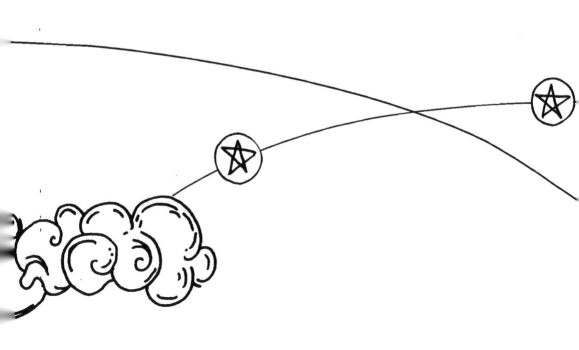

Chapter 4

THE SUIT OF WANDS

The suit of Wands consists of 14 cards from the Ace to the King. Wands people thrive on action and activity. Their vitality and sheer enthusiasm for life makes them excellent sportsmen and women, successful business people and keen travellers.

If there is a mountain to be climbed, a snowstorm will not deter them. In sports, games and in everyday life Wands people are naturally competitive, keen to embrace a challenge and to be first. The best way to motivate Wands people is to tell them that they cannot do something or to dare them to do it.

In astrology Wands people are the Fire signs: Aries, Leo and Sagittarius. They tend to exhibit a fiery temperament, and they are passionate, active and impatient. Conflict, physical challenges and sports help Wands people to feel alive. These people usually prefer to die in a skiing accident or while climbing a mountain than in a retirement village.

Suited to careers in sales, sports, fitness, teaching and coaching, Wands people enjoy jobs where they can travel or work hard on a project that provides tangible results at the conclusion. They enjoy careers where there is plenty of action and activity. Sitting at a desk all day is a recipe for depression for Wands people. When upset, Wands people are forthright, assertive and unafraid of conflict. Negative Wands people regularly seek conflict to help them feel alive.

'What you see is what you get' is how one Queen of Wands friend describes herself. When she spies a man she likes she will give chase until she receives a firm 'no' or a firm date. If you seek sympathy from Wands people you may be wasting your time. Recently I witnessed a King of Wands supervising his three children in the park. A young boy limped up to him after falling over and received this response. 'Is that it? That's the whole cut? And you've been limping around for how long? It's just a graze. You'll live.'

The Ace of Wands

General meaning

A hand protrudes from a cloud clasping an upright wand. The cloud represents spirit or the source of inspiration. The Wands Ace represents ideas translated into action. It indicates enthusiasm for your plans and passion in undertaking new ventures. It can signify impatience to see some results from your efforts, or simply that you enjoy action and activity.

This card describes initiating action. It is a card for travel, starting a new project or doing something physical to realise your goals, however, the ace shows that planning is being ignored in the rush to see rewards.

Reversed

When reversed, this ace highlights the need to complete outstanding projects before you attempt new ones. Your energy may be drained by other projects at this time and more focus is required on these projects before you can proceed. You need to return to the lesson of the Ten of Wands (a card of responsibilities and multiple projects), to delegate some of your responsibilities before proceeding.

Finances

This ace describes a need to seize the day and push ahead with your financial plans. You have the energy required to begin new projects. Risk-taking may appeal to you now. Worthwhile opportunities are available presently, so act on your plans immediately.

Reversed

The Wands Ace suggests that you are pursuing a new project before you have completed current enterprises. It is wise to defer your plans until you have completed or delegated existing responsibilities and projects. Financial delays are to be expected when the Ace of Wands appears reversed in a financial question.

Health

Your physical energy levels are high when the Ace of Wands appears in a layout as it suggests vitality. You have sufficient energy and enthusiasm to embrace life fully, so enjoy. Be aware not to tackle too many projects at once, and take advantage of this Wands vitality through sports, walking, running or the great outdoors.

Reversed

This ace suggests that you may become hyperactive, restless and impatient when opposed by others. It's time to take a long walk to discharge some energy and to reflect upon your circumstances. Your physical vitality may be low due to scattered energy or too many demands on your available time.

Two of Wands

General meaning

The Two of Wands describes a decision about physical location, usually related to home or work. You are deciding whether to remain where you are or to move forward into a new home or work environment. Wands types relate to life in a physical way, so there is actually no pressure to make a move now, but the desire to experience new locations and opportunities is increasing.

Reversed

When a card appears reversed it signifies that you need to return to the previous card (in this case it is the Ace) to master that lesson before tackling the lesson of the present card. When reversed the Two of Wands suggests prolonged indecision. It is necessary to return to the Ace and act. You may be bored or dissatisfied as no new challenges have presented themselves for some time. Perhaps fear of loss prevents a close examination of the available opportunities. Instead of looking to new horizons, you may be ignoring the journey forward in favour of becoming comfortable in the present location. It is time to search actively for new opportunities instead of justifying why you need to remain where you are in life.

Finances

Although still describing a decision regarding a home or work move, the Two of Wands in a financial question suggests that you are asking if you can afford to make a move at this time. When upright it is time to move forward as you are likely to be able to afford to make the change you desire.

Reversed

The reversed Two of Wands suggests that you cannot move forward until you have paid off a debt or reduced your financial outgoings. It is time to return to the upright Ace of Wands in order to concentrate on one direction. New financial opportunities are available to you, but you need to look beyond your immediate physical home or work environments to see these.

Health

The Wands Two signifies a time of deciding on more activities and a positive approach to your health. Perhaps you are deciding whether to join a gym, take up a sport or to take regular walks.

Reversed

When reversed, the Two of Wands can indicate that ignoring your health alternatives or current physical circumstances may be adversely affecting your health. It is time to return to the upright Ace of Wands in order to act, or to embark on a new direction in your health plans.

Three of Wands

General meaning

A figure clad predominantly in deep red and green grips one of three wands which protrude from the ground. He overlooks three boats in a bay reflecting the golden rays of the sun. This card signifies travel and progress with plans. The figure may be about to board a boat and travel abroad, or to meet a boat to collect goods hc has purchased. The arrival of goods suggests progression with plans and few obstacles, so acting on your plans is likely to reap rewards.

Reversed

When reversed, the Three signals a need to return to the upright Two of Wands to decide on a suitable physical location. It may be time to change your home or work environment or to spend less time travelling and more time at home. You may be frustrated with the slow progress of your plans. This may continue until you return to the Two in order to make important decisions.

Finances

Financial plans are progressing and may include local or overseas travel. The clear skies shown in the card suggest an easy time ahead financially as you put your plans into action. You can act on your past decisions (made in the Two of Wands) as you have the financial support to move forward now.

Reversed

This three can herald delays in financial plans and the need for a new physical location (job or home) before real progress can be made. It is time to return to the upright Two in order to decide which financial path is most suitable.

Health

Improved health, perhaps as a result of travel or a holiday. This is a stress-free time where improvements in health can be made. As an answer to a question about a health procedure, this three suggests you will be on your feet again soon.

Reversed

In a health reading, this three can describe delays in a return to health resulting from an overdue decision. You need to return to the upright Two of Wands in order to decide how best to approach your health. Perhaps you have been postponing a medical procedure or embarking on a strict diet. At this stage health difficulties or obstacles are likely to result from indecision, or avoiding making an important health choice. In some cases travel may be cut short due to your health or the health of a close friend or relative.

Four of Wands

General meaning

Four wands stand upright, supporting a wreath of flowers while people dance and celebrate. In the background a castle stands firm in the noonday sun, no shadows are visible. The fours in the Minor Arcana represent consolidation, the act of making plans real, solid and tangible. The Wands Four suggests a move to a new home or work environment, or the act of settling into your current home after renovations. It depicts a stable period; a rest on the path of the Wands lesson as you make your way towards the Ten of Wands. This four describes the act of making yourself comfortable for life's journey.

Reversed

When reversed this is a card for temporary circumstances, such as visiting friends or working in a casual position. It suggests that it may be time to revisit the Three of Wands in order to move forward to a new home or work location or simply to experience the freedom that stems from owning few possessions and the ability to live in the moment. Perhaps temporary work may suit you now, giving you time to decide what type of position or corporation is for you.

The reversed Four of Wands sometimes appears when you are leaving a job or moving from a permanent home into temporary accommodation. The reversed Four suggests that it is time to return to the upright Three of Wands, a card you might expect to see if you were about to set out on a long journey. In a relationship question the reversed Four suggests a lack of commitment to consolidating a long-term relationship.

Finances

Stable, healthy financial circumstances are indicated by this card, and you are likely to share this successful period with others. It may signify a time of consolidation financially. Perhaps this is a time to focus on one or two financial investments, including the family home. The Four appears when you are enjoying a stable job or home environment, reflecting how financial stability can lead to stability in other areas of life.

Reversed

This four describes a period of unsettled finances. Although it does not suggest disaster, few solid steps can be taken now. You may require a more permanent or stable home or work situation before you can make financial progress. It can also describe temporary or casual work.

Health

Good health and vitality are evident when the Four of Wands appears upright in a health reading. A harmonious home or work life lends security and stability to your health now. This may be a time to establish healthy fitness routines, such as daily walking, stretching, yoga or jogging to maintain fitness and vitality.

Reversed

This four suggests that your health may reflect your physical environment, both being inconsistent at this time. Overindulgence during celebrations may unbalance your physical health. Perhaps you do not have the opportunity to maintain your usual health routines due to temporary circumstances, such as travel or work demands.

Five of Wands

General meaning

Five people are locked into a struggle, pitting their energy against one another without an obvious purpose. Their efforts are contrasted with a tranquil blue sky and a perfect day. This is a card indicating scattered energy; are you undertaking too many projects at once or being a willing participant in office, family or local conflicts? Energy which is expended in petty conflicts might be directed towards a sporting conquest where opponents maintain strenuous efforts in pursuit of a trophy, a reputation or fitness.

Group activities result in conflict now, as each participant struggles to be heard and acknowledged. The Five can signify a group of individuals who are experiencing difficulty negotiating a workable solution. In business this card represents chaos, revealing the corporation as merely a huge dysfunctional family. In a relationship it signifies conflict arising from two people with different lifestyles, interests and friends.

Reversed

The Five is a more positive card reversed, as it suggests that after disagreement common ground can be found. It is a card of change, usually physical change (home or work environment) as the Wands suit deals with the physical world. Perhaps you are leaving a job or a love relationship but, if so, you are not being forced out. Instead you are returning to the upright Four of Wands to enjoy the stability it offers.

After a period of struggle comes cooperation and cohesion. This Five reversed can indicate leaving behind a period of scattered focus. Fewer new projects are undertaken now, improving focus on those goals already being pursued.

Finances

Finances are usually stretched when this five appears in a layout. Too many demands or projects scatter your focus now, resulting in limited success. This card can describe a small business where one person has to do everything, from sales and marketing to service and stock control. They are too busy rushing around to make a practical plan for success.

Reversed

The Five of Wands reversed indicates the chances of success are improved due to an increased focus on the tasks at hand. Instead of competing with each other, those involved are learning to cooperate on common goals and to share success. This card can also suggest that internal conflict is subsiding now, allowing for a concentrated effort towards goals.

Health

The upright Five is an example of the urgency with which Wands people like to pursue their goals. A hard-won achievement is more appealing than an opportunity which falls into their hands. Wands people are passionate about beating the competition. The result from such prolonged exertion can be exhaustion or a collapse into bed with a cold or influenza.

Reversed

This card describes a more balanced lifestyle, increasing the chances of maintaining good health. It can also represent the act of refocusing on your health after a period of prolonged physical effort. The reversed Five suggests a return to the upright Four of Wands, which signifies stable, balanced health.

Six of Wands

General meaning

A man rides a horse which has been covered in a green cloth. His red robes present a regal air as he holds a wand with a wreath tied to it in one hand. Another wreath rests on his head and five other wands are visible. These are held by men who walk beside him. This procession suggests a victory parade. Wands people can enjoy many victories when they harness their fiery passion and direct it towards a particular purpose. Blue skies await those who triumph over the obstacles in their paths. After the chaos depicted in the Five, all six wands here are upright and synchronised, suggesting energies harmonised towards a goal or an agreed purpose.

The conflict of the Five has been replaced by a negotiated team effort. Progress becomes more rapid as all of the wands (all of your energies) are focused in one direction. This is a card of success in your plans. You may receive a promotion at work, secure a new job, graduate from a course or settle into a long-term love relationship. The Six indicates the realisation of your plans.

Reversed

The Six of Wands reversed suggests a lack of success with your plans. You may be retrenched, fail to graduate from a course, separate from your partner or simply give up on your plans. It is time to return to the upright Five of Wands to determine where your focus is right now. Perhaps you are scattering your energies in too many directions to effectively pursue your plans.

Finances

The Six of Wands suggests financial success. If this card appears in the answer position in a layout for a financial question, it confirms a victory. With discipline and focus you can enjoy a successful conclusion to your plans. It exemplifies the act of harnessing your energies (the six individual wands) and focusing on the task at hand.

Reversed

This six reversed suggests that you may have undertaken too many goals simultaneously, scattering your energies beyond your capabilities. Success is unlikely now as you may give up too soon, ignore your opportunities or be forced to concentrate on another enterprise, as you have too many projects on your plate at once. It is possible that you have lost confidence in your ability to realise your goals. In some cases the reversed Six in a financial question suggests that you have too many backup possibilities in case you cannot achieve your primary financial goal. These may be distracting you from concentrating on the main goal.

Health

Balanced health is suggested when the Six of Wands is found in a health reading. If you ask whether a particular health approach is wise, the upright Six offers a clear 'yes', unless contradicted by surrounding cards. When Carla nervously asked if her forthcoming surgical procedure would be successful, the upright Six confirmed a successful outcome.

Reversed

This card reversed describes poor health due to scattered energies. It suggests a return to the Five of Wands and the accompanying chaos. When you tire of the chaos of the Five, the stability of the Six will once again beckon. Perhaps it's time to eliminate those demands or goals you have which are draining your energy without hope of reward. It may be that you don't realise that age has diminished your capabilities. When Lazlo chose the Five of Wands at his reading I suggested that being a full-time bricklayer at his age may no longer be a wise choice of career. Being a fit, muscular, outdoors type, Lazlo thought that he was still 23 years old but admitted that a possible pinched nerve in his back was reminding him that he was 51.

Seven of Wands

General meaning

A person stands alert to the advances of six others carrying wands. Situated on the high ground, he staunchly defends his position. He wears one shoe and one boot, suggesting that he may have dressed in haste. The footwear also suggests that he is torn between the stability of the Six of Wands and the freedom of the Eight. Does he dress for a stable situation or for a challenging one?

Blue skies indicate that this is a chosen conflict and not one that has been forced upon him. Perhaps it is the result of his desire to expand a business, be selected for a sporting team, successfully complete an exam or it is simply a time when he is juggling work and study commitments in order to secure a better job in the future.

Reversed

The Seven of Wands reversed describes becoming overwhelmed by the obstacles before you. Perhaps too many demands on your time and attention have depleted your physical or mental energy, and it is time to return to the stability of the upright Six of Wands where a stronger structure enables the smooth flow of proceedings. Rather than holding on to the many goals you are pursuing now, it is better to release some, retaining only those goals you are certain that you need.

Finances

The Seven of Wands describes a time when you thrive on the challenges presented to you. It also suggests a need to remain aware of your financial obligations and responsibilities. Although life is challenging now, you can afford the lifestyle you seek. This card indicates a time when you may increase your range of financial investments or expand your current investments successfully.

Reversed

Your financial obligations are likely to be too much for your current income. It is necessary to reduce your expenses by returning to the Six of Wands. It is time to concentrate on the things that you can afford in order to return to a stable financial lifestyle. You may feel overwhelmed by financial demands at present so it is important to eliminate some of those demands.

Health

The Seven of Wands represents stress resulting from overcommitment. Although you have health issues under control, your life is currently filled with challenges. Generally the upright Seven shows that you have a strong focus on your goals and are harnessing your energies effectively.

Reversed

This seven reversed suggests low reserves of physical energy, possibly due to strenuous long-term obligations. Perhaps you have been trying to balance relationship or family commitments and long working hours. When Elaine selected this Seven reversed it turned out she had been working 45 hours a week in an office and tending to her aged mother who was in the early stages of dementia. Most week nights Elaine cooked and cleaned for her mother before returning home to do the same for her her own family.

Eight of Wands

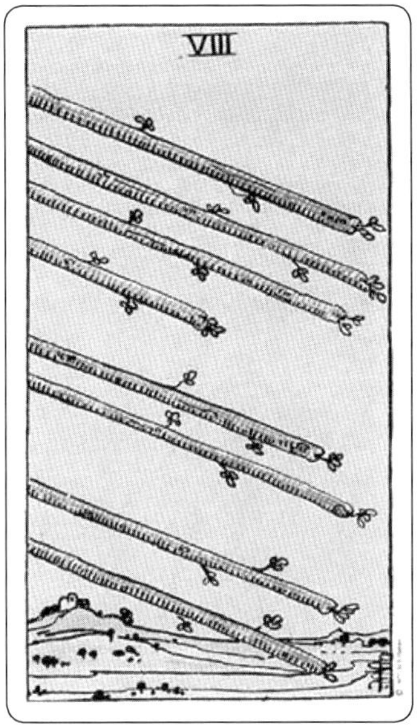

General meaning

Clear skies illuminate eight wands that travel through the air unrestrained. A castle is situated on a hill in the background, beyond a gently flowing river. This is a card which highlights the Wands person's dream of freedom. Wands people are at their best when unfettered by obligations and responsibilities. When freed from life's daily restraints, Wands people feel life is brimming with glorious possibilities, challenges and conquests.

This Eight represents travel overseas, free-flowing energy and a clear path to your goals. Past efforts have cleared the way for you to travel freely through life now. This is the summer you are likely to remember for years. The rich reds of a slow Mediterranean sunset, or afternoons spent sailing in azure blue seas remind you that your efforts were worthwhile.

Reversed

This card reversed suggests some delays to your plans or travels, but not enough to significantly reduce your enjoyment of your freedom as the sky remains blue. When this card is reversed the image shows the earth above the eight wands, suggesting that earthly concerns demand your attention. Perhaps your travels are halted as you organise sufficient funds to proceed. Often the reversed Eight of Wands describes a peaceful period when life rolls uneventfully between triumphs. Such times can seem interminable for feisty Wands and curious Swords people, but creative Cups and practical Pentacles people appreciate these periods. The reversed Eight suggests a return to the upright Seven, and the need to discharge your responsibilities and obligations.

Finances

The Eight can describe a financial summer time when you can easily afford the material possessions you need and desire. It also represents travel and the carefree manner in which you might spend your time and money while on holiday. Financial opportunities are more readily available to you as you enjoy financial abundance.

Reversed

Financial circumstances are stable but not necessarily exciting. It may be time to return to the Seven of Wands in order to get your expenses under control or to establish beneficial financial routines that will allow you to return to the upright Eight to feel free again.

Health

This is a positive card in a health reading, both upright or reversed. You now have sufficient energy and enthusiasm to pursue your life goals with passion. It is a time to appreciate good health and ample reserves of energy for healthy living. In a question about surgery, this Eight describes a speedy recovery. It generally signifies good health and an enthusiastic approach to living.

Reversed

This card can describe a slow but steady recovery. Generally the reversed Eight of Wands indicates a period of stable health, however, you may desire the vitality and enthusiasm evident in the upright card.

Nine of Wands

General meaning

A person stands in front of eight wands, clutching a ninth. He glances uneasily over his right shoulder at his past. A head bandage suggests that he was not victorious in all of his pursuits. This is the first time in the Wands suit that someone contemplates the past.

Used to looking towards the future for solutions to existing problems, this person now looks back to past actions to determine how he came to be where he is today. He is becoming aware that actions have consequences, just as he is currently living with the consequences of past actions, in the future he will have to live with what he decides and does now.

This card indicates a growing awareness of how important it is to focus one's attention on commitment and intentions. Instead of planting 500 mixed seeds and hoping for the best, he is contemplating planting seeds of only a particular kind, and tending them carefully in order to enjoy reaping what he sows.

Reversed

The reversed Nine presents a review of the past in search of fulfilment. Instead you find obligations, stress and continual strenuous efforts. This card reversed suggests you are overdue for a rest or a refreshing holiday (the upright Eight of Wands) to rekindle your enthusiasm for life. A reversed Nine may also suggest you are being too critical when reviewing the past, tending to overlook your successes by concentrating on your failures or those obstacles you encountered in your progress. A return to the upright Eight of Wands offers you the chance to rest, relax and recuperate before you tackle the challenges offered in the Ten of Wands.

Finances

The upright Nine is a time when you are cautiously reassessing your financial commitments. It's time to move forward slowly, conscious of the financial consequences of your decisions and actions. Perhaps financial setbacks have made you more aware of how easily your money is lost if you don't invest wisely.

Reversed

You may feel overwhelmed by financial circumstances after a long period of struggling to make ends meet. It may be time to take a break or to reward your continual efforts with a weekend away or a short holiday. You may be anticipating endless hurdles followed by paltry rewards when this nine appears reversed. A rest is likely to help you clarify your goals and rejuvenate your enthusiasm for the future.

Health

After setbacks with your health you are acutely aware of how much energy you have squandered in the past. It is time to guard your reserves of physical energy and set a comfortable pace for the future. Health problems affecting the head area (signified by the bandage) may be the result of past decisions and actions.

Reversed

You feel drained of energy and exhausted by past activities. Perhaps you have been attempting too much at once and it is time to seek a simpler, less stressful lifestyle. Ongoing health difficulties may have drained your resilience and a short rest may rejuvenate you and improve your confidence in the future. A return to the upright Eight of Wands offers you a chance to rest and relax, and to rebuild your reserves of physical energy and vitality.

Ten of Wands

General meaning

A man carrying ten wands lumbers towards a house in the background. Blue skies suggest that his burdens are of his own choosing, and these have most likely been steadily increasing over the previous months or years.

'I can do this. It will be easy and it won't take long', is the attitude which leads to situations shown by the Ten of Wands. The 'easy' project turns out to be more complicated than first imagined and this person is burdened, unable to delegate any of the load. This card is often selected when you are self-employed or running a small business. Having several roles at once, you may feel that it is impossible to hand over control to anyone else.

Despite the burdens, the Ten signifies success in your ventures after you have made great effort. You may benefit from delegating some responsibilities which will reduce stress and allow you to spend time pondering your long-term vision. You can be justifiably proud of your achievements when you realise your goals because this ten confirms the tenacity and effort required to make your dreams a reality.

Reversed

Chances of success are slender now, as you sink beneath the burdens that you presently face. It is time to return to the upright Nine of Wands in order to reassess which goals are worth pursuing and which can be delegated to others or abandoned. The attitude that 'if you want a job done, do it yourself' is likely to restrict you in the pursuit of your goals now. It is time to allow an accountant to complete your tax return, a graphic designer to draw up your new brochures or website, or a lawyer to help you with business contracts.

Finances

It is time to introduce a sound financial system as you are struggling with too many demands. Although you may feel that stopping to learn new habits may deflect you from your goals, acting now can help you with your longer term purpose. Financial success is confirmed by the Ten of Wands (depending on the surrounding cards in the layout) but this success is not without strenuous effort.

Reversed

You may feel financially burdened and unable to delegate your financial concerns or responsibilities to anyone else. It is time to return to the upright Nine of Wands to determine what expenses can be trimmed, or removed entirely, to allow you to pursue your goals more efficiently. The reversed Ten usually indicates physical exhaustion accompanying financial burdens.

Health

Health areas indicated by the upright Ten include shoulder tension, back troubles and general fatigue due to over commitment and demands upon your time by circumstances. Delegating some of your responsibilities now may ease your physical tension. Time spent on creative projects or recreational activities may also release the sense of being burdened.

Reversed

This ten reversed suggests that your reserves of energy are being depleted. You risk a physical collapse if you continue at your current pace. It is time to return to the upright Nine in order to determine which parts of your life can be effectively streamlined or simplified, and what activities can be removed so that you have more time and energy for yourself.

Page of Wands

General meaning

This young person is usually outgoing, sporty, enthusiastic, forthright and easy company. He or she enjoys sports, physical pursuits and the outdoors. The Wands Page tends to be noisy and messy around the house, and is self-motivated from an early age. This page responds well to rewards offered and is not discouraged by competition as this only serves to sharpen his or her focus on the desired goal.

As an aspect of you, the Page of Wands can describe the act of feeling young when beginning a new venture. Filled with passion and enthusiasm yet nervous about the possibilities ahead, this person is keen to explore available experiences and embark upon new adventures.

Reversed

They can be demanding, impatient, loud, reckless and clumsy. This is the Page who arrives home from school with their leg in plaster after a sporting incident. The negative aspects of the Page reversed mean this person is naturally untidy and sloppy. He or she is likely to be bossy and competitive with friends. The negative Page can present as the loud-mouthed teenager that many of the local adults secretly want to lynch.

The reversed Page of Wands suggests delays in beginning new projects, perhaps being distracted by present demands. It sometimes signifies a fear of beginning new projects is making you hesitate before acting.

When opposed

When the Page of Wands feels thwarted he or she can give up pursuing a goal, preferring instead to switch to another objective. This is the noisiest of the four pages when thwarted. They are likely to shout loudly when life is perceived as unfair. The positive types seek other goals or become more determined to achieve the original goal, competing with themselves.

This Page makes a positive first impression, being quick to tell newcomers of their current goals, yet dissipating all reserves of energy in the discussion and not in the pursuit of the desired goals. When thwarted the Page of Wands depicts passion without purpose. Instead of rising above obstacles they may succumb to anger, lashing out at those close by. Alternatively, restlessness may cause this person to abandon desired goals at the first hurdle.

Knight of Wands

General meaning

This Knight is usually impatient, enthusiastic, eager to explore the world and forthright. Capable of short bursts of hard work, the Knight of Wands tires easily of routine and longer term objectives. He is goal oriented, outgoing, cheeky, bold and loves a challenge. He enjoys travelling and outdoor work where he can feel free. Young women often find this Knight attractive, despite his admission that he has no interest in emotional commitment. He is usually confident, positive and outgoing. He will flirt just because he can and he is usually generous with his time and energy.

The Knight of Wands can also represent the need to act quickly in order to seize an opportunity while it is available. It is a card for travel and for being free to embrace a variety of choices. It is a card for the astrological sign of Sagittarius and when it appears in a layout with the Major Arcana card Temperance, a Sagittarian (male or female) person may be significant for you.

Reversed

The Knight of Wands reversed can enjoy the chase more than the rewards. He often lacks commitment and takes on too many projects at once. He can be competitive, especially with close friends. Women are sometimes drawn to the wild, rebellious side of him, hoping to tame him. He resists domestic life, preferring to move on to the next relationship when it is presented. He can make running away look like searching for his place in the world.

This knight reversed indicates a need to keep moving in search of the right opportunity, increasing the likelihood of ignoring opportunities when they are presented. There are also delays or impatience with plans which results in few projects being successfully completed.

When opposed

The Knight usually abandons his goals in favour of another goal, often in another location, when he is thwarted. He tends to repeat his unlearned lessons in new situations. He can reveal a competitive streak when thwarted, working hard for a goal against opposition, only to abandon it once he has achieved it. The positive Knight tends to push harder when frustrated. Delicate negotiations are not his preferred approach.

Sometimes the Knight will need to find himself as an escape from a situation which doesn't allow him all the freedom he desires. He will abandon a relationship, a job or a home with the hope that another location will offer him a better chance at fulfilment. It usually does until commitment is again required or someone thwarts his plans, and the road out of town beckons. Wands people often live in the future, unaware that when they arrive at their destination they bring with them unfinished business from their past. This is especially the case when Wands court cards appear reversed.

Queen of Wands

General meaning

The Queen of Wands is usually generous, courageous, forthright, passionate, bold and independent. She is hardworking, capable of inspiring others and spontaneously intuitive. Her reserves of energy keep her going long after others give up, and she is an excellent coach or role model for those around her. A natural teacher and explorer, the Queen thrives on challenges and enjoys reaching beyond established limitations. She can be a model for assertiveness and often displays courage in the face of adversity. She is usually cheeky, forthright and strong willed.

The Queen can describe success through inner strength and self-confidence. Your courage against the opposition is likely to help you to realise your goals. This card represents the astrological sign of Leo, and when it appears in a layout with the Sun and/or Strength cards, a Leo person (male or female) may be significant for you.

Reversed

This Queen reversed can be competitive, reckless, ruthless in business, aggressive and hot-tempered. If this woman was represented by a dance, it would be the tango. She finds drama attractive and will create it around herself if she doesn't have enough worthwhile goals to pursue in her life. She often doesn't know when to stop, consequently she can collapse with physical or emotional exhaustion occasionally.

The reversed Queen will readily give you advice which she should apply to herself, point out your flaws and advise you as to how to fix them. It is probably in your best interest not to treat her the same way in return.

A lack of success is indicated due to a lack of courage or self-confidence. Behind the bold exterior of the queen are doubts, self-criticisms and unfaced fears. Perhaps a lack of courage or self-confidence makes you hesitate in the pursuit of your goals.

When opposed

When thwarted, the Queen of Wands is quick-tempered, forceful and outspoken. Sometimes she explodes before she has all the facts, making an apology necessary afterwards. Generally she will push harder for results when thwarted, if she can harness her temper to push her forward. If not, she can react with fury, lashing out at those around her and alienating them in moments. This is the person you want at the forefront of a demonstration, as she will carry the flag, using it against the opposition if the need arises.

King of Wands

General meaning

The King of Wands is enthusiastic, passionate, excitable, honest, forthright, capable of seeing the bigger picture, hardworking and generous. His straightforward manner endears him to people easily. He has few pretensions and enjoys a challenge. He is usually cheeky, passionate, keen to flirt openly with those he finds attractive, and he is competitive in sports, business and in life generally. He is usually a good teacher or coach as he enjoys motivating others.

The King of Wands represents success through self-discipline. It is a card representing the astrological sign of Aries and, along with the Emperor card, it can suggest that an Aries person (male or female) is significant to you. The King has mastered the passion and enthusiasm of the Wands suit, and is able to harness this energy towards practical life goals.

Reversed

The King of Wands can be competitive, impractical, blunt, reckless, aggressive, hot-tempered, quick to rescind commitment and incapable of completing his plans. His need for instant gratification usually makes him a poor negotiator. With his desire for immediate results he can overlook the long-term consequences of his actions. He usually resents authority and lacks self-discipline. When he repeatedly acts without self-control others usually intercept to discipline him. Thus he may lose his driving licence, be dismissed from his job or asked to leave his home or relationship as a consequence of his actions.

In general terms the reversed King can describe a lack of success due to lack of self-discipline. Enthusiasm combined with a lack of patience can result in too many projects being undertaken simultaneously, each being abandoned without sustained effort.

When opposed

The King can be short-tempered when thwarted. When angry he is likely to shout and rant because he understands that throwing a big enough tantrum usually encourages others to give him what he wants. They may despise him, but they will meet his immediate demands. The positive King, however, tries harder when frustrated in his plans. He will work all night if necessary to complete the task at hand.

Like the Knight of Wands, the King can abandon current plans in pursuit of new opportunities when thwarted. He tends to repeat his mistakes until he develops self-discipline. Because the Wands people learn through direct experience rather than through observation, repetitive mistakes only make the King more angry and impatient with himself and his circumstances.

Chapter 5

THE SUIT OF CUPS

This 14-card suit, ranging from the Ace to the King reveals a path to understanding through love, creativity and imagination. By nature Cups people are often kind, gentle, compassionate, patient and sentimental. Whereas Wands people seek competition, Cups people prefer union as they realise that competition only separates us from each other. Understanding that humans are already alone and isolated, Cups people seek the ways we are connected to each other on our individual paths to fulfilment. While Wands people possess the physical courage to climb a mountain, Cups people exhibit great emotional courage.

In astrology, Cups people are the water signs Cancer, Scorpio and Pisces, although people represented by Cups cards are not restricted to these signs. They tend to exhibit a soft, sentimental nurturing temperament. These are the people you contact when you need sympathy and understanding. Cups people, usually good listeners, are capable of nurturing those they love. They value inner peace and calm, and sometimes find their Wands counterparts too restless and competitive for their liking. They appreciate tranquil afternoons spent by the sea, reading a book or watching a romantic film.

Suited to careers in nurturing, creativity, counselling, psychology, art therapy, energetic healing and music, Cups people avoid highly competitive businesses in favour of cooperative ventures. They sometimes seek spiritual and emotional fulfilment through meditation, yoga, writing or painting.

When out of temper Cups people tend to sulk or emotionally withdraw from situations. They avoid conflict and are easily hurt by the thoughtless words or actions of others. Naturally private and sometimes secretive, Cups people need time to be discovered, revealing themselves only slowly to others. They are naturally intuitive, sensitive to the moods and feelings of others and are often kind to animals.

When negative, Cups people sometimes use alcohol or drugs to dull the emotional emptiness or pain they are experiencing. They tend to be melancholic when negative, and are unable to release the past or to live fully in the present. Cups people sometimes escape from life through romance, fantasy or by daydreaming of a better life.

The Ace of Cups

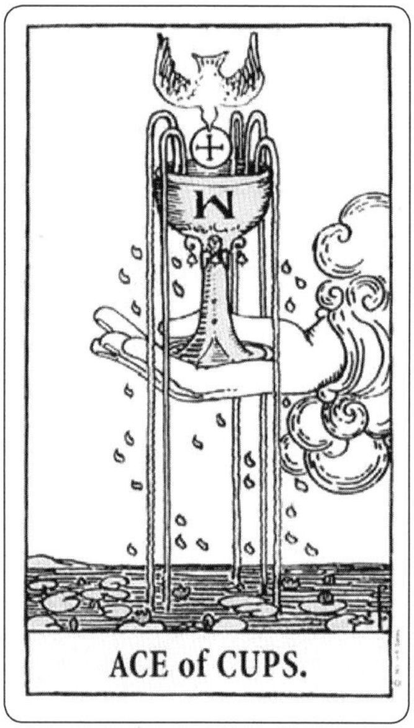

General meaning

In this card a hand holds a cup which is overflowing. The Ace of Cups highlights the creative imagination required to dream up new ideas. When this ace appears in a layout it signals a time when you are spiritually and emotionally fulfilled and connected to life, through your relationship, your work or your creative projects.

In a relationship question this card suggests a new love relationship or a new stage of an existing relationship. It offers a rewarding connection to another human being.

Reversed

Connection to spiritually fulfilling people, opportunities and circumstances is intermittent now. In a relationship layout the reversed Ace suggests periods of emotional fulfilment between periods of emotional hunger. A return to the upright Ten of Cups offers a group of like-minded people who can help you to reconnect spiritually. In a question about whether it is worthwhile pursuing a particular goal, this Ace reversed highlights a lack of fulfilment if the goal is pursued.

Finances

The Ace of Cups in a financial layout can indicate that you are content with your financial circumstances. It also suggests that you may earn an income from creative endeavours or pursuits which give you deep fulfilment. Loving what you do or the company you work for is shown by this card.

Reversed

The Ace describes an intermittent connection to your sources of financial stability. Perhaps you are struggling with a job which you usually find fulfilling. It can describe doing too much of something you like, reducing the enjoyment normally derived from the process.

Health

A positive card in a health reading, this ace describes balanced health and a sense of emotional equilibrium. Spiritual connection to life and a sense of contentment are the result of this balance.

Reversed

The Ace of Cups reversed suggests that any current health difficulties may have emotional or spiritual causes. It may be time to examine your sources of spiritual and emotional fulfilment in order to restore your physical and emotional health.

Two of Cups

General meaning

The Two of Cups describes a balanced friendship, partnership or love relationship. It shows two people standing facing each other. The indication is that they are equal, complementary and responsive to each other's needs. Positive ideas flow easily from this partnership—to the world and between partners—as this couple work harmoniously together. In a question about career, this two describes working closely with someone you respect who also values you.

Reversed

When reversed the Two of Cups portrays two people who want control over one another. This friendship or relationship will be a constant power struggle until each party returns to the Ace of Cups to reconnect to life and an inner spiritual source of joy. This card reversed also indicates two people, each person searching for fulfilment through the other, which places unnecessary demands on the partnership.

Carrie felt bored and unchallenged by life when she came for a reading. Tired of shopping, travelling and lunching with friends, she complained that her love relationship with Nikolai wasn't fulfilling. The reversed Two of Cups indicated that Carrie expected her partner to be her sole connection to life. Nikolai cooked for her, entertained her, shared his friends with her and pampered her when they travelled. The reversed Two suggested Carrie was placing a strain on the relationship and that it was time for Carrie to find her own spiritual and emotional connections to life rather than depending on Nikolai to do this for her.

Finances

In a financial question the Two of Cups represents a harmonious partnership or love relationship in which both parties are generous, compassionate and unlikely to seek advantage over each other financially. In a business question, this card suggests an amicable business partnership, while in a career question it can indicate that you are working closely and harmoniously with a work colleague.

Reversed

The Two reversed suggests that personal differences in a partnership may be draining your finances. Proper attention to financial concerns has been diverted to the problems between the partners. Sometimes the Two reversed indicates former partners wrestling over possessions after a separation.

Health

When the Two of Cups is found upright in a health layout it indicates you are experiencing good physical health that stems from emotional balance. Being loved and valued by someone significant to you can help you towards a harmonious, healthy life.

Reversed

The Two reversed may indicate that your relationship or a work partnership is draining your energy and adversely affecting your health. Perhaps your partner demands more from you than you realise. In order to maintain good health, you need to ensure that someone close to you is not relying on you to the extent that your health is affected.

Three of Cups

General meaning

Three women dance in celebration during the harvest, each one holding a cup above her head. This three suggests a time of celebration, a gathering of like-minded people or simply a party to mark an important occasion. In a career question it can describe a compatible group of people working together. In a question concerning love relationships, it often describes a harmonious family or a supportive group of friends. If you are single, the Three of Cups can indicate several love relationship opportunities approaching at once.

Reversed

The Three of Cups describes disharmony within a group of people. Perhaps now work colleagues compete with each other or a relationship is marred by the negative influences of a friend, a relative or a secret love affair. It can indicate a child, perhaps from a previous relationship, that is adversely affecting the stability of the current relationship.

Finances

Shared financial success is suggested now, with three or more people enjoying the fruits of their combined labours. This card shows three or more people working or investing together and sharing the rewarding results. Sometimes this three indicates that several rewarding opportunities have arrived and that you need to choose the most suitable one.

Reversed

The Three of Cups reversed portrays a conflict within a group of people that may be the result of differences of opinion over the way finances are used, or because someone feels that the financial rewards are not being equally divided. If you cannot agree with everyone in the team, it is time to return to the Two of Cups upright, finding one person who shares your perspective.

Health

Good health enjoyed amongst friends is shown with the Three of Cups. It signifies a time when you may be celebrating or holidaying with friends, while appreciating your good health. Time spent with like-minded people contributes to feeling balanced and appreciated.

Reversed

A time when you feel isolated or left out of the group. This requires a return to the Two of Cups in order to find someone special who values and appreciates you. Health concerns related to emotional issues can be shown with this card. In rare cases, the reversed Three can signify a group of people who share patterns of behaviour which adversely affect the health of those involved. When Colin complained at a reading of lacking vitality, the reversed Three of Cups indicated his social habits were part of the cause. Colin spent five or six nights a week playing pool in a local bar, drinking four to six glasses of whiskey each night. It also created conflict in his relationship because while Colin saw it as entertainment, his partner Shaz perceived it as a house deposit lost to the bar owner.

Four of Cups

General meaning

A man sits cross-legged and with his eyes closed in meditation in the shade of a tree. He dreams of the Ace of Cups which is extending him opportunities from other dimensions. Before him stand three upright cups containing real opportunities. The Four of Cups is a reminder that unless you have a spiritual and emotional connection to life, few opportunities seem appealing or fulfilling. The man depicted sits quietly, balancing his inner and outer needs.

Reversed

This person is discontented, unable to maintain a link within and to those opportunities around him. It is time to revisit the Three of Cups in order to meet people who remind him of or awaken him to the joys of life. Fulfilment seems fleeting when this card is reversed. The man sits reflecting on lost opportunities while present opportunities are ignored.

As current circumstances do not allow your inner needs to be met, look elsewhere for spiritual and emotional nourishment. It might be helpful to join a meditation group, a car club, a regular stretch class at the local gym or a nature conservation society.

Finances

Consider how much happiness you derive from your work now, as success is measured in more ways than financially. If success means that you end up with the money but not with the respect of those you deal with on a daily basis, perhaps it is time to reconsider other paths to success.

As an answer to a financial question, this four suggests that you can take a step back to reconsider your path in life if you choose. This may mean that you are financially secure enough to do so without feeling pressured. It is time to recognise that the current path may make you money, and to ask yourself if you will feel fulfilled at the end of it.

Reversed

Discontent overshadows any financial success now. It is time to revisit the Three of Cups to reconnect with people. Play is as important as work, and the reversed Four usually appears when work consumes you and play is merely a distant memory. A lack of financial fulfilment is indicated by this four reversed. In re-connecting with people you may be introduced to new, more rewarding opportunities.

Health

The upright Four can suggest that meditation can go some way to restoring your physical, emotional, mental and spiritual energies. Alternatively, some time spent resting, reflecting or relaxing will reward you with powerful insights.

Reversed

You may be feeling depressed or disconnected from life due to working too hard. It is time to return to the upright Three of Cups in order to play with others who know how to enjoy themselves. The reversed Four can signify a loneliness resulting from disconnection from those people and activities that feed you emotionally and spiritually.

Five of Cups

General meaning

Clad in black, a mournful figure with head bent ponders his or her circumstances. Three overturned cups lie in view while two upright cups stand behind the figure. A river, which represents emotion, separates this person from stability, represented by the castle in the background. A bridge leads across the river to the castle, but this person is more focused on what he or she has lost than a path to stability.

This is a card of loss, sadness and regret brought about by a change in circumstances. This person retreats into themselves to cope with these feelings. The fives represent a state of narrow-mindedness, which in this card is shown by grief. In grief, opportunities for happiness elude us as we focus on the source of our pain.

Reversed

In reverse, this five is a more positive card; it indicates the gradual release of grief and a recognition that the bridge nearby leads back to emotional stability and fulfilment. It represents the growing awareness of opportunities for emotional and spiritual nourishment.

After a period of loss or sadness, you recognise new paths to fulfilment. You are again open to the possibility of love. A return to the upright Four of Cups offers a chance to experience inner stillness before you seek happiness from people and surrounding circumstances.

Finances

Financial loss is shown by the Five of Cups. It indicates a lack of concern for financial demands as you focus on emotional matters. As the answer to a question about a business or a financial investment, this card signifies disappointment with the outcome. Sometimes when you are ending a long-term love relationship, you are too distraught to care about financial issues. There is a risk that the more level-headed partner may end up with most of your possessions and you need sound legal or financial advice.

Reversed

The Five reversed can indicate a healing from past financial and emotional disappointments, along with a return to the emotional stability of the upright Four of Cups. It offers an awareness that money cannot substitute for emotional and spiritual emptiness.

Health

The Five of Cups can suggest health issues resulting from emotional loss or grief. Powerful or prolonged difficult emotional states can lead to depression and other health issues, yet honest grief is often only briefly tolerated in western society. Instead, you are admired if you get back to work the day after you bury your dead and your heart. Take time now to accept loss or grief and your health may improve as a result.

Reversed

The Five reversed is a more positive card in a health layout. It indicates a return to a more balanced outlook after the grief subsides. The castle represents stable health after you cross the bridge, leaving your pain behind. This card indicates someone receiving support from family and friends or seeking refuge from emotional loss in a stable, routine life.

Six of Cups

General meaning

Pale blue skies illuminate a garden that surrounds a couple as they examine the flowering contents in a cup. They appear safe and protected from the outside world and in the background a guard patrols their domain. Despite their adult appearances they are dressed as children.

This card represents the emotional stability which a solid home environment offers. It shows a loving couple enjoying simple pleasures such as gardening and sharing a home. In general this six can suggest a period of tranquility, harmony and emotional stability. It can also represent a rest period between the change offered in the Five of Cups and the growth offered in the Seven.

Reversed

This card reversed suggests a return to the Five of Cups, where you may revisit your grief and loss. Stability doesn't last forever, and can be broken by periods of grief when loss occurs. The reversed Six offers a period of growth before the next period of stability and rest.

There is an opportunity to break free of comfortable routines and experience life more directly. Change offers new perspectives, understanding and opportunities for those who are willing to relinquish the current routines and explore.

Finances

A stable financial time is indicated by this six. The emphasis here is not on finances but on the emotional security afforded you by this financial stability. This six highlights your community spirit of tenderness and harmony stemming from solid financial circumstances.

Reversed

The Six of Cups reversed can describe limited intimacy and cooperation between people due to a lack of financial stability. Emotional security may be threatened by a weak financial foundation when this card appears reversed in a financial layout. A return to the upright Five brings change and loss, but also growth.

Health

The upright Six of Cups portrays balanced health mirroring a harmonious emotional life. Congenial surroundings relieve health pressures and allow for rest and recreation. This card sometimes indicates that you are taking a relaxing break in familiar surroundings to restore themselves.

Reversed

This six reversed can suggest that current health concerns are the result of emotional loss or instability. A return to the Five of Cups offers a reminder that nothing is permanent in life and that loss and pain are inevitable. This change in wellbeing may be an opportunity for growth, leading to new and more supportive health routines.

Seven of Cups

General meaning

A person gazes at seven cups in order to determine how to balance life for spiritual fulfilment. Each cup offers an important aspect for a rounded life, yet favouring one cup over another can make life lopsided. Energy must be devoted to the persona (the cup containing the face), home (the castle), material wealth (the jewellery), personal goals (the wreath), subconscious desires (the demon) and sexual and creative goals (the snake) before you can meet your deeper spiritual needs (the shroud).

This card describes thinking about what is important in life. It shows the process of reviewing your circumstances to ensure you are on a path to fulfilment. The Seven indicates reflection on the inner life for either a spiritual or an emotional review.

Reversed

When reversed the Seven of Cups indicates that there is a compulsion for you to fill your life with routines or obligations in order to avoid contemplation. There may be a fear of what might surface as a result of a period of contemplation, or that work or hectic routines are preventing reflection.

A return to the upright Six of Cups is necessary to enjoy the stability offered there. After a while you are likely to become restless for change, growth and emotional development, and this is when the upright Seven of Cups is likely to represent itself. Enjoy the routine offered by the return to the six until you decide that you need greater emotional fulfilment.

Finances

Do not give up on your financial goals now, as you are aware that they will contribute to your lasting material and emotional fulfilment. Take time to ensure that your financial needs are not diverting your attention from emotional, mental or spiritual needs. Contemplating your deeper needs may enable you to determine whether your current financial goals will meet these needs.

Reversed

This seven reversed suggests that you may need to return to the upright Six of Cups in order to enjoy a period of stability. When you are ready you can move forward again to the upright Seven of Cups. Release current financial goals as you are unlikely to be fulfilled by these goals long term.

Health

This is a card for seeking deeper spiritual or emotional causes to current physical health symptoms. Health is balanced if you meet all of your needs, so take time to reflect on your inner and outer needs.

Reversed

The Seven of Cups reversed describes a tendency to overlook spiritual and emotional needs in pursuit of financial stability. It is time to return to the true stability offered in the upright Six of Cups until you outgrow it naturally and decide that you are ready for growth.

Eight of Cups

General meaning

Eight cups are arranged in a manner that allows for the ninth cup to be added later. A person clad in a red cloak and boots leaves the eight cups behind in search of the ninth cup. The moon covers the sun, forcing a more thorough search. This card represents the renunciation of one source of fulfilment to seek another. Perhaps you are leaving your job to find something more rewarding, or you are retreating from your love relationship to find a deeper source of happiness.

The eights are cards of strength. The Eight of Cups represents emotional courage prompting you to look for a deeper source of fulfilment. There is a risk that you won't find it, and that in searching you will lose the existing source of happiness. There is the hope that in finding this deeper source of fulfilment, that you will have more to offer others and more to contribute to your existing circumstances.

Reversed

The reversed Eight of Cups describes being torn between the urge to search for deeper fulfilment and the fear that you may lose everything that gives you joy at present. Your alternatives appear equally matched, resulting in confusion and indecision. It is time to return to the upright Seven of Cups in order to recognise and identify your needs. Then can you make the best decision when returning to the upright Eight.

Finances

You may be considering leaving your job or walking away from an investment or a source of income when this eight appears in a financial layout. For continual growth and fulfilment, take time now to consider new possible income streams or a new job.

Reversed

You may be trying to decide whether to leave your job or to remain. During a recent reading 27-year-old legal assistant Arianne explained she learned that her company was involved in a merger with a larger organisation. Talk of redundancies and job duplication spread immediately. Arianne was unsure whether to ride out the merger or to find more stable employment elsewhere. It was important for her to determine her own needs before making this decision. After consideration (a momentary return to the upright Seven of Cups) Arianne decided that job security was more important than familiarity. She searched successfully for a position with a new company.

Health

A new approach to health is suggested by this card. You are likely to depart from familiar approaches to your health wanting new, possibly more effective health alternatives. The eights are cards of strength and the Eight of Cups suggests emotional and spiritual strength. This spiritual and emotional strength forms a solid foundation for balanced physical health.

Reversed

This card indicates there is confusion about the best approach to maintaining or improving your health. After Charmaine was diagnosed with cancer she was torn between mainstream treatments and their side effects (possible loss of hair and hearing, liver damage) and alternative medicine and its consequences (possible loss of health or even death if it didn't work). Her life depended upon the choices she made and the reversed Eight of Cups appearing in her health layout reflected her indecision. Her return to the upright Seven of Cups involved reading and researching her alternatives before making an informed decision. She discovered microwave therapy, which was considered alternative by mainstream doctors yet mainstream by natural health practitioners. Charmaine returned two years later to say that her health was fine again.

Nine of Cups

General meaning

A man is seated before nine cups, placed out of immediate reach. He sits with folded arms, at ease with himself. The bright yellow in the card signifies clarity of thinking while the rich deep red of his hat, feather and socks show his passion for life. Beyond this passion for living is the blue cloth, suggesting a spiritual awareness of his true worth.

This card suggests that you understand your true worth, and the value of what you bring to a situation. There is a sense of fulfilment derived from your present career. Life flows more smoothly when you avoid people and situations which may deplete your energy with no hope of reward. Nines are cards of reflection. This man sits reflecting on what he has to offer others in friendships or in love relationships. His tunic is grey because his love is only worthwhile when he gives it away to someone deserving. His tunic is a reminder that he has not yet reached the Ten, the completion for the suit of Cups.

Reversed

The fulfilment you desire proves elusive, making you snatch at it wherever it may be found. This can lead to addictions, obsessive or compulsive behaviour as you search for short-term fulfilment and lasting inner peace eludes you. It is time to return to the upright Eight of Cups in order to walk away from people, situations and habits that offer you no long-term nourishment.

The reversed Nine of Cups describes clients who insist that they have many unfulfilled needs when in fact they have only one, deeper unsatisfied need. Addressing this deeper spiritual or emotional need often takes care of all the smaller, surface needs.

Finances

This card often represents fulfilment resulting from sound financial decisions. It heralds a time when financial pressures are behind you. You may be earning your income in a creative or fulfilling manner. You may experience a sense of personal wealth and financial contentment when the Nine of Cups appears in a financial question.

Reversed

The reversed Nine of Cups suggests a desperate need for financial wealth which masks deeper, more spiritual needs. It may be that you dislike the way you earn your income and compensate for this by spending a great deal of money to cheer yourself up. Perhaps it's time to return to the upright Eight of Cups in order to free yourself from financial habits which keep you stuck or unfulfilled in your life.

Health

Balanced physical, emotional, mental and spiritual health is shown by the upright Nine of Cups. This is a period where you appreciate your health and your life. Balanced health results in a balanced attitude to life and a sense of wellbeing when the Nine of Cups appears upright in a health layout.

Reversed

This nine can suggest addictive behaviour is negatively affecting your health. It is time to examine your routines for the sake of your long-term health. Addictions to cigarettes, alcohol, drugs or simply to unhealthy foods are shown by the reversed Nine of Cups. It is time to shed old habits through a return to the upright Eight of Cups.

Ten of Cups

General meaning

A couple stand together, each with an outstretched arm as though to embrace their surroundings. Two children play together beside them. A stream flows gently past the house through established gardens and ten cups are visible in a rainbow above them. The Ten of Cups offers a mature version of the love relationship that appeared in the Six of Cups. The difference is that fulfilment is derived from within and from each other. Now the children, nature, their home and life itself nourish each person emotionally and spiritually.

This ten represents a group of people working together harmoniously, such as a group of friends, a sports team or a collection of employees. When this ten appears upright each person in the group feels that he or she is part of the team and contributing something worthwhile to the process.

As the outcome or answer card in a question about a love relationship, the Ten of Cups suggests a rewarding outcome offering long-term fulfilment.

Reversed

This ten reversed shows a group of people no longer working together as a team. There is a need to return to the upright Nine of Cups to recognise what you can contribute and the value of this contribution. Sometimes the reversed Ten of Cups describes a lack of confidence in what you offer to those around you. You may feel insignificant in comparison to others in a group, perhaps at home or at work.

When reversed this card indicates you feel excluded from the group or are excluding yourself from the group process. In relationship questions the reversed

Ten of Cups indicates that you are attempting to avoid repeating past relationship patterns. Perhaps you have left an unsatisfactory relationship or have grown up witnessing a dysfunctional union between parents, and you are keen not to repeat this in a present relationship.

Finances

The upright Ten of Cups suggests more attention is being paid to emotional fulfilment than financial stability at this stage. Sufficient financial stability exists for you to be able to focus on enjoying life.

Reversed

This ten reversed suggests that you are experiencing feelings of poverty that may be the result of emotional emptiness rather than of a lack of money. It can also suggest that attention has been diverted from financial issues towards securing emotional stability and fulfilment. If this continues financial problems are likely. It can signify a need to return to the upright Nine of Cups in order to reassess the value of what you bring to your job or to your love relationship.

Health

Good health is confirmed by the upright Ten of Cups in a health layout. You now have supportive friends and family, and a balance between work and play. Many sources of love and emotional enrichment combine to keep you balanced and fulfilled.

Reversed

When the Ten of Cups appears reversed in a health reading you may feel a deep sense of emptiness in your home, your family or your love relationship which may be an underlying cause of health problems. Depression is sometimes portrayed by this ten reversed, confirming that you have become disconnected from the people with whom you live or work. It is time to return to the upright Nine of Cups in order to meditate on who you are and what you offer to those around you. It may be necessary to seek out a more suitable group of people in a new home or work environment.

Page of Cups

General meaning

This card represents a dreamy young person whose romantic view of life sometimes leaves him or her open to the hidden motives of others. Creative, sensitive, shy and kind-hearted, this person is content to write or draw on a rainy day and probably loves reading or films.

As a situation, the Page of Cups represents an emotional offer. Perhaps a friendship, a love relationship or a creative offer is presented now. In a career question it can indicate an emotionally rewarding job proposal. It can also suggest restoring balance through meditation.

Reversed

The negative Page of Cups can be painfully shy, fearful of new experiences and exhibit a tendency to hoard mementos of more harmonious times. Clingy and timid among new people, he or she usually warms to strangers slowly. As a child, this page has only a few close friends, preferring to be with them one at a time rather than in a group.

When opposed

There is a tendency for the Page of Cups to sulk or to use tears to control circumstances when they are frustrated. This page has a long memory for emotional hurts and they can usually quote back to you verbatim conversations relating to events years ago. The positive Page of Cups sometimes cries quietly to release frustration.

Knight of Cups

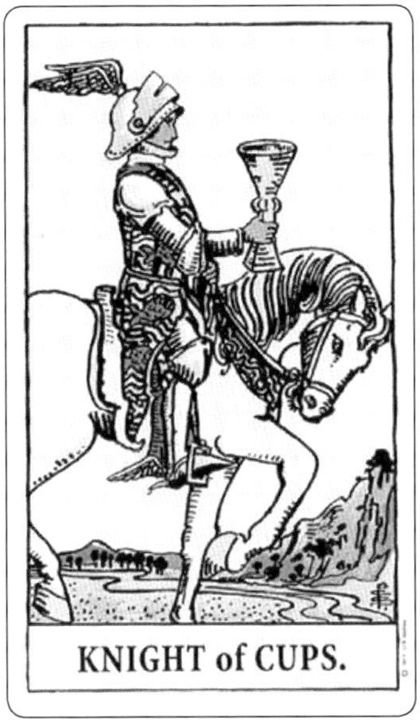

General meaning

The Knight of Cups is enthusiastic yet compassionate. Women are attracted to him for his ability to compete and his capacity for sensitivity and understanding. He listens to those around him when they are troubled and consequently he usually has many friends to help him when he needs assistance. He can be alternately restless and then patient, as he is a combination of the elements of fire and water. Sentimental and romantic, love is rarely far from his thoughts.

Reversed

When negative this knight is continually falling in and out of love. He is emotionally immature, often shaping each new relationship in the form of a previous one. He begins projects without any idea of how he will complete them. His fertile imagination offers him plenty of ideas which rarely amount to anything tangible.

When opposed

The Knight of Cups can despair when frustrated, believing that he may not feel loved or happy again. Like a sensitive artist or a poet, his emotions determine the path he takes in life. He may seek refuge in the promise of a new love relationship when life frustrates him. The positive Knight of Cups searches for the spiritual meaning behind frustrating events to learn and to move forward on his path.

Queen of Cups

General meaning

The Queen of Cups is intuitive, compassionate, kind-hearted, sensitive and nurturing as she has great emotional depth. This queen needs to avoid emotionally turbulent work environments, as she is easily overwhelmed by the emotions of those around her. Her need for peace and harmony may find her giving too much of herself in order to maintain a sense of accord. She is likely to keep confidences and offers an ear to those who want to unburden themselves of their troubles.

Reversed

The reversed Queen of Cups can be secretive, unable to forgive or forget the past and melancholic for no apparent reason. This queen is more a burden to herself than to others when negative as she withdraws from life, effectively starving herself emotionally and spiritually. If you upset her and don't apologise, it won't be forgotten. Every factor will be recalled at the appropriate time, with the accuracy of a digital image. The negative Queen can become a martyr, living with an intolerable situation instead of changing it or leaving it behind.

When opposed

The Queen of Cups is easily diverted from her purpose when frustrated as she does not have the righteous indignation possessed by the Queen of Wands. Instead of demanding her rightful share, she hopes that others might notice that she needs assistance. The positive Queen of Cups tends to await another opportunity patiently.

King of Cups

General meaning

The King of Cups is sensitive, compassionate, creative, patient and a good listener. Capable of great depths of feeling, this king has a big heart, is usually kind to children and sentimental by nature. This is the man who remembers anniversaries, enjoys the ocean (even if it is simply staring out to sea from a headland) and prefers a career which is creative or spiritually meaningful. He is intuitive and avoids competition whenever possible.

Reversed

When negative, the King of Cups is the 'King of Sulking'. He harbours grudges and may have a tendency towards alcohol or drugs to smooth over emotional ups and downs. Secretive, moody, often despondent and melancholic by nature, this king lists his pastimes as brooding, wallowing, sighing and recounting past misdeeds.

The negative King of Cups is often creative but unable to pursue his creative endeavours due to current obligations or past negative experiences surrounding creativity. Deep down this man dreams of a creative life, but recognises that he has already travelled too far down his chosen path to go back to start again.

When opposed

The King of Cups can hold a grudge for a lifetime and although he avoids confrontation, he can display passive-aggressive tendencies. When you are in a hurry to get to an important occasion, he will decide to service the car or he will lose the keys for an hour. When thwarted he is the master of withholding.

The positive types forgive easily and enjoy spending time by the sea, listening to soothing music or talking to friends in order to rebalance. Creative activities equalise them emotionally and restore their faith in humanity.

Chapter 6

THE SUIT OF SWORDS

This 14-card suit ranging from the Ace to the King, shows a path to understanding by using the mind. Swords people are usually talkative, social, curious and unsentimental. They seek answers to life's questions, love to read, to discuss important issues with others and to make sense of the world rationally.

Swords people are effective administrators, planners and organisers. If a problem arises at work, the Swords person can usually find a quick solution or contact someone who can rectify the problem. Being sociable people, they normally have a wide circle of friends and business contacts.

In astrology Swords people are the air signs Gemini, Libra and Aquarius, although the Queen of Swords can also represent the sign of Virgo. Swords people are not limited to these signs, and they can be any sign of the zodiac. It is the inquiring mind and desire for rational answers to life's questions which reveals a Swords person. While Cups people offer nurturing, Swords people offer ideas, concepts, quick minds and good conversation.

Suited to careers where they can meet people, communicate ideas or talk on the phone, Swords people can become depressed if there is not sufficient change in their work routine. They thrive on new horizons, short-term projects and sharing responsibility for an outcome with a team. They are natural teachers and are rarely shy.

When out of temper Swords people can become sarcastic, curt and sharp-tongued. They may freeze out those around them emotionally or ask pointed questions and verbally back others into a corner. They answer your questions with clipped tones, leaving you well aware that you owe them an apology.

When negative, Swords people can take on too many projects at once, becoming mentally scattered and complete nothing. They can talk incessantly about nothing as though afraid of silence. In extreme cases, negative Swords people cannot fall asleep at night without a radio or television playing beside them. Negative Swords people need the company of others, with little regard for the quality of their companions. Negative Swords people can be slanderous gossips, terrible at keeping confidences and enjoy prying into the affairs of others.

Swords people in negative mode prefer to plan and to talk about their intended adventures rather than take the necessary steps to realise their goals. Whereas negative Wands people can be 'all torque', their Swords counterparts are often all talk.

Ace of Swords

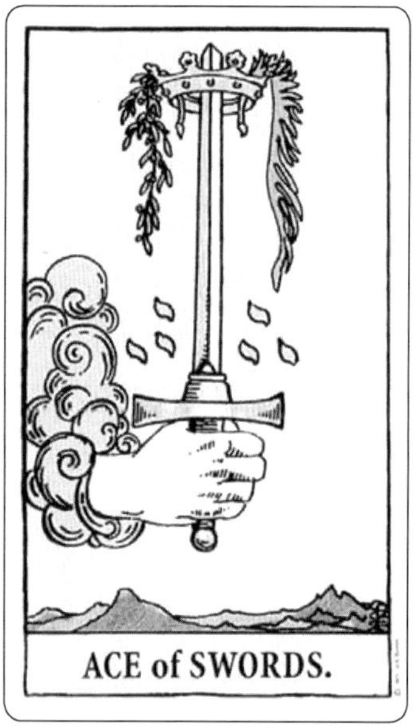

General meaning

The Swords Ace represents the planning part of new projects, when ideas, concepts, measurements and designs are balanced against objectives before the commencement of a new venture. The card contains a hand protruding from a cloud. The hand clasps an upright sword that pierces a crown and partial wreaths. This is the sword of understanding piercing the illusion of reality. The double-edged sword highlights both the rewards and the responsibilities that come with worldly achievements and success.

Reversed

The reversed Ace of Swords indicates impatience to move forward without a clear plan or destination. It is time for you to return to the upright Ten of Swords in order to examine your beliefs about life and all the mental demands currently placed on you. With careful reassessment, out of confusion can come one clear idea or plan, that can be used as a starting point for a new project or goal.

When the card is reversed, the cloud in the illustration is now above the hand, suggesting that mental confusion reigns. It is time to concentrate on one project or plan at a time, in order to recognise the steps ahead that will lead to the desired goal. It is difficult to move forward as your thinking is clouded. Clarify your purpose before taking any steps and success is more likely.

Finances

The Ace of Swords can represent careful financial planning preceding action. You are vigilant to changing circumstances and able to adapt when required. Success through careful planning is shown when the upright Ace of Swords appears in the answer position to a specific question.

Reversed

The reversed Ace of Swords suggests delays in beginning new financial projects due to careless planning or too many confusing ideas. In returning to the Ten of Swords you are challenged to examine your beliefs about finances before proceeding. The reversed Ace describes lack of success due to lack of forethought.

Health

The appearance of the Ace of Swords suggests you have a clear understanding of your health weaknesses and strengths. It can also represent an operation (the sword being the surgeon's knife) because the sword is inverted (blade down) as a knife is before it is applied to the body. In tarot cards surgeons are often represented by the King and Queen of Swords.

Reversed

In a health reading the reversed Ace of Swords indicates it may be necessary to rethink your current health plans and consider the longer term consequences of your actions. Take time now to consider all your options before acting. A surgical procedure may be likely with this card reversed.

Two of Swords

General meaning

A blindfolded woman is perched on a grey stone seat, with a sword in each hand. Her hands are folded across her chest with the two swords extended diagonally. Calm waters (representing emotions) separate her from the rolling hills in the background, and a crescent moon shines overhead. The yellow of the moon matches her slippers, representing intellect and imagination. Each of the swords represents an alternative and she dispassionately weighs up her choices. As a reader, you can request that the client select two extra cards to go on each side of this two. Each additional card relates to one choice or sword.

Reversed

When this two is reversed the water on the card appears above the swords, suggesting that emotions are clouding your thoughts at this time, making decisions more difficult. Perhaps it is time to examine one at a time those attitudes or concepts which have been avoided. By clarifying each unfaced issue, you are free to return to the upright Ace of Swords so you can arrive at one clear, viable alternative.

The reversed Two of Swords suggests that there is really only one viable option available to you now, so it is necessary to choose it realising also that emotions and logic were involved in the decision-making process.

Finances

A choice between two alternatives. The Two of Swords indicates a time to weigh up your financial choices mentally before considering your feelings on the matter. You may have limited vision of the consequences of your choices at this point. Perhaps you are considering two job opportunities, one of which is in another city. You are deciding without an overall view of your circumstances or the consequences of your final choice.

Reversed

Two or more choices now, none of which is outstanding or appealing. Perhaps the act of hedging your bets has left you scattered in your financial focus. It is necessary to release one alternative in order to pursue the other. A return to the upright Ace offers you the chance to use your mind to cut through the hopes and fears surrounding each choice so that you make the best decision for long-term financial rewards.

Health

The Two of Swords indicates you are retreating from life in order to reflect upon your health. Perhaps you are considering your options, or contemplating how your thinking might be affecting your physical health. The crescent moon appearing on the card indicates that dreams at night may offer you solutions or viable alternatives. It also confirms low reserves of physical energy at this time.

Reversed

The Two of Swords reversed suggests you are struggling with unappealing choices regarding your health. It may be time to return to the upright Ace in order to clarify your health plans. Unresolved emotional decisions may be draining your health.

Three of Swords

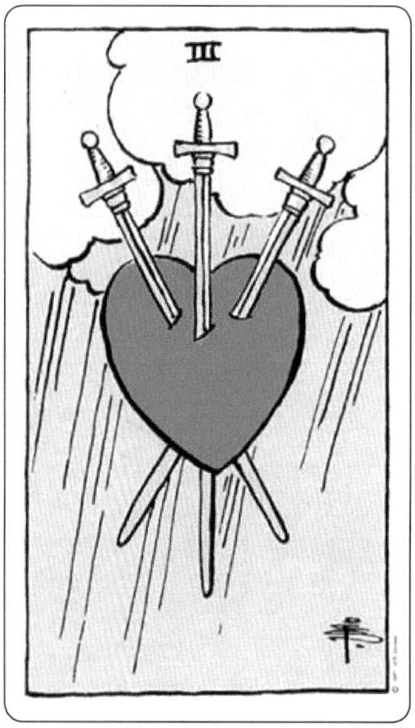

General meaning

Three swords pierce a heart as a storm rages in the background. It is said that into every life a little rain must fall. This card describes one of life's emotional storms, revealing pain, loss, grief and despair. Although the causes may vary widely, the feelings are universal. From the small child who has lost her favourite toy rabbit to the businessman who has lost control over his financial empire, despair descends upon us all at one time or another. For some these visits are fleeting, while for others despair is present for prolonged periods.

The three swords are at conflicting angles, indicating that no sense can be made of circumstances at this time. It can be tempting to ask why when experiencing such deep, searing pain, but answers usually prove elusive when the Three of Swords appears. Instead it may benefit you to still your mind and allow the pain to sweep through you and subside. Although minutes may feel like hours while you are in the eye of the emotional storm, this pain will pass. Then is the time to search for the causes of the recent distress.

Reversed

The reversed Three of Swords points to suppressed pain, resulting in fears and phobias or chronic depression. To regain a sense of vitality, past pain must be examined and released now. Surrendering to this pain may seem impossible, but it can allow the pain to pass through you and dissipate.

Past circumstances required that you get back on your feet to survive but, in doing so, you have had to suppress your grief and pain. It still awaits you. Take time soon to let these feelings sweep through you, as this will allow you finally to experience deep peace again. It may be necessary to return to the upright Two of Swords in order to choose a suitable path back to a more rewarding life.

Finances

In a financial question this three can mean serious financial loss or disappointment. Perhaps you have not received the promotion you feel you deserved, or you have been unexpectedly made redundant. This card described the sense of loss Silvia felt when a house she wanted was sold to another buyer. To Silvia, this home represented the life she had dreamed of living. Losing this property meant that she was losing her chance at the life she desired. Silvia would find another house, however, the Three of Swords in her layout signified real grief resulting from a disappointment.

Reversed

The reversed Three of Swords indicates that past financial disappointment haunts you still. This pain or lingering sense of discontent may serve to sharpen your awareness of the consequences when making current decisions, or it may cloud your thinking leaving you feeling less hopeful about financial possibilities. Determine if the current situation is a repeat of a previous set of circumstances before proceeding.

Health

Grief and pain that affect your physical and emotional health are signified by the Three of Swords. This level of grief can cause sleep problems, reduce your appetite and impair your judgement. This card represents depression as a reaction to recent loss or current circumstances.

In physical terms, this three can represent heart problems such as angina or heart disease, but more often it signifies deep emotional pain affecting your physical body.

Reversed

Unresolved past emotional pain may be adversely affecting health now. Perhaps the loss of a partner, a parent or close friends has left you depressed or less optimistic about life. General health areas for this card include the heart and chronic depression.

Four of Swords

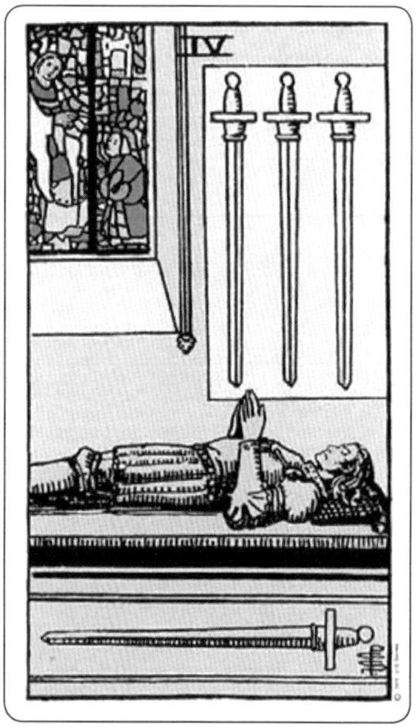

General meaning

In the privacy of a church a man lies in quiet repose. The yellow colouring suggests an active mind despite outward appearances of languidness. The only vivid colours in this card appear in the stained glass windows, which are specifically designed to evoke noble or spiritual thoughts within the congregation.

This is a card for reflecting on past actions and future plans. It illustrates mental consolidation: the act of making sense of past actions and eliminating those thoughts and beliefs which have proved inaccurate or destructive. In this way it is possible to use past experience for future success. After the pain of the Three of Swords comes a deeper understanding of yourself and of life.

Reversed

A return to the upright Three of Swords offers an opportunity to grow through surrendering to pain or grief, allowing it to dissipate and subside. While the desire expressed by the upright Four of Swords is for consolidation of thinking, the emotional urge is to act now without careful plans. Perhaps an opportunity has arisen that requires an immediate decision or action. It is also possible that the need for continual action masks a deeper grief stemming from past loss or disappointment.

If learning is a combination of action and reflection, the reversed Four of Swords shows the action part of this equation, while the upright card describes the reflection. Thought is still apparent when this card is reversed, as the colour yellow now appears across the top of the card, however, this thought may lack some of the contemplative qualities shown by the colourful leadlight in the upright card. The man is falling away from the coffin when the card is reversed, suggesting that past losses or deaths are less significant now.

Finances

It is time to reflect on past financial endeavours, in order to recognise which future opportunities are sound and which are merely ephemeral. Perhaps your endeavours have not yet led you to the financial success you desire. It is time to examine your thinking, your past actions and your beliefs about success.

Reversed

You may be feeling restless now, hoping that bigger risks might lead to greater rewards. You recognise what hasn't worked effectively for you in the past and you are eager to try new approaches. This attitude might lead you back to the upright Three of Swords, with the accompanying pain or loss. This pain is likely to be a powerful teacher.

Health

The upright Four of Swords heralds ill health, a period of recuperation after an illness or an operation. Life has forced you to lay down and reflect upon your chosen path. This offers a last chance to change direction before you realise at a later date that it is now too late to change course. Sometimes this card signifies a period of low physical energy.

Reversed

This card reversed can suggest the desire to avoid reflection by taking hasty action. Although your actions might distract you from past hurts, they may also bring you back to the upright Three of Swords and new pain. Sometimes the reversed Four of Swords simply means a return to activity after a period of reflection or ill health as replenished physical energy stirs a desire to become more involved in life.

Five of Swords

General meaning

A man stands in the foreground clasping three swords. Two opponents walk away, nursing their wounds. The existence of five swords suggests that there were originally five combatants. The person clad in red, orange and green has won the battle but not necessarily the war.

This card describes arguments, disagreements or clashes with those around you. Jagged cloud formations mirror the tension below as five different beliefs (swords) meet in difficult circumstances. It can also describe inner chaos, confusion and scattered mental energy. Perhaps you are struggling with different needs or opposing desires within. It can also describe a forceful attempt to have those around you agree with your point of view. The Five of Swords appeared in Ted's layout when he came to find out why his staff were leaving. Ted had purchased a major share of an accountancy practice. The Five revealed that he had attempted to force those around him to change the direction of the practice, which was why the staff were departing to more harmonious working environments.

Reversed

The reversed Five of Swords reveals that there have been initial arguments or disagreements and that those have passed, leaving room for negotiation. Those involved realise that they have to continue to live or work with each other, despite having said and heard statements which cannot be retracted. A workable compromise is possible now, with those involved agreeing to disagree on certain subjects.

Finances

There are arguments, disagreements and bitterness over financial matters when this card appears here. As the outcome to a business venture, it is unlikely that those involved will be speaking to each other in a civil manner after the venture is completed. Blame, recriminations and resentment are the probable outcome if you insist on pursuing your intended course of action without taking into consideration the viewpoints of others who are involved.

Reversed

The Five of Swords reversed indicates a period of tension which can be overcome if handled with tact and mental agility. As an outcome to a financial question, you are likely to feel disinclined to repeat your actions as this is not a card signifying financial rewards. A return to the upright Four of Swords may give you an opportunity to reflect on your decisions to determine the real value of the confrontations described in the Five.

Health

Stress due to unresolved issues with others is represented by this card. It can also suggest that your health will remain unbalanced until you resolve your differences with those around you or leave those people behind.

Reversed

The Five of Swords describes a return to a more restful state after reaching inner or outer resolution. It suggests that it may be time to revisit the upright Four of Swords to reflect upon your life. It can sometimes signify a return to the Four and to a period of ill health that will enforce a period of reflection.

Six of Swords

General meaning

A man guides a water taxi from turbulent waters towards the stillness ahead. A mother and child are huddled together in the boat, surrounded by six downward pointing swords. Cloudy skies reflect their feelings, as this scene emphasises the act of moving from troubled times to more peaceful circumstances.

The six swords are the shared beliefs about the life of these people, as they struggle to understand what is real and what is the result of negative thought and behaviour patterns. The Six of Swords describes the act of moving from old beliefs about life towards a new understanding of yourself, your life and life's possibilities. This can represent the process of moving away from blaming others for your circumstances to taking responsibility for where you want to go in life.

Reversed

When reversed, this six suggests quarrels and disagreements within yourself and others in an attempt to break free of old patterns. It shows someone attempting to steer themselves (the vessel) away from old behaviour patterns and beliefs but instead effectively moving towards those beliefs. Change can only be achieved by thinking about patterns of behaviour and understanding your part in current circumstances. You may feel inclined to speak out, however this energy needs to be channelled into thinking about what you are responsible for and what you can change. When the six is reversed, the water is at the top of the card, suggesting you may be emotionally charged about your beliefs.

Finances

The upright Six of Swords suggests a time of rest after a period of upheaval. Perhaps you can repay debts and save towards your goals when the Six appears in a financial layout. It can also signify a realisation of how your actions have led you to current financial circumstances. It offers a chance to allow financial matters to settle down, providing you time to reflect on your actions and their results. Beliefs about money are slowly changing now. An overseas job may be offered now or overseas travel related to work as the boat in the six carries its passengers over water.

Reversed

This six reversed describes more financial chaos and strife ahead. A return to the Five of Swords may take the form of arguments with creditors or with those around you. It may be time to use the swords' ability to analyse issues to plan a way out of the current strife. Emotions are clouding your thinking when the reversed Six appears. If you can detach emotionally from current circumstances you may find it easier to make effective decisions.

Health

After a period of stress, the upright Six heralds a time of healing and a chance to think about yourself and your life direction. It is time to consider if you have formed debilitating habits such as worrying or stressing over unimportant issues or problems over which you have no control. It may be time to ask yourself the following question: 'In 100 years from now, how important will this be?'

Reversed

The reversed Six of Swords indicates that increased stress and tension are evident now, and it may be necessary to find ways to rise above it all through meditation, prayer or practising detachment. Mental stress relayed into your physical body can result in poor health. Beliefs about yourself and life generally are negatively affecting your health, so examine your thinking.

Seven of Swords

General meaning

This card shows a person stealing away from a military camp with five swords. It is not clear if this is an opportunistic theft or if he is increasing his chances of surviving another day by plundering his enemy's arsenal. The use of stealth, lateral thinking and the nerve to oppose a formidable adversary suggests that he is not giving up.

This is a card for utilising your strengths in order to achieve your objectives. Through careful planning (Swords) and not giving up (the sevens) you are able to achieve more. The mind offers solutions that may require less strenuous effort than you are currently devoting to an important issue.

Reversed

Holding on to old methods and attitudes is preventing your progress. A refusal to be adaptable may result in a return to the upright Six of Swords and to a period of reflection. During this you may discover alternative approaches to circumstances. In a relationship layout, the reversed Seven of Swords can describe two people avoiding addressing the real issues. By tiptoeing around their problems they extend the peace encountered in the upright Six of Swords, but this tact can soon lead to dishonesty or a lack of positive communication.

Some words and ideas (swords) may cut into you now, just as your harsh words have cut deeply into others in the past. Perhaps self-criticism prevents you from revealing yourself to others. A return to the upright Six will distance you from the situations that may have caused your pain so that you can gather your thoughts and determine a better approach if circumstances are repeated.

Finances

The Seven of Swords heralds a time to be adaptable in order to achieve your financial goals. It can also suggest theft or deceit around finances. As an answer to a question about financial investments, this seven suggests that you need to examine the investment more closely before committing any money.

Reversed

Reversed, the Seven of Cups can suggest that fear of deceit is restricting your financial development. Perhaps you have made a small fortune from real estate investments and now it is time to put some of that money into the stock market. With the reversed Seven in the layout you may be clinging to the tried and trusted methods instead of investigating other alternatives. Perhaps it is time to educate yourself about viable financial opportunities before making any decisions.

Health

It is time to examine alternative ways to improve or to maintain your health. Perhaps a yoga class or a regular remedial massage will help you to reduce stress, or a natural therapist may offer you a solution to a chronic health issue. This was the case with Kevin when, after several years of using lotions to control the symptoms of psoriasis, he read about the possible side effects of their prolonged use. The Seven of Cups revealed that Kevin was torn between his need to have smooth, healthy-looking skin, and his desire to live a long and healthy life. He looked for an alternative and consulted a herbalist who ignored his symptoms and sought out the possible causes of his psoriasis. Within a year of taking this new approach, Kevin had few skin issues as his psoriasis had become a rare occurrence.

Reversed

The reversed Seven of Swords suggests that you may be resisting viable health alternatives for a chronic condition. It is time to learn about other possible treatments, if only to allow yourself some choices. Holding on to old methods may be restricting your health and limiting your vitality. Asking others how they might deal with your current circumstances can allow you to perceive the situation in a new light.

Eight of Swords

General meaning

Surrounded by downward pointing swords, a woman stands bound and blindfolded. Grey skies reflect her inner world and her limited perception. A castle is visible on a distant hill.

The eights are cards of strength, and for the woman in the Eight of Swords this strength lies in her ability to listen to her inner voice. Prevented by the blindfold from judging through sight and limited in her ability to walk away from her circumstances, she appears to be powerless. Those who live in the nearby castle see clearly and keep her restricted to serve their purposes.

What at first appears to be a hindrance is in fact a help. That which hinders this woman's ability to make decisions about herself and her surroundings enables her to go within to listen to her inner voice and to heed its directives. It is time to heed your higher self now if you want to make effective decisions.

Reversed

When reversed the Eight of Swords represents a need to return to the Seven of Swords in order to be adaptable in your search for solutions. Perhaps you are 'playing the game' with those around you, telling them what they want to hear while secretly doing what you want to do. The reversed Eight may be the stirring of your intuition and the opening of your eyes. You may be ready to challenge those beliefs you were taught to value, as Riba was when the reversed Eight appeared in her reading. Riba's desire for material possessions had kept her on a treadmill for 40 years. She finally decided to step away from the constraints of her friends, her family's expectations and her superficial lifestyle. She resigned from her job, sold her house and moved to the country. It was a decision that has brought her a new lifestyle, friends and rewarding opportunities.

Finances

Money is tight when this eight is selected for a financial layout. Perhaps you have lost your job or your expenses are rising against a static income. It is time to still your mind and heed your inner voice or intuition. This can be almost impossible when you are faced with continual financial stress or debt collectors, but it is necessary nevertheless.

Reversed

You are returning to the upright Seven in order to find solutions when the reversed Eight is chosen. You may find yourself avoiding people calling for payments. It may be time to shave some of your expenses or design a payment plan which satisfies your creditors. Look within (away from the restrictions and distractions of financial debt) and find a suitable long-term solution. When reversed the Eight can suggest that the worst is over now.

Health

In a health reading the Eight of Swords represents asthma, chest complaints and depression. It is natural to become depressed when faced with few alternatives and mounting pressures. You may feel restricted by circumstances now, but inner strength and peace can be found through meditation or techniques which quieten the mind enabling you to heed your intuition.

Reversed

The reversed Eight of Swords indicates that you have passed the lowest point with your health and improvements are likely. It is time to return to the upright Seven in order to find new solutions or improved ways to approach your health and wellbeing. Being open-minded about possible health alternatives is important.

Nine of Swords

General meaning

In the Nine of Swords, a person is sitting up in the dark, unable to sleep due to worries and fears. She mentally searches for solutions to her current dilemmas but her racing mind prevents her from resting for the day ahead. Her concerns are real, the alternatives plenty and yet the viable solutions are few indeed. She covers her face in anguish.

Rational thought may not provide the right solution now, so she may be better off falling asleep and recalling solutions offered through her dreams. This is a card that signifies strong dreams at night, broken sleep and continual worries and concerns.

Reversed

The reversed Nine of Swords suggests a stronger connection to your dreams, often resulting in more clarity in choosing a workable solution to your concerns. Powerful dreams at night are more likely to be remembered now, as the link between the conscious and subconscious mind is strong.

Returning to the upright Eight of Swords may enable a retreat from worldly worries to contact that part of you which already knows the perfect solution to your current problems. Contacting your higher (or spiritual) self through meditation, contemplation or through dreams may enable you to ease your worries and find a suitable path to your goals.

Finances

Fear and worry over financial matters is suggested by this card. You may be rightly concerned about your ability to repay your debts and sleepless nights are exacerbating the situation. Make a list of your debts and your anticipated income. Then list ways to increase your income or decrease your expenses to rebalance your financial situation.

Reversed

You may find viable solutions through dreams so be prepared to act on the information you are receiving during your sleep. A return to the upright Eight of Swords may help you to understand the necessity of disciplining your spending. Poor sleeping patterns may result from financial stress when the reversed Nine appears in a layout for a financial question.

Health

Broken sleep or inability to fall asleep easily due to difficulty releasing your daily concerns are signified by the upright Nine of Swords, all of which affect health. Headaches, neck difficulties and upper back problems (those areas on the card where the swords penetrate the body) are other possible health concerns now.

Reversed

You may be finding it easier to fall asleep now after a period of restless, broken sleep. Contemplating the message in the upright Eight of Swords may remind you that it is okay to sleep and forget your concerns at night in order to approach the new day refreshed. The reversed Nine of Swords in a health question can signify improved sleep patterns after a period of stress.

Ten of Swords

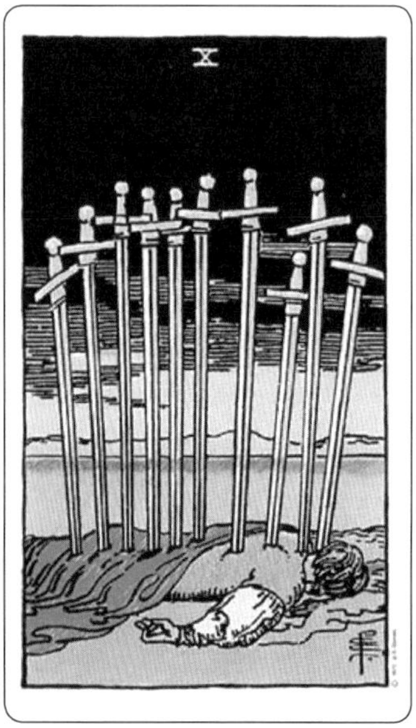

General meaning

A man lies face down on the ground with ten swords in his back. At this point he is no longer counting the swords for he is already at his lowest point, being firmly staked to the ground. His beliefs about life have him cornered now, and yet these beliefs are not readily visible. He may be able to determine his beliefs or better understand himself by examining the circumstances, which led to his predicament.

The night is beginning to disappear, as dawn approaches, indictating that from this low point life will improve. Some readers prefer to gloss over this card, put off by its gruesome image but this is unfair to the client. If the client has reached the lowest point in a situation they deserve to know this. If the worst is yet to come, the client may need to be forewarned so that they may prepare for the winter ahead. Winter eventually gives way to spring and it is important to tell the client how and when they can expect spring to arrive.

This ten can represent a loss of a job, the ending of a love relationship or suddenly feeling overwhelmed by life. You can expect to feel confused and exhausted mentally and physically. Although this is undoubtedly a difficult time, the good news is that it will pass.

Reversed

The Ten of Swords reversed offers a chance to return to the upright Nine of Swords in order to heed your intuition through your dreams. It suggests that the worst is over now, but that you need to stand up and shake off those old beliefs (swords) before you can proceed.

The reversed Ten suggests that you are being restricted by your thinking. The difficult times are behind you now, yet you still cling to your fears and outmoded life attitudes. Sometimes the reversed Ten describes the act of suppressing your fears during the day, only to have to face them in dreams when you return to the upright Nine of Swords at night. This pressure is not altogether negative. It may serve to force you to clarify your thinking and update old negative beliefs.

Finances

The upright Ten in a financial layout suggests financial ruin or at least the collapse of a situation. When Akmed was about to file for bankruptcy he came for a reading. Despite 17 years as a successful small trader, Akmed's family grocery business was forced to close after a large shopping centre opened nearby. He had struggled to make ends meet for 12 months before closing his doors burdened with debt. The upright Ten in the answer position suggested that Akmed was at his lowest point. The appearance of the Three of Pentacles in the outcome position suggested that new financial opportunities awaited Akmed in the future. If the Ten of Swords appears in the outcome position, select an extra card, which you place beside the Ten. This additional card is often a more positive one, offering you hope and reminding you that this winter won't last forever.

Reversed

The Ten of Swords suggests that the worst is over now and that finances will improve once you shake off your old beliefs and make plans to deal with your financial obligations. It may take some time to repay debts and to re-establish yourself financially. It is important to use this time to prepare yourself mentally for the financial challenges ahead. Sometimes the reversed Ten can describe poor health restricting your ability to earn a living.

Health

The Ten of Swords represents the lowest point in a situation, and in a health reading it can suggest death, but only in combination with a minimum of three other cards (Death, the Tower, Three of Swords, the World, Judgement, the Six of Swords and the blank card). Usually it describes reaching a point of exhaustion or a collapse before you give your health the attention it deserves.

Back and neck pain are shown with the appearance of this ten in a health layout, along with headaches and exhaustion. It is time to plan how you intend rebuilding and maintaining your health for the future.

Reversed

Having come through a difficult time with your health and energy levels, you need to return to the upright Nine of Swords to heed your intuition through dreams. Perhaps your dreams are urging you to change your life, or it is possible that you suffer with insomnia. The lack of vitality arising from poor sleep may result in long-term exhaustion.

Page of Swords

General meaning

This quick-minded young person enjoys words, ideas, new concepts and the pairing of ideas that don't belong together. Bizarre stories and conversations appeal, along with books, films and telephone conversations. Even as small children, Swords Pages don't cling to parents when a babysitter arrives. They are usually too curious about the new person to be shy. They may experience difficulty with early schooling, as their minds wander and they have low boredom thresholds.

Reversed

When negative this page can experience a constant desire to talk, driving those around them crazy. They easily become scattered mentally and possess a short attention span. This page can whinge when negative, understanding that the squeaky wheel gets the oil. The attention span improves if this young person is encouraged to exercise more. To quote a Queen of Wands to her 14-year-old Page, 'If your feet got as much exercise as your mouth, you'd be an Olympic marathon runner'.

When opposed

This page tends to escape into his or her mind when frustrated by life. It becomes easier to imagine success than to achieve it. Instead of searching for a viable solution they daydream. In some cases a centred Page of Swords negotiates concessions, assistance and another chance at the desired goal. The gift for communication coupled with a rational mind allows this young person to search rapidly for new solutions when frustrated by circumstances. When arriving home late one night my ten-year-old son asked 'Can I watch a video?' 'Absolutely not,' I replied. 'The first half of a video then?' he countered, opening negotiations. I realised that if he were permitted to watch even ten minutes of a video this time, he would negotiate 20 minutes next time. Eventually I would be up all night with him, as he forced me to keep promises made without regard to their consequences.

Knight of Swords

General meaning

He is enthusiastic, quick-minded and restless. This is a young man who knows how to 'seize the day'. His mind is constantly searching for new opportunities, fresh pathways and innovative ideas. He is capable of taking several unrelated concepts and combining them to form something new. He is usually talkative, curious, animated and keen to understand more of life. He asserts that the way to a woman's heart is through her ear, and he is keen to practise an imaginative turn of phrase.

Reversed

When negative the Knight of Swords has yet to learn that words have power. He recklessly throws around ideas and concepts without fully comprehending their significance. He may promise something one day and then abandon his promise the next. Whimsical, erratic and capricious aptly describes this reversed knight. He is unreliable, unpunctual and likely to forget previous commitments when swept up in current circumstances. Easily diverted from his train of thought or his short-term purpose, he does not yet realise that words do not make deeds. He doesn't yet understand that an idea is worthless until it is applied in a tangible manner.

When opposed

The young Knight of Swords may turn in a completely new direction, or launch into a verbal tirade at those who thwart his plans. This knight is quick to explain away his responsibility when situations fall apart, that is in those rare cases where he waits around long enough for issues of blame to arise. He is fleet of foot when affairs go wrong, leaving others to take the blame as he pursues his next urgent opportunity.

Queen of Swords

General meaning

The Queen of Swords is articulate, quick-minded and organised. Armed with a pen, paper and a telephone she can arrange anything from a wedding to a funeral in less than an afternoon. She loves reading, studying and usually excels in any career where she can use her mind and her organisational skills. She is the person to ask when you need a discount on a car or a good lawyer, as she will know most people in her community. As a researcher, investigator or small business manager, she ensures that life is smooth yet always interesting. The butterflies in her crown signify the mind's ability to transform our understanding of life. Her perfectly straight upwardly pointing sword reveals her to be the most perceptive member of the swords suit. The tassle on her left hand is a reminder of the restrictions she encountered in the Eight of Swords.

Reversed

When negative the Queen of Swords can be self-critical, mentally scattered and a perfectionist. Instead of using her powerful mind for learning, she turns it against herself, inwardly criticising her best efforts. She loves gossip and often displays a limited attention span. She can be talkative without any purpose to her conversation. Being a Queeen (the watery part of air), when positive she is a deep river, winding silently to the sea. When negative she is a stream, noisily splashing over rocks and pebbles.

When opposed

When the Queen of Swords is opposed in her plans she can be verbally critical or she will write a stinging letter of complaint. When dealing with those who know her she will raise one eyebrow to signal her disbelief or disgust at the situation. Sometimes she will carefully plan another route to her goals while pretending that she has abandoned them.

When frustrated by circumstances this queen can become sharp-tongued and precise in her argument. It is difficult to win an argument with her because she quickly seeks out and exploits any weaknesses in your position. Frustrated by more than 1500 changes required to a manuscript I fired off a critical letter to my editor one afternoon, demanding to know why so many changes were required so late in the editing process. My letter was faxed back to me, edited. The Queen of Swords had changed the spelling of a word, queried a few terms and pointed out that I had ended a sentence with a preposition. I was suitably chastised while she remained calm and composed.

King of Swords

General meaning

The King of Swords is a quick-minded, analytical, facts-oriented man. He possesses an inquiring mind, is curious and can usually express himself verbally with ease. Because his mind is capable of collecting, storing and recalling a wide variety of facts, he is suited to a career which uses his mind or his communication skills rather than his hands. He is quick with a story or to ask questions and his curiosity overcomes shyness.

Reversed

The words flow as easily when the King of Swords appears reversed in a layout, only they are not necessarily based on facts. The King convincingly makes verbal commitments he has no intention of honouring and, in the mood of the moment, he actually believes what he is saying. Although he knows what to say to make the right impression, he doesn't realise that promises without delivery can cause great pain. When negative he can become mentally scattered, undertaking too many projects at once.

The reversed King of Swords has the limited maturity of the Knight, and completing projects undertaken in the mood of the moment can prove difficult, sometimes impossible. When new opportunities beckon, he is reluctant to persevere with those tasks at hand.

The reversed King of Swords is reluctant to make a lasting commitment to a love relationship, afraid that he might miss a better opportunity.

When opposed

The King of Swords is likely to become sarcastic and sharp-tongued when thwarted. He asks pointed questions or writes furious letters of complaint. His words become his sword as he slashes away at yielding, often unprepared opponents. When frustrated, the positive type negotiates a new path to his goals or seeks a solution mentally. The positive King is quick to seek new solutions or an alternative path to his desired goal if thwarted.

The negative King of Swords is quick to rationalise away his guilt or his responsibilities and to justify his actions. He is a convincing speaker and effective in securing your commitment while not making any commitments himself.

Chapter 7

THE SUIT OF PENTACLES

These 14 cards ranging from the Ace to the King, show a path to understanding through practicality and taking care of the physical needs in life. Pentacles people are usually practical, hard-working, conservative, resistant to change and they thrive on routine.

A pentacle is a five-pointed star contained within a circle. The five points of the upward star represent the head, the hands (on outstretched arms) and the feet (standing with legs apart). The circle which surrounds the five points of the body (star) contains the energy of a person. The upright star suggests that the mind governs the passions and desires. In this way the hands and feet coordinate to fulfil the plans in your mind. It is through doing something practical that a plan becomes a tangible product or a visible, measurable outcome.

When a pentacle card is reversed the feet are above the head. The reversed pentacle indicates that desires govern your head. This can translate into financial poverty if you allow your desire for material possessions to drain you financially. When the pentacle is upright, your rational mind can assist you in deciding whether you need a new car or to pay outstanding bills, whereas when it is reversed your desire for new possessions outweighs your current financial obligations or long-term financial goals.

Pentacles people understand that lasting success takes time to achieve. They are usually prepared to make prolonged efforts to accomplish their long-term goals. Reputation is important to people of this suit, making them reluctant to do anything spontaneous which might threaten their good name. Being consistent planners, Pentacles people recognise at an early age that with the right effort and careful planning they can ease the journey through life. Money is the most obvious way to make the journey comfortable so they pursue money with tenacity. Money equals choices for Pentacles people, and the more money they have, the more choices they have in life.

While Wands people make choices without the necessary financial backing, Pentacles people do not like to commence a project without having an achievable ending in mind. Stability is essential for these people, and inner peace comes from having sound financial investments, low debt and money set aside for emergencies. Sometimes even in emergencies, Pentacles people are reluctant to reach for the 'emergency fund' as having it offers them peace of mind.

Suited to careers in business, real estate, farming, banking and finance, Pentacles people thrive on a solid career structure. In astrology, the Pentacles are the earth signs Taurus, Virgo and Capricorn, however this suit describes the nature of a person more than their astrological sign.

When negative, Pentacles people control others by controlling the money. They may be the chief breadwinner in a relationship who uses their income to control their partner or children. Sometimes negative Pentacles people who lack self-worth live in poverty. This is very difficult for people of this suit, as they are prepared to work hard to secure a comfortable lifestyle. While Cups and Wands people can overlook financial restrictions, those of the Pentacles suit feel constantly frustrated by inadequate financial circumstances.

Seeking routine for a sense of continuity, negative Pentacles people can release a love relationship, a family or their children before they will surrender their work routines. When offered a choice between career or relationship, they will usually choose career without hesitation or regret.

Ace of Pentacles

General meaning

The Pentacles Ace shows the beginning of a new venture which is well-financed and often one which has been methodically planned. This ace shows the calm, deliberate pacing which stems from the realisation that the venture is more likely to be a marathon than a sprint. In general terms this ace suggests that you are well-funded for the journey ahead.

Reversed

Money is disappearing as you display an inability to grasp it firmly. Perhaps your expenses are temporarily greater than your income, or this may be an example of poor spending habits. Career or financial opportunities slip through your fingers when this Ace appears reversed.

Finances

The Pentacles Ace offers a most promising beginning to a business venture, suggesting that the necessary funds are available to carry you through those first few months until the project is self-sufficient. Pentacles cards suggest that you will begin as you intend to finish: carefully, methodically and at a comfortable pace. As an answer to a question about a financial investment, this ace usually confirms financial success (depending on the surrounding cards).

Reversed

The Ace of Pentacles reversed heralds delays with beginning a new venture, probably due to financial constraints. It can highlight financial difficulties, the loss of a job or a source of income. As the answer to a question about an investment, it suggests financial loss.

Health

The Ace of Pentacles indicates that you have a practical approach to your health. It suggests that you have a moderate approach to life and as a result you enjoy good health. This is a time when you have the financial resources to improve and to maintain your health. It also suggests a balanced, relatively ordered life, allowing for stable health. It can also describe investing in maintaining your health, such as joining a gym, a walking group or consulting a natural therapist.

Reversed

The Ace of Pentacles reversed suggests that financial worries are underlying your current health issues. Alternatively the reversed Ace can indicate that present health concerns are the result of how you earn your income. This ace appeared reversed when Colin, a removalist, had dislocated a vertebrae when lifting a sideboard onto a truck. As a result Colin had two weeks without his usual income.

Two of Pentacles

General meaning

A man carries two large golden pentacles, carefully contemplating one. An infinity symbol surrounds these pentacles, suggesting that they circulate constantly. Two boats sail turbulent seas behind the man, serving as a reminder that, like the tides, money comes and goes. The person is clad in red and orange, passionate earthy colours. These colours suggest that he is grounded in the physical world and focused on his money. His green shoes match the green of the infinity symbol, suggesting that his money flows in and out according to where his feet take him. This indicates that certain locations will benefit him whereas other places may cost him dearly. For example, in a nearby strip of shops on a six-lane highway, the turnover of businesses is constant, partly because passing customers have nowhere to park. When driving past these shops, even if you wanted to turn around and grab a bargain it is impossible to turn for five kilometres. In ten years 20 businesses have opened and closed in those four shops.

Reversed

Inability to determine which of two opportunities offers the most practical rewards is shown when the Two of Pentacles appears reversed. It is time to return to the upright Ace in order to pursue one clear path (opportunity) to fruition. The reversed Two indicates a financial decision or the need to juggle finances in order to make ends meet. Perhaps your desires are stronger than your mental discipline, and this is costing you financially.

Finances

The Two of Pentacles shows a man focused on his finances. He has decisions to make but there is no great financial pressure on him at this point. It is a case of deciding which bills to pay first. Because the boats on the card are both seen on the crests of waves, it suggests that this is a time of surplus income, some of which might be carefully invested or set aside for the inevitable approaching winter.

Reversed

The Two reversed suggests that winter has set in; you need to reduce your expenses in order to make ends meet. This is a time to decide which bills to pay now and which can wait. It is also a time to decide on ways to reduce your outgoings in the future. It offers a return to the upright Ace of Pentacles in order to improve your focus on your income. Perhaps it is time to write up a clear budget and to stick to it tenaciously.

Health

Financial decisions around health are shown with the upright Two of Pentacles. Perhaps you are deciding to invest in your health through a gym membership, improved health benefits cover or a series of visits to the dentist. It may describe the act of deciding when to take time away from work to have an operation. Weighing the balance of work and health can be shown by this card.

Reversed

The reversed Two of Pentacles suggests that your work or the pursuit of money might be adversely affecting your health. Perhaps you have two jobs and it is time to return to the upright Ace in order to pursue one job more effectively. You may be deciding how much you can afford to spend on your health, juggling current expenses against a costly surgical procedure. It can describe poor health that is restricting your ability to earn an income.

Three of Pentacles

General meaning

A tradesman, an architect and a clergyman are gathered together as the tradesman makes alterations to a church. The architect and the clergyman discuss the plans. Three pentacles appear in the edifice above them. This card represents the act of transforming plans into concrete results. Something solid and tangible develops as a result of careful plans and physical effort. The Three of Pentacles represents a solid foundation for spiritual worship but this can be translated to any other area, according to the question asked. It can signify study through courses or on-the-job training. It can also describe a love relationship which has solid footing for long-term success.

Reversed

The Three of Pentacles reversed suggests a lack of success due to poor foundations. More study or experience may be required to ensure the best outcome. Repetitive patterns are emerging which hamper success, and it is time for you to ask what you need to learn from current circumstances to avoid repeating past negative patterns.

The reversed Three can describe abandoning a course or training without thought of the consequences. A return to the upright Two of Pentacles offers the chance to decide on one clear worthwhile course of action. You can then pursue this course of action to its conclusion.

Finances

Solid foundations are in place for long-term financial success. Perhaps study or direct experience helps to ensure that your plans can progress smoothly. A solid structure or organisation exists to support you with your financial plans now. This is a card of growth, progress and success in financial ventures.

Reversed

Success is impaired by weak foundations. Perhaps you don't have sufficient experience or knowledge to make your plans real at this point. A return to the Two of Pentacles is necessary to decide where to invest your time, effort and money wisely.

Repetitive patterns emerge, causing you to fail in a manner you have failed previously. Perhaps your new job brings out the same issues as the last job, or a business venture fails due to shaky foundations. Vanessa started a business without any real idea of how to generate sales. The reversed Three of Pentacles in her reading suggests she was headed for trouble. When questioned she revealed she had no business plan and assumed customers would just appear. Despite her strong desire to work for herself, Vanessa had few practical ideas of the way in which a business must work to survive. Two months later she closed her business and now contracts to a large organisation. She plans to begin again, and the upright Three suggests that she is currently studying small business management.

Health

The upright card represents balanced wellbeing due to healthy patterns of behaviour. With a balance of the fire (the tradesman), water (the clergyman) air (the architect) and earth (the building) good health results. Perhaps you have positive health patterns learned in childhood which will contribute to your sound health in the future.

The Three of Pentacles describes a patient, methodical approach to health, as Pentacles people usually enjoy life in moderation. The Pentacles approach is to remember that you are growing older and will have to live later with the health decisions you are making now. The upright Three suggests that you have a solid health foundation. It can also represent a course of study or learning which is health related.

Reversed

The Three of Pentacles reversed can suggest that bad patterns of behaviour are undermining your health. Perhaps the six spoons of sugar in your coffee and the four cigarettes before breakfast suggest you have formed some habits which don't contribute to good health. It may be time to return to the Two of Pentacles in order to decide where to put your energy and attention for best health results. Repetitive health problems are shown by the reversed Three.

Four of Pentacles

General meaning

A man sits on a grey stone seat clutching a golden pentacle. Two pentacles rest beneath his feet and another rests on top of his head. A crowded city is visible in the background yet he faces away from this, intent only on thoughts about money. The Four of Pentacles is a card for saving money, accumulating wealth and planning how to make money work for you. It shows an awareness that financial security is important, and that cities offer solid opportunities for improving financial circumstances.

Reversed

The reversed Four of Pentacles warns that money is being spent more readily than it is being accumulated now, and debt will result. It is the act of spending money freely and generously, without regard for maintaining your sources of income.

'The wages of sin is debt', declared a King of Pentacles recently. This card appears reversed when you are living on borrowed money, such as credit cards or an extended home loan that has been used to pay for a holiday. Be wary of allowing your outgoings to become greater than your income for extended periods if you plan to remain financially solvent.

Finances

The Four of Pentacles is a positive card financially, describing having sufficient income to feel secure, to fund new projects and to put some aside for retirement. As an answer to a financial question, this card suggests that you will end up with a solid financial return on an investment of money or time.

Reversed

The reversed Four of Pentacles indicates a venture which involves spiralling costs and limited income. With constant financial demands your resources may steadily dwindle, forcing you to return to the upright Three of Pentacles. This presents you with the opportunity to re-establish solid financial foundations for further growth and development. This opportunity might mean that you undertake more study in order to specialise and charge more for your time, or simply that you make a more practical financial plan.

Health

One of the cards for the sign of Taurus, the Four of Pentacles can indicate problems with the neck, throat and shoulders. In some cases it simply means that your work or your pursuit of financial freedom is affecting your health.

Reversed

The Four reversed represents generosity, but it can sometimes signify a lack of personal boundaries that leads to your being emotionally or psychically drained by others. It can also suggest that underlying your health concerns is a fear of financial loss. Perhaps you are unable to afford proper health insurance or ongoing health maintenance.

Five of Pentacles

General meaning

Despite the church window showing them a sanctuary, the man and woman in this card are cold, tired from ongoing struggles and isolated from each other and from life's bounty. The cold weather, his ill health and financial poverty conspire to force changes upon this couple for which they are ill-prepared.

The Five of Pentacles is a card of hunger, either spiritual or financial. You are burdened with life when this card appears in a spread. You might be unemployed and feel excluded from society, or it may signify the struggle to provide a basic living for yourself and your family.

Reversed

The personal winter is subsiding now as opportunities approach once more. This change heralds a return to the upright Four of Pentacles which provides opportunities to save money and to enjoy the physical comforts that material wealth can provide. It offers you the chance to live comfortably within your means.

After a period of financial hardship, money flows to you more freely now, offering you the chance to repay debts and save for a worthwhile goal. The fives represent change, and the reversed Five of Pentacles describes improvements in financial circumstances, offering more choices and an improved lifestyle.

Finances

The Five of Pentacles shows financial hardship, poverty or a severe financial loss. As an answer to a question about a business or a financial project, you are ill advised to pursue this direction. When James came for a reading he was considering taking a voluntary redundancy. He had been offered a partnership in a start-up company and felt that it was a good time to take the risk. He was comfortable in his present position and he asked if it was wise to stay on in the company for another two years. The answer was the Five of Pentacles, which suggested that leaving now was likely to be a change that he would not regret. He took the redundancy and three months later his previous company went into voluntary receivership. Many of those who still worked there lost their entitlements and their jobs.

Reversed

When reversed the Five of Pentacles suggests that the worst of a financial winter is behind you now, and that improvement in circumstances is likely. It sometimes suggests that you might be walking away from a business venture or an investment before it costs you more than you can afford.

Health

Poor health is shown by this card. Beyond the physical symptoms is often a spiritual and emotional emptiness that makes it more difficult to endure the physical health limitations. The Five of Pentacles can indicate that your health is affecting your ability to earn an income. Perhaps you are unemployed due to ill health.

Reversed

The worst of your ill health is behind you now. Support is likely to be forthcoming from those around you if you are open to receiving it. Feeding yourself emotionally and spiritually can help you to enjoy improved health when this five appears reversed in a health layout.

Six of Pentacles

General meaning

A wealthy man holds a set of scales in his left hand while with the right hand he drops some coins into the open hands of a person beneath him. The fact that those before him are beneath him signifies that he has control over this situation due to the control he has over his finances. The man standing understands that money equals choices. The better he is able to manage his financial affairs, the more choices he has in life.

This card can indicate that you are about to purchase a new home or a car, or that you are commencing a new job, as new sources of income or serious purchases are shown with this card upright. It is not clear whether the kneeling figures in the card are his employees or beggars. The scales indicate that he has weighed up the payment against the goods or services offered, or perhaps he has weighed up how much he can currently afford to give them. This six can describe securing start-up funds for a business venture. Financial stability exists now so with good financial management, success is likely.

Reversed

The reversed Six of Pentacles suggests disruption to a stable financial situation. Perhaps you have lost your job, a home loan has been declined or your overheads have increased beyond your income. It is time to return to the upright Five of Pentacles in order to reflect on the consequences of your income and spending patterns. The reversed Six suggests a loss of control over finances, the result being the experience of the hardship and poverty of the Five.

Finances

In a financial question, the upright Six of Pentacles indicates success. This could be from the sale of a home or a business, the securing of a new source of income or a new financial backer for your venture, or from success due to diligence in the handling of your financial affairs. Basically you are likely to have a reliable source of income and have your spending under control when this card appears upright.

Reversed

The Six reversed can indicate that you are leaving your job, selling a home or a car or simply that you are experiencing a period of financial constriction. At this point you may have less control over your income or your finances than usual. It can indicate that you feel trapped by your current financial obligations. This sometimes occurs when you purchase a new home before you settle into the routine of loan payments.

Health

The upright Six of Pentacles can indicate that you are spending money on your health. You may be investing in a gym membership or structuring your life and work to allow for improved health. Stable health is indicated by the upright Six in a health layout.

Reversed

The Six of Pentacles reversed can describe ill health that is restricting your earning ability. You may be unemployed for a period due to ill health, or stressed due to financial concerns. It can also highlight the need to examine how your job might be adversely affecting your health. In some cases the reversed Six indicates that you are presently unable to afford to maintain your health as you might prefer.

Seven of Pentacles

General meaning

A man stands patiently, resting on his staff before a money tree. The fruits of his labour are ripening before him as he ponders what he might do with them. He wears different coloured boots, suggesting that he is torn between the financial stability of the Six of Pentacles and the opportunities available in the Eight.

This is a card for allowing the efforts of your labours to bear fruit, such as an investment steadily growing, a good reputation widening among the business community which will lead to more customers, or simply the opportunity to take some time to reflect on your financial plans. The stability of the Six of Pentacles has given way to the expansion of the Seven as a larger investment of time, money or experience increases your worth more rapidly.

Reversed

You may need to return to the stability of the Six of Pentacles in order to ensure a strong financial structure is in place in your life before proceeding to the upright Seven again. When the Seven of Pentacles appears reversed in a layout it is most likely because you have not tended to your financial investments or stability (the money tree) and you need to return to the Six in order to be an employee (one of the beggars) until you learn how the wealthy man in the card became financially secure and independent.

In general terms the reversed Seven describes working too hard to have time to plan for financial independence. It may be necessary to simplify your life so that you have time to reflect on your financial and career plans. If you cannot step back from your work or your business, perhaps it is time to engage a consultant or someone with a fresh perspective to assist your progression towards the Ten of Pentacles.

Finances

Your efforts are about to bear fruit so don't give up yet. It is time to consider your financial options and to plan for stability and long-term success. The man in this card is not just contemplating his future, he is also keeping a close eye on his crop to ensure it receives sufficient water and nutrients. He recognises that success stems from continuous effort, not simply a good plan or a short burst of enthusiasm.

Reversed

The reversed Seven of Pentacles indicates that you may have left a job or closed a business at the point where people knew you for the work that you did. Having established a solid reputation, you abandoned your source of income to begin anew. You have effectively planted a crop and moved on before harvest day. This card can also describe closing a business to take a job or contract work with an employer.

Health

The Seven of Pentacles may indicate that you are considering spending some money on your health, or that you are thinking about how much money you will need to live comfortably in retirement. When the Seven of Pentacles came up in Simone's reading she was about to have a spinal operation that required a six-month recuperation period. She saved for the operations and planned it to coincide with a quiet period at work. She organised home delivery of videos and fine dark chocolate to make her rest period more comfortable.

Reversed

Your pursuit of financial stability may be adversely affecting your health. Perhaps it is time to simplify your life by returning to the upright Six of Pentacles to give yourself time to catch up financially. Then you can proceed to the upright Seven to think about your long-term health and financial issues.

Eight of Pentacles

General meaning

A man sits, hammer in hand, focused on the work at hand. Six completed pentacles are on display while another lies beneath his seat awaiting his disciplined hands. This man's red tights highlight his enthusiasm while his blue tunic reminds us that the physical work he completes also has spiritual significance. His work improves his skills, his discipline and his ability to translate ideas into physical form. As this man represents spiritual energy manifested in physical form, so are his ideas (the pentacles) made tangible or real.

This is a card of commitment to and focus on the task at hand, with a longer term goal in mind. The man works diligently to complete his task which will earn him an income to support his family and himself. If the discipline he uses in his craft is applied to his income, he will prosper as he will be able to live within his means and invest any surplus income to ensure security in old age. Thus his devotion to his task will benefit him now and in his future retirement.

Commitment to work, to a love relationship, to health and to life generally is shown by this card. Commitment and focus can make seemingly impossible goals achievable. The areas you pay attention to are the areas that will yield results. If you focus on problems they will grow, and if you focus on finding solutions they will become visible to you. During a recent business coaching session Karen complained that her massage business was slow. It turned out that Karen's focus was on having fun; she took time off every day to walk in the botanical gardens and as soon as she received payment from a client she would leave the office to shop. The Eight of Pentacles in her reading indicated that if she focused her attention on a set number of clients being booked each day, her business would thrive, which it did. The Eight of Pentacles illustrates how what we focus our attention on expands.

Reversed

The Eight of Pentacles reversed describes a lack of commitment. It is time now to return to the upright Seven of Pentacles in order to remember what you expect as long-term rewards for all your efforts. The Seven offers a chance to think about life ten years from now, and to plan the steps that will take you towards your desired goals. Perhaps you are bored with your work, your love relationship or your life generally and your lack of devotion manifests as boredom and restlessness. If you don't return to the upright Seven to clarify your goals, an impoverished old age will allow you plenty of time to ponder a lack of financial forethought in youth.

Finances

This is a card of commitment to financial stability and growth. It describes someone who loves their work and consequently the quality of their work is outstanding. At a recent lunch for 12 people I attended, the waiter obviously loved his work providing unobtrusive yet outstanding service. He made table waiting an art form, even discreetly suggesting that some of the men might like to take a stroll along the beach with a glass of brandy and a cigar after lunch. The offer was embraced enthusiastically by five non-smokers who parked their shoes and socks at the door, rolled up their trousers and took off along the pale cream sands, cigars in hand. The waiter's commitment was appropriately rewarded with generous, well-earned tips.

Reversed

The Eight of Pentacles reversed can suggest a lack of commitment to long-term financial success. Perhaps you feel that financial issues and decisions will take care of themselves. When Sandy came for a reading, her failure to take control of her finances showed when the Eight of Pentacles appeared reversed. Sandy carelessly squandered every cent she earned because she knew that when her parents passed on, they would leave her a generous inheritance. When her father died Sandy's stepbrother contested the will and secured the entire estate. Sandy couldn't afford to pursue her rightful share through the courts. Possessing few career skills and having made no financial provision for old age, the time had come for Sandy to decide how much commitment she had to living a fulfilling life and how she was going to fund it.

Health

There is a commitment to improving and maintaining your health, especially physical health, because the Pentacles suit indicates a focus on the physical world. The Eight of Pentacles implies a measured, practical approach to maintaining your health for the long term.

Reversed

You are not giving enough thought or commitment to physical health concerns. Either your health is fine and you expect it to remain so, or you may be in denial about your poor health. Perhaps your commitment to increasing your income has come at the cost of your health. The reversed Eight of Pentacles indicates that health is a low priority at present.

Nine of Pentacles

General meaning

A woman stands serenely in a fruitful garden, with a hooded bird resting on her gloved hand. Bright skies suggest good times are likely to continue and a snail in the base of the card confirms that this success has been steadily achieved. Some might see it as a long time coming, but Pentacles people understand that solid success takes time.

This woman's current success is the result of careful planning and past efforts. She has time to contemplate her future, secure in the fact that those nine pentacles at her feet will help to shield her from any cold winters ahead. When immediate needs have been taken care of and income set aside for investments, your wealth will increase with careful planning.

In general terms the Nine of Pentacles describes a comfortable life resulting from past efforts. When 55-year-old Eric asked about his impending retirement from work, the Nine of Pentacles suggested that his lifestyle was financially secure. He confirmed that for the past ten years he had earned more from his investments than from his paid job. In typical King of Pentacles fashion, Eric had planned ahead to secure an income for his retirement.

Reversed

The Nine of Pentacles reversed can describe the pursuit of money dominating everything else in your life. Too much exertion is being put into earning a living to enjoy the rewards of your efforts. Perhaps it is time to return to the Eight of Pentacles to gain additional skills to increase your income or your ability to handle the salary you presently receive.

Despite the reflection offered in the Seven of Pentacles and the commitment to particular financial and career directions offered in the Eight, you are burdened with the daily financial and career grind when the Nine is reversed in a layout. It is time to decide what paths warrant your commitment and which directions can be safely abandoned. The reversed Nine of Pentacles can describe working evening or weekend shifts in an underpaid job. It is time to return to the upright Eight of Pentacles to undergo more training so that you can secure a better paid job.

Finances

Financial success is evident when this card appears as an answer to a financial question. Life is organised and stable as you contemplate the next step in securing your financial future. The pentacles either side of the woman in the card suggest that she has diversified her investments so that if one avenue of income falters, she has others to support her through lean times.

Reversed

The reversed Nine of Pentacles indicates that you may be working and studying or perhaps working two jobs. The financial rewards do not match your efforts now, so if you are not studying something which may lead to an increased income, perhaps it is time to return to the upright Eight of Pentacles in order to focus your attention on mastering skills that can bring you great wealth.

Health

Balanced health is suggested by the Nine of Pentacles upright. You have time to contemplate life between your working hours and your everyday commitments. Keeping the long-term view of health maintenance is likely to improve your health in the years to come. Your current good health is probably the result of sound past health practices. You may have the added joy of fulfilling work which rewards you financially, emotionally and spiritually.

Reversed

Your work or the efforts you are currently devoting to the pursuit of income may be adversely affecting your health. Long working hours, dangerous working conditions or not enough time to rest between shifts may be depleting your energy. It is time to return to the upright Eight of Pentacles to commit yourself to a balanced diet and an exercise routine to ensure sustained health benefits. Lack of commitment to health is indicated by the Nine of Pentacles reversed.

Ten of Pentacles

General meaning

Through the archway of a solid family home, a factory and blue skies can be seen. An elderly man sits with a pair of attentive dogs at his feet while a couple talk together as the male partner gazes at the factory. Family crests containing a castle (also shown in the King of Pentacles) and a set of scales (seen in the Six of Pentacles) adorn the walls. In the extreme left of this card a tower is visible on a tapestry. This tower is a reminder that if those involved lose sight of their circumstances by living removed from the workings of their business, they risk eventually losing everything (as shown in the Tower Card).

The Ten of Pentacles depicts a stable financial situation offering comfortable routines and rewards for past and present efforts. In a career question it can suggest that you are employed in a large organisation, a government department or that you work in big business. Even if this card appears for a client who is self-employed, they may be under contract to a large organisation.

Pentacles people strongly identify with career, so a successful career equates to a successful life. In a general reading this ten indicates the good life: a large home on a generous plot of land filled with the rewards of accomplishment. Although Pentacles people tend to work diligently, they also reward themselves for their efforts. Pentacles types are easily identified by the expensive watch, car or jewellery, or perhaps by an exquisite collection of rare coins, books, stamps or vintage cars.

Reversed

The Ten of Pentacles reversed represents difficult financial circumstances. Perhaps you are living beyond your means, working hard to maintain a lifestyle you cannot afford. Swamped by payments on credit cards, personal and home loans, you are sinking deeper into debt. This card reversed can describe someone attempting to maintain an expensive lifestyle long after their income has diminished.

In a career layout this card can indicate a company struggling to survive in a shrinking market or downsizing and retrenchments due to financial constraints or mismanagement. When Umberto asked if it was wise to purchase a new sports car this ten appeared reversed as the answer. I told him that he could not afford it yet, and that it was wise to wait at least another year before borrowing the money for the car. This seemed only to incite him to immediate and radical action. Ignoring the advice, Umberto purchased an $85 000 car which was repossessed seven months later after his business slumped and he couldn't afford the repayments.

Finances

The upright Ten of Pentacles indicates financial stability and growth. This is a time of plenty, resulting from your past efforts and a solid, practical financial structure. As an answer to a question about starting a new business, this ten suggests success. In a question about borrowing money for a new venture, it indicates that the money will be forthcoming.

Reversed

Finances are likely to be tight when the Ten of Pentacles appears reversed in a layout, so ensure that the client is forewarned. In a career question you may lose a job or be unable to gain suitable, well-paid employment for an extended period. When economies go into recession this card appears reversed for months at a time in career and financial layouts. It can be found in layouts as a prediction up to 18 months ahead of time. As a reader, if several clients a week select this ten reversed you are being warned that a general financial downturn is predicted in the longer term, and it is advisable to reign in your spending over the coming months.

When this card is reversed, it is time to return to the upright Nine of Pentacles in order to look after your own needs. The reversed Ten of Pentacles suggests a large company that is losing staff but not hiring replacements, leaving those remaining to do the job. You may find yourself completing the work of several people but not being paid for your extra efforts. Perhaps it is time to return to the upright Nine in order to determine what your needs and responsibilities are in this situation.

Health

Balanced health is shown by the Ten of Pentacles upright. The Pentacles approach to health is one of continual maintenance and practical health routines, ensuring balanced health in the future. It can sometimes suggest that gym membership or health insurance is included in your salary package.

Reversed

Your career may be adversely affecting your health at this time. Perhaps you are working long hours, or the location is contributing to bad health. When the Ten of Pentacles is reversed in a health layout financial constraints may be a source of continuous stress which, in turn, may lead to health problems. Poor health may prevent you from earning an income when this ten is selected reversed.

Page of Pentacles

General meaning

This young person is practical, conservative and usually a committed student. This is the youth who raises an eyebrow in horror at the King or Queen of Wands parent who is dancing wildly at a party. The Pentacles Page constantly fears embarrassment, preferring the well-trodden path rather than attempting anything risky and untried. He or she usually matures early and can be trusted with responsibility at a young age. This page is likely to have a part-time job early in life, as young Pentacles people equate money with freedom. As a young person this page understands how the practical world works. They are capable of managing finances, study and life routines easily. This is the child to put in charge of the family pets, as they will be fed regularly every day.

As a situation, the Page describes a practical commitment to study or to career. You may be studying or learning new skills in your daily work life. The Page of Pentacles describes being attentive and serious in your approach to mastering new skills.

Reversed

When negative, Pentacles Pages usually desire money and material possessions continuously, without possessing the commitment necessary to build wealth. They measure those around them by what they own rather than who they are. They are less committed as students and can become obsessive with food as a compensation for inner hunger. They can also be materially competitive.

When describing a situation the reversed Page of Pentacles suggests a lack of commitment to mastering new skills. In a work or study question, you have limited commitment to a positive outcome and may leave the job or discontinue study before completing the course.

When opposed

This Page of Pentacles often resorts to food when frustrated by circumstances. Usually patient, he or she works hard at tasks which can be completed while awaiting opportunities that are not yet forthcoming. Sometimes even at an early age these pages attempt to buy their way out of difficult circumstances. When 16-year-old Robert (a Page of Pentacles) accidentally kicked a ball through the living room window early one afternoon, he had the window replaced immediately, paying for it out of his own money to avoid being chastised by his parents.

Knight of Pentacles

General meaning

The Knight of Pentacles is wiser than his years, practical in approach and hardworking. It is likely that he has his career life mapped out until retirement, if not on paper, then in his head. This knight desires a comfortable passage through life, yet he quickly realises that hard work in the early years can lead to time off with money to spend in maturity. He is a serious student and eager to undertake responsibilities at work. While his fellow knights are out partying, he is planning his business or real estate empire. Shy and aloof when it comes to potential partners, he admires those who work hard and show a sense of self-discipline. This young man is usually offered responsibility early on in life, becoming the youngest state manager or the youngest board member of a large organisation.

When representing a situation, the Knight of Pentacles describes contemplating a lengthy commitment, probably to career. It indicates an awareness of the hard work involved in the pursuit of a long-term goal. It describes an undertaking to pace yourself until the goal has been realised. Although others may offer assistance occasionally, it is regarded by you as your goal requiring your determination and effort.

Reversed

The Knight of Pentacles reversed describes someone who can be ambitious without the ability to work hard or to remain constant in his purpose. He resents authority (often due to unresolved issues with his father) and yet lacks the self-discipline to work for himself. He can be unsociable, aloof, and in constant need to control those around him. This knight fears change and losing control over himself and his life. Preferring books to people, he can be a keen student. He has a sense that time is running out and that he may miss his chance to do what he has come into this life to do. This leaves him feeling restless and frustrated at his lack of purpose.

As a situation the reversed Knight of Pentacles indicates a lack of commitment to goals. Your thinking is short-term and as a result you may not find the longer term repercussions of your current plans enjoyable. The reversed Knight also describes feeling burdened by responsibilities and obligations and seeing no respite.

When opposed

When weighed down by circumstances, the positive Knight of Pentacles usually becomes more determined, working even more diligently towards his goals. To redress the escalating tension he feels, he might benefit from a long walk alone among nature. This young man truly rests only when he is away from people and responsibilities. If he has savings or valuable investments he usually copes more positively with the frustrations of life, as financial stability lends emotional stability to Pentacles people.

Queen of Pentacles

General meaning

The Queen of Pentacles is usually a practical, warm-hearted woman with a love of nature, gardening and animals. She is often a successful business owner or manager and is not afraid of hard work. This is a person who enjoys work and has a sense of pride in making her own way in life. If her partner owns a business, this queen usually has a valuable role in the enterprise. She enjoys routine and is usually patient and realistic about life's possibilities.

As a situation, the Queen of Pentacles describes a person being patient while waiting for opportunities to arise. It can signify a connection with nature, walking and gardening. When feeling flat or frustrated by circumstances, time spent among nature is likely to restore this queen.

Reversed

The Queen of Pentacles reversed can feel restless in her career and unable to settle down to a particular purpose. Often ambitious, she is usually unable to fulfil her ambitions due to her changeable nature. Life in the country or time spent among nature may help restore her equilibrium. The negative Queen of Pentacles is sometimes torn between the need to find a wealthy partner to support her and the desire for financial independence. She worries about financial stability yet spends continually to compensate for the inner hunger she is experiencing.

If this queen appears reversed you might be identifying too strongly with your career or financial standing, forgetting that soon after you depart this life your footprints fade. Those possessions you worked so hard to own are then given away or sold. It is important to take a break from your unceasing workload to notice the seasons and to spend some time with those whose company you value.

When opposed

When surrounded by opposition this queen sometimes throws herself into her career, preferring to work hard than to be still in the face of obstacles. 'I left my marriage and took a second job. It pays better than he ever did', is how one frustrated Queen of Pentacles described it. The Queen of Pentacles may reward herself with expensive trinkets but her initial instinct is to work her way out of current circumstances. If thwarted for long periods of time she may reach for food as a consolation. Unresolved frustrations usually manifest themselves as physical health symptoms with the Pentacles types.

King of Pentacles

General meaning

This patient, practical man displays a realistic approach to life, preferring routine and stability to adventure. He usually works hard and rewards his efforts with a few material possessions such as an expensive car or watch. He is the type of person who prefers to holiday in the same place each year and is content if he owns his holiday accommodation. In this way he can renovate a cottage in the country annually over twenty years and eventually retire in it. He understands the need for financial stability in the pursuit of a rewarding life.

When describing a situation, the King of Pentacles represents success through practical effort. By tenaciously pursuing one career direction or personal goal, there is slow, steady success as practical efforts bring financial success. The rewards of maintaining a stable purpose include financial stability.

Reversed

When the King of Pentacles is reversed he can be materially greedy, running a business and his employees on a tight budget while paying himself handsomely. He is sometimes unsuccessful if he has been forced into a career by his parents or by circumstances. This is the man who awakens one morning to realise that his dream of pursuing another path is over because it would cost him too much to commence a new career from scratch. He desires money but doesn't have the inner stability to hold onto it. He can be inconsistent financially, being alternately generous and then miserly.

A lack of financial success or mediocrity may be the result of pursuing a career which was not in your heart. Following in your father's footsteps despite a calling to pursue a different path is shown by this king reversed. It is likely that you have had to reward yourself with material things regularly over the years to compensate for the emptiness experienced in a career that does not inspire you.

When opposed

When the Pentacles King is frustrated by circumstances he usually works harder. He seeks the fulfilment that comes from seeing a job completed to his standard, as this gives him a feeling of control over his circumstances. When continually frustrated by life he hoards money, planning his escape from his relationship, career or obligations. He sometimes controls those around him through finances. He may withhold financial support from a child until his child agrees to undertake a particular career or act in an agreed manner. When opposed this king sometimes attempts to buy his way out of situations.

Chapter 8

UNDERSTANDING THE MINOR ARCANA

Now that you are more familiar with the 56 cards of the Minor Arcana here are some exercises to help you to remember these cards and the significance of their numbers. Firstly, let's examine the numbers and their meanings.

Ace The aces represent *beginnings*. They each show a different approach to commencing something new.

Two The twos represent *decisions*. They also represent the blending of opposites, which can be how you arrive at a decision. You may have a need for familiarity yet a desire to move forward into uncharted waters. You must weigh up your opposing needs and make a decision.

Three The threes represent *progress* after decisions have been made.

Four The fours represent *consolidation*. This is the act of making something solid from your ideas and beliefs.

Five The fives represent *change*, either chosen or enforced. Change pushes us out of complacency towards new opportunities.

Six The sixes represent the return of *stability* after the changes experienced in the fives. The idea of stability differs according to each suit. For

Wands people, stability lies in opportunities, while Cups people find it in emotions. For Swords people stability exists in life unfolding according to plan or expectations, while Pentacles people seek financial stability.

Seven The sevens signify the return of *struggle to expand ourselves*. They show us in the act of not giving up until we realise our full potential. This struggle manifests in different ways, according to the suit.

Eight The eights show us displaying our *strengths*. These strengths vary according to the suit, and in each we have a glimpse of ourselves at the end of the journey. For Wands people strength lies in overcoming challenges and being free to travel. For Cups types it is found in being able to leave behind past emotional troubles and to be still. For Swords people strength is found in understanding those people and circumstances which have previously restricted them. For Pentacles types, strength is found in career success and maintaining worthwhile future goals.

Nine The nines show *reassessment*. Each nine represents someone reassessing the past before committing to the future. Wands people reassess past actions while Cups people reassess emotional experiences. Swords types reassess the path to knowledge and understanding of life, while Pentacles people reassess the path towards financial stability.

Ten The tens show the *completion* of the lesson contained in each suit. With the *exception* of the Ten of Swords, each ten shows the full potential contained in the seed of the ace. In the Swords suit, the Ten portrays the results of continual negative beliefs while the Ace shows clarity of thinking.

Having revisited the numbers one to ten it is necessary to examine each of the four suits as a whole. By knowing the meaning of each number and the significance of each suit, you can piece together the meaning of any individual card when it occurs in a layout.

Wands

The Wands path is one of action, activity, passion, movement, travel and quests. Many goals tempt Wands people and they usually have the energy and vitality to pursue the ones most important to them.

Wands people:

- Are most alive when doing.
- Live in the future, where possibilities exist.
- Enjoy striving for a goal.
- Are passionate, enthusiastic and forthright.

Cups

The Cups path is one of emotion. These people seek stillness, nurturing, harmony and a connection to others. Shared goals are more rewarding to Cups people who need to love and be loved. Creativity, sentimentality, romance and imagination are highly valued by Cups people.

Cups people:

- Need time to be still and to reflect.
- Like to reflect on the past, when times seemed more emotionally rewarding.
- Shy away from competition.
- Enjoy creativity and are often soft-hearted.

Swords

The Swords path is one of understanding life. Why, what, when, where and who are the questions Swords people ask continually. This is a path of ideas, concepts, comparisons, exactness and memorising facts.

Swords people:

- Enjoy solving life's puzzles.
- Are attracted to those with unusual or eccentric minds.
- Are curious, communicative and love to increase their knowledge.
- Are usually tactful and enjoy thinking, planning and discussing life.

Pentacles

The Pentacles path is one of being. Pentacles people plan ahead so that they can make life's journey comfortable. These people enjoy being present in daily life, so it makes sense to them to make life as comfortable as possible. Sometimes Pentacles people confuse being present and balanced for possessing material things. When this happens they strive to make themselves secure through ownership. Pentacles people are hardworking, slow to embrace change and steady in friendship.

Pentacles people:

- Thrive on stability and security.
- Enjoy routine and are reliable.
- Are not afraid of hard work and often work for themselves.
- Are constant, practical, thorough and patient.

The Chart of the Minor Arcana (see the colour charts section of the book) summarises what each card means. Use it to see what you know about each card by covering portions of the chart, then try to remember the meanings.

With regular reading experience you can appreciate the deeper meanings for each card. This enables you to give your client a more detailed reading.

A part of being an effective tarot reader is being able to apply card meanings to the questions being asked. If the Two of Wands upright represents making a decision regarding physical circumstances, what does it mean as the answer in a relationship question? The formula is Two (decisions) + Wands (location) + relationship = meaning. It may mean

- the client is deciding whether to live with their partner

- the client is deciding about moving home and how this will affect their partner (perhaps an interstate move or a move to another suburb)
- the client is deciding about moving forward into the next stage of a relationship (marriage or having a child).

To be effective in applying a meaning to a question or a set of circumstances is simple when you have a solid understanding of the four suits and the meaning of each number. The numbers even apply to the Major Arcana cards one to nine. For example, the fours represent consolidation and the number four card of the Major Arcana, the Emperor, represents a solid, reliable, practical man.

The court cards as combinations of the elements

Each court card represents a combination of the elements of fire, water, air and earth. Understanding these elements can help you to recognise the issues your clients are dealing with when you read for them. The Pages represent air because they exhibit the natural curiosity which is associated with the air signs. Knights represent fire as they display the abundant enthusiasm of fire. Queens represent water as they are receptive, intuitive and adapt to their surroundings more readily than the others. Kings represent earth as they are relatively steadfast and practical in their approach to life. See the Court Cards as Combination of the Elements chart in the colour section of the book.

Chapter 9

PERSONALITY TRAITS AND THE MINOR ARCANA

By understanding the humour of the four suits, their approaches to life when positive, frustrated or upset, you are able to present your readings in a manner which is readily understood by your clients. This enables you to relate to those people around you who are of different suits from yourself.

You can learn to determine a person's suit more easily when you know what to look for. When a Wands person opens their mouth and states aloud what others were secretly thinking, they usually respond to the glares or stares of surprise with 'What?! What did I say?'

From improving relationships with co-workers or family members to streamlining your tarot readings, knowing how to relate to others by recognising their approaches to life can be invaluable.

Some students of the tarot are confused as to which court card represents them. On a good day you can be the best that the upright kings and queens can be, but on a bad day, when stressed or opposed by others, perhaps another side of you emerges. When a Queen of Wands friend was asked how she was, 'Bloody reversed; that's how I am today!' she replied. The lists below detail how each of the four suits deals with setbacks and humour.

Attitude to setbacks

Wands Defiant, outwardly angry, spoiling for a fight, telling anyone who will listen the events of the day. Wands seek a physical way to discharge their pent-up aggression. Competitive sports or exercise often help to dissipate the tension.

Cups The silent treatment, lethargy, retreat to cry in order to release tension, quiet resistance to offers of help. Cups people can possess a diploma in sulking and can resort to passive-aggressive behaviour when negative.

Swords Argumentative, sharp-tongued, plan to outmanoeuvre those who oppose them, scheming for advantage. Swords people can freeze you out emotionally, using a cold stare, clipped tones and sarcasm to ensure you understand that you have offended them.

Pentacles Retreat into work, eat rich, sweet foods, and return to a routine which restores their sense of control over circumstances. When negative, Pentacles people can consider theft, such as embezzling from a company which they feel has overlooked their prolonged efforts.

How they act when upset

Wands A depressed Queen of Wands friend recently ceased sobbing long enough to begin an argument. Sympathy at how she must have felt at not being productive, produced the response 'Unproductive? I've been flat out and I'll prove it to you. I've renovated a house from the floorboards up in six months. What have you done this year?' Wands people soon forget their troubles when a fresh challenge presents itself.

Cups Cups people tend to cry quietly, becoming wistful or melancholic. The melancholic periods can extend to days, weeks or even months at a time. If Cups people are reminded that they are loved and appreciated, they usually perk up again. Given some fresh flowers, a card or an animal to hold, the water types become immersed in nurturing and feeling wanted.

Swords When upset the Swords people usually repeatedly review events mentally in an attempt to understand. Their reasoning is that when they understand what was said and why they feel more at peace with themselves. This can lead to circular thinking, which requires a patient ear and sometimes a persistent friend to remind them to let things go for awhile. If encouraged to partake in physical activities (a walk, sports or a swim) Swords people may relax again.

Pentacles Being essentially patient types, it takes a great deal to upset Pentacles people. If a King or Queen of Pentacles has worked hard and feels unappreciated they may spend some money to reward themselves for their efforts. Alternatively, Pentacles people regain equilibrium by a walk in nature or an hour working in the garden. When deeply upset, Pentacles people suffer physical ailments. This type tends to manifest frustration in the physical body.

When out of temper Wands people tend to shout, storm about or argue. They promptly forget their troubles once they have discharged their feelings. Others don't necessarily forget however, especially if the Wands person has been throwing a tantrum in a public place. While dining out in a restaurant one evening, I heard a fellow diner bellowing in his full Shakespearian voice at the waiter. This Montague-like person was able to bend others to his will. He also instantly united the entire restaurant in a shared sense of loathing of his company. While waiters leapt to meet his needs, fellow diners glared at him for interrupting their meals.

Wands people seek immediate resolutions when issues arise for, when frustrated, their limited patience evaporates rapidly. They can make circumstances so difficult for those around them that friends and colleagues are soon prepared to give them anything to restore peace. Of course if they cause too much trouble they risk being arrested, but when angry or frustrated Wands people have a limited capacity for rational thought.

When incensed, Cups people are not necessarily forthcoming with their grievances. They may be hurt by the words or actions of others, but retreat to somewhere private to re-establish their equilibrium. Usually company-loving, the frustrated Cups person prefers solitude, so that they might write down current troubles or reflect upon circumstances. If frustrated by life, Cups people become pessimistic about life's possibilities and may reach for drugs or alcohol to numb internal pain. If prolonged frustrations occur, Cups people can sink into depression, becoming lethargic, despondent and invisible to those around them.

When irate, Swords people prefer company, if only to have an opponent for an argument or a strenuous discussion. They need to talk about their circumstances to prevent themselves from becoming wound up by circular thinking. Others may offer a different point of view, enabling the Swords person to make sense of circumstances. When extremely angry, Swords people possess tongues which cut through defences like a hot knife through butter. They can become emotionless, employing glacial logic. They use the minimum number of words to inflict the maximum pain as they execute their delivery like a swordsman lunging with his blade.

If an opponent cannot be found, the frustrated Sword may phone a few friends, write a stinging letter of complaint or prepare an argument well in advance of meeting with those who have thwarted their plans.

When angry, the Pentacles types tend to revert to a familiar routine which will re-establish a feeling of effectiveness. 'If I can't have the new photocopier set up by the technicians today, then I'll get through that pile of invoices instead', is the rationale. Because Pentacles people are very connected to their physical bodies, food usually appeals when frustrations mount. They need to guard against this as a habit, as they will put on excess weight.

Sometimes when Pentacles people are thwarted financially, they may punish financially. They drag their feet when payments are due, complain about the product or service as a hint for a discount, or simply refuse to pay the agreed amount. When prolonged frustrations occur, Pentacles people can suffer physical health problems as they are the most physical of the four types. For a compartive understanding see the Court Cards as People chart in the colour section of the book.

Sense of humour

Wands Wands people enjoy physical humour such as slapstick. When you trip and fall into the mud just before the photo shoot, the Wands person is too busy laughing to help you up. They enjoy the shock value of a gag and the negative types resort to practical jokes that often have an underlying aggression or include a put-down.

Cups The humour of Cups people is more gentle than that of the Wands type. If may involve a photo of a small child with a grinning face covered in chocolate or the family dog eating an ice cream from the hand of grandad as he sleeps. The negative Cups people enjoy an entirely darker sense of humour. A friend who had two dogs was heartbroken when one of them died of old age. On inquiring over her loss she said she had been too busy to miss him, in fact she said with a wry smile, 'very busy indeed. I've reburied him four times this week. The other dog keeps digging him up and dragging him around the garden to play.'

Swords Swords people love words so any humour which twists words is usually enjoyed by these people. A friend recently declared that he had graduated from the School of Hard Knocks and moved on to the University of Adversity. The night before my wedding, my best man, a King of Swords, thrust a glass into my hand as he asked if I was nervous. 'A bit,' I confessed. 'You have a right to be nervous,' he said calmly. 'Getting married is a big commitment. It's the sort of thing you only do two or three times in your life.'

Pentacles Pentacles people often share a dry, understated sense of humour. Not easily given to excess emotion, their deadpan delivery can be overlooked if you are not paying attention. During a tropical downpour James took shelter under a shop awning one afternoon, in awe at the staccato sound of huge raindrops pelting the surfaces around him. The deafening rain sounded like bursts of machine-gun fire exploding above him on the steel awning. The splash back of those drops hitting the ground steadily soaked his legs and shoes.

Puddles formed in minutes, while small rivulets gushed in every direction as a group of people stood gazing at nature's fury. The calm voice of a stranger beside him stated drily, 'Looks like it's turned out nice again.'

Compatibility

The four suits or groupings of court cards represent the growth and development of the four personality types. Overall, the pages represent boys and girls with the qualities of each suit. Knights represent young men in their twenties, more developed than they were as young children but not yet fully mature. A male page grows into a knight before maturing into a king. A female page develops into a queen. As boys take longer to mature than girls, a queen can be a woman in her twenties whereas a man in his twenties is usually a knight.

When a king or a queen appears reversed in a layout, the reader needs to decide if that person is habitually reversed (usually displays the negative qualities of the king or queen), or if that person occasionally exhibits these qualities such as when exhausted, ill or overwhelmed by life. The person described by the reversed card may be frustrated by current life circumstances or may habitually seek the easier path and avoid the lesson of the card.

It is worth being aware of social trends when reading the cards. As more young adults stay at home longer, which can delay the onset of maturity, people up to the age of thirty can appear as pages instead of knights or queens. Two generations ago those at the same age might already have had a family of four.

Certain suits pair well with each other, forging lasting friendships and love relationships easily. Any king, queen or knight is capable of enjoying a fulfilling long-term love relationship with any other type.

Compatibility chart for the four suits

Although someone from your own suit is likely to perceive life in the same way as yourself, this may not help you to grow and develop as a person. Opposites attract but opposites can find relationships difficult unless they make allowances for their partner's different view of life. Each suit is naturally compatible with another, and this pairing of suits is Wands with Swords and Cups with Pentacles.

Wands people enjoy a passionate if short-lived friendship or relationship with other Wands types. This is a relationship which can burn itself out rapidly.

- Wands people sometimes find Cups partners too slow, sensitive and dreamy for their liking.
- Wands and Swords people are usually mutually compatible because Wands types enjoy adventures while the Swords types thrive on change.
- Wands people often find Pentacles people too staid, routine and practical for their tastes.

Cups people often feel that the Wands types are too active, feisty and unpredictable for a long-lasting friendship or relationship. Cups people can be easily hurt by the direct approach preferred by Wands people.

- Cups people enjoy the company of other Cups types, sharing memories, emotions and romantic ideals together.
- Cups people sometimes find their Swords counterparts too intellectual and unemotional for their tastes.
- Cups and Pentacles people are often compatible because Cups people enjoy security while Pentacles people enjoy providing a solid structure to life through routines and wealth building.

Swords people enjoy the company of the Wands types as they travel easily together, they both enjoy meeting new people and both types rapidly become bored with routine.

- Swords people often feel that Cups types are stuck in the past, layered over with sentimentality or unresolved emotional hurts. They also find Cups people are not talkative, and almost conversation resistant.
- Swords people enjoy the company of other Swords types as conversation flows easily into gossip, rumour, conjecture and slanderous humour.
- Swords people can find the Pentacles types too slow, plodding and routine for their tastes.

Pentacles people soon become exhausted by the passionate approach to life possessed by the Wands types. 'Where's the fire?' is the response when a Wands person arrives, full of enthusiasm and restlessness.

- Pentacles people often enjoy an easygoing and complementary relationship with Cups people, as one provides financial security while the other offers emotional nurturing and a chance to dream.
- Pentacles people usually find Swords types too quick-minded, restless and changeable for their liking. When Pentacles people suggest that they holiday in the same location as last year, Swords people shudder at the thought of a regular destination and the forming of routines.
- Pentacles people often enjoy the company of other Pentacles types as both understand the value of working hard for their long-term goals. Both enjoy structure, routines and smooth-running, ordered lives.

Wands people usually seek adventure while Swords people strive to understand life. This often translates into Swords people accompanying their Wands friends on adventures and travels, meeting new people along the way. New people can offer a different perception of life, which Swords people enjoy.

Cups people shy away from adventure, preferring a comfortable set of routines to provide time and space to reflect on their feelings. Pentacles people are well suited to providing this stable and routine environment. At the same time Pentacles people usually enjoy the tenderness and devotion offered by their Cups counterparts. Cups people cannot understand why Wands people forgo the pleasures of a comfortable home and work environment to explore untamed places.

Generally Swords people find their Cups counterparts too shy and retiring while the Cups people eventually search for an escape from the incessant talking of the Swords types. Swords people can find Pentacles people too routine, restrictive and predictable while the Pentacles people find Swords types changeable and unreliable.

Wands people sometimes find the Pentacles types too fearful of change and lacking in passion, while Pentacles people sometimes perceive the Wands' passion as a waste of energy. Pentacles people can see passion as drama and a distraction from serious matters. Drama leaves them feeling insecure, and security is of paramount importance to Pentacles people.

- Wands people dance a tango. It's passionate, intense and can be exhausting.
- Cups people dance up close to a sentimental song, with her head on his shoulder.
- Swords people join a group dance where partners change every 60 seconds.
- Pentacles people dance a slow waltz, preferably with a partner who took lessons with the same dance instructor.

Chapter 10

SPIRITUAL PURPOSE IN THE PHYSICAL WORLD

Each of the four suits of the Minor Arcana offers a unique journey through life and a chance to fulfil your spiritual purpose while maintaining your connection to the physical world. Keeping a balance between your physical needs and your spiritual purpose requires vigilance, and each of the four suits struggle with this human dilemma in different ways.

The Wands path

Key: To pursue life's opportunities with passion and courage.

Harnessing passion and applying discipline to enthusiasm is part of the lesson of the suit of Wands. The challenge is to do this without extinguishing the fires of passion within. Too much passion and energy dissipates in too many directions, usually without success. Too much discipline wilts passion. Many great ideas have been lost to committees, extinguished by unimaginative people in the lead-up to morning tea.

When Wands children are raised by Pentacles parents conflict can arise between the child's quest for excitement and adventure and the parent's insistence on order and safety. There is a risk that in keeping the Wands child safe and secure, the Pentacles need for order and routine can stifle the natural Wands creativity and spontaneous enthusiasm.

When five-year-old Jake wanted to put on a play for his parents, he was seeking to express himself. His parents, the King and Queen of Pentacles were too busy managing a business ensuring that Jake was afforded the right school, to take the time to sit with him. Later in high school Jake continued acting in and producing plays, while his parents tried to encourage him towards a stable, financially secure career. His father negotiated a deal whereby if Jake reached a particular score in his exams, he'd be allowed to attend a theatre workshop in the summer holidays.

For Wands people learning to harness natural passion and enthusiasm, this is usually done through direct experience. Unlike Swords people, who can learn by observing others, those of the Wands suit usually burn their fingers in order to discover that the stove is hot. For Wands types, their path involves learning to pace themselves to reach some of their goals. This includes not taking on too many new goals when they don't have the time, money or energy to see them through to conclusion. It includes understanding how important preparation is in the realisation of your goals.

Being essentially impatient, Wands people often want to fly before they can walk. They thrive on seeing plans take shape, which is why so many of them are found in the construction industry. At the end of a project they can see what they have built. A home, office block or a shopping centre stands as evidence of their efforts. They don't like the tedious planning process, which is why it is Swords people who are usually the architects, designers and project planners.

Jake learned about planning the hard way. At eleven years of age he asked if he could produce a play at the end of year concert. Unaware of how important the planning and rehearsal stages are to the final success of the venture, Jake was still rewriting the play on the afternoon of the performance. It was a dismal failure, with Jake and his friends being clapped off stage half way through their performance. If Wands fail dismally through lack of planning they are depressed initially, but they are not deterred. Instead of hiding away they take time to plan and prepare for future successes.

Wands people need to have a series of worthwhile goals ahead in life which are attainable yet not too easily achieved. There is often a sense of mild disappointment after a long-term goal is achieved, so that unless a new goal holds promise of fulfilment, Wands people can feel flat soon after their most recent achievement.

Being essentially competitive and passionate people they can perceive spiritual nourishment and inner harmony as something to be ticked off their list of important things to achieve this lifetime. Queen of Wands Beth listed off her spiritual quests, which were essentially a list of travel destinations.

'I've done Nepal and Tibet, the Incas, a few ashrams in India, Lourdes, that pilgrims walk in Southern Europe and a meditation retreat in the Gobi desert,' she said proudly. The whole list sounded like a marathon run with a stop watch. It was reminiscent of Groucho Marx boasting that his band could play 'The Minute Waltz' in 53 seconds.

The Wands path involves discovering what is humanly possible, whether it be the four-minute mile, a long distance swim, a trek up the Himalayas with your guide dog or a night parachute jump into the ocean under the light of a full moon. It involves pushing yourself past your previous best, to discover your new limits. The reasoning is that, 'Even if I die trying, I'll discover my limitations'.

Deep within, the Wands people have a sense of urgency. They want to achieve as much as possible before they die. Tackling each goal with passion and enthusiasm they discover unchartered places, invent new gadgets, discover shipwrecks in waters deeper than others have previously ventured or start new businesses. Wands people perceive life as a series of conquests, and their challenge consists of living in the present while having an awareness of the future.

Wands people need to keep an eye on future goals while remembering that it is what we do today that shapes tomorrow. When they haven't mastered self-discipline (the lesson of the King of Wands) they can make running away from current circumstances seem like pursuing a quest. Running away is still only running away, even with a new coat of paint or a multimedia presentation. Prone to exaggeration, they can make building a tree house sound like construction of the palace at Versailles.

When Wands people harness self-discipline, they can extend their success rate tenfold. They continually find new ways to expand their horizons, an example of this being entrepreneur and businessman Richard Branson. When Wands people manage to live in the present while harnessing their passion and enthusiasm for unrealised goals, they build businesses, coach sports teams, write songs, construct houses, motivate others to realise their own goals and generally inspire those who follow them. They possess natural leadership qualities, although others may have difficulty keeping up with them.

Wands people have a passion to be like the gods of ancient times. They push themselves to achieve more and more, until one day they find themselves in competition with their gods. Easily motivated to action, these people are not the tactful diplomats keen to hear the group consensus. They thrive on challenges, compete with those around them and eventually raise their gaze from short-term physical goals to the longer term spiritual goals in the pursuit of deeper fulfilment.

Be aware of

- impatience with plans which take time to reach fruition
- becoming short-tempered with those who are not as energetic as yourself
- competing with those on your team
- competing with your relationship partner or your children
- being tactless in your dealings with others.

The opposite to the Wands energy is the Pentacles energy. For a more balanced approach to life, you might consider embracing some of the Pentacles attitudes to life, exchanging some of your spontaneous passion for effectiveness, which will result in a focused effort towards your goals.

Try to cultivate

- an awareness of what needs to be done today to take you closer to your goals
- patience with the process of life and other people
- an awareness of the present
- an understanding of how worthwhile team efforts can be
- the concentration necessary to complete current projects before tackling new ones
- a sense of pride in your past achievements without always having to look forward to new possibilities.

Taking the Wands path

If you are taking the Wands path through life, you might benefit from developing an awareness of the following:

- A need for an important long-term life goal.
- Mid-range (three-to-five year) goals.
- Achievable short-term goals.
- Surrounding yourself with practical people who are capable of helping you turn your goals into reality.
- Others who may perceive you as competitive; try to realise that a team effort can improve a project.
- You may need a hobby or a sport which allows you to discharge some of your pent up passion each week.

The Cups path

Key: To nourish yourself and those around you spiritually and emotionally while you share a spiritual path through life.

The Cups path involves a search for people and activities which nourish the heart and soul. From meditation, writing, painting and playing music or doting on someone special, Cups people thrive where they can share their warmth and kindness. While the Wands people seek separation through competition, Cups people seek union through group activities.

Cups types need like-minded people who share their spiritual perspective so that the journey through life is more gentle. The existential aloneness we each experience can be difficult for Cups people. Meditation can dispel this sense of aloneness. For Cups people, meditation allows them to glimpse how we are all interconnected on a spiritual level. Cups people are usually compassionate. They remember that we are all treading unique paths in life with similar destinations.

Avoiding competitive projects, Cups people search for stillness in order to reflect. They tend to be sentimental, reviewing past experiences repeatedly. One of the reasons that Cups types partner naturally with Pentacles people is that those of the Pentacles suit provide the structure and stability for Cups people to daydream and reflect on life's possibilities. It is difficult to reflect on life when you are working hard to secure your next meal.

The Cups path is one which involves the question, 'Where are we going together?' The 'we' may be a love relationship, a family or a spiritual group of like-minded people. Cups people instinctively understand that pairing their steps in life with another person involves give and take. Cups people adapt easily to circumstances as water adapts itself to the environment.

The challenge here is to believe in the power of unity with others despite the pain which can accompany it. Overcoming past emotional hurts can be difficult for Cups people because they remember emotional experiences with great clarity.

Cups people are more romantically inclined, needing to guard against falling in love with a partner's potential, realising that some people never reach their potential. Cups people intuitively anticipate their partner's needs and meet these wants regardless of the sacrifices required. This works if the partner is also sensitive to the Cups person's needs, but in the case of the King of Wands, he may well expect a partner to speak up when they have needs, like he does. Cups people rarely speak up, preferring instead to wait patiently, hoping that eventually the partner will acknowledge their needs.

The Cups path includes creative discipline (the lesson for the King of Cups). The process of being inspired with an idea, and then taking the practical steps necessary to make that idea into a song, a painting, a book or some other work of art requires discipline if you are to remain faithful to the original idea. While Wands people passionately embrace new ideas, abandoning them when another concept is presented, Cups people can prefer the dream part of the equation, finding the practical steps too daunting or tedious.

Helping others to pursue their spiritual paths in life can be a rewarding career for Cups people. In career, Cups people are drawn to spiritual healing, psychology, the arts, music and child care. They are also often suited to infant school teaching, the human resources department in a large company, customer service, natural therapies, aged care and beauty therapy. The Cups types usually thrive in any career which nourishes others and encourages them in the pursuit of spiritual and emotional happiness.

Harnessing creative inspiration and channelling it into a worthwhile career or lifestyle is the preferred path of the Cups types. Whereas Wands people actively pursue an idea, Cups types can be easily dissuaded from their creative purpose. Criticism, a lack of tolerance, or a series of setbacks can stop a Cups person.

Repeated frustration in the pursuit of creative endeavours can leave these people sullen and resentful.

With a kind, patient approach, Cups people gradually pursue their creative endeavours. They are suited to partnerships or group activities, but must guard against allowing the needs of others to displace their own needs for creative expression.

Wands people are nourished by future possibilities. Cups people are nurtured by past events. Through remembering how those around them supported and encouraged them in the past, Cups types can find strength to pursue their dreams.

Cups people realise that when the needs of certain members of a community are ignored, the whole community suffers. Theirs is an inclusive mentality. They seek a suitable place for each member of the community so that everyone contributes something meaningful to the group. Pursuing a path in life which causes the least amount of conflict with others is essential to Cups people.

Be aware of

- any tendency to live in the past
- your propensity to romanticise possibilities
- your compassion for others overriding your better judgement
- the need to have time alone to reflect upon life
- any reticence to speak up when you feel that circumstances are unfair.

The opposite of the Cups energy is the Swords energy. It may help you to cultivate some of this energy for a clearer, more balanced perspective on life. Cultivating the thinking processes familiar to swords people may help you to shake off overwhelming emotional states.

Try to cultivate

- a pragmatic approach to your life goals
- methods to prevent those around you from draining you emotionally
- your mind so that you can think clearly about your feelings and gain a clearer perspective
- clearer judgement of others through analysis combined with intuition or feelings so that you don't make decisions based on clouded emotions

- an appreciation of the value of emotional nourishment in long-term happiness.

Taking the Cups path

If you are taking the Cups path through life, you might benefit from developing an awareness of the following suggestions:

- If you have close friends, you are less likely to rely on a love relationship partner for your emotional fulfilment.
- It is important to have creative hobbies or creative outlets which you can enjoy every week.
- You need some regular quiet time for personal reflection. This may be time for meditation, reading, watching a sentimental film or time spent daydreaming.
- Spiritual nourishment is easily found in helping others, as long as you are not taken for granted by those you are helping.
- For a more fulfilling life, learn from the past, let it go and live in the present.

The Swords path

Key: To seek answers and understanding of life and its purpose as you discover the innate order within the universe.

Swords people need to understand life, and any spiritual purpose which makes sense to them is considered. These are not people who can exhibit faith in things which they cannot comprehend or explain to others. These are the people who want to meet God or Buddha directly, in order to ask some pertinent questions.

This path offers a successful life when the mind has been disciplined. Clarity of thought results in a precise, ordered life, at least intellectually. In physical terms the Swords people can be changeable with jobs, locations and partners but once they establish a workable perception of life, Swords people are organised and precise.

The Swords question is 'Why?' Why are we here on earth? Why do we live in a physical world? Why do we accept linear time? Why would one person completely believe this while another person believes entirely the opposite with equal intensity? How can people be spiritually nourished with completely different religions or spiritual beliefs?

Harnessing mental energy while preventing your thoughts from becoming scattered is part of the lesson for Swords people. As children, they have quick minds which are easily diverted from their purpose. In maturity, Swords people recognise that although many alternatives can offer you useful choices, once you determine which choice to pursue, you need to focus on your chosen path if you want to succeed.

Swords people are naturally curious about other people, different countries and about life itself. This is the child in the school yard who approaches the new pupil to begin a conversation simply because the new pupil is foreign or different. Curiosity forces Swords people to begin conversations, open a new book, collect a few brochures, travel to new locations and explore new ways of thinking.

A Swords student needs to know why they are learning the way that they are. Rarely short of a conversation, Swords people are suited to careers where they can meet the public. Sales, teaching, public speaking, presenting a radio or television program, or a career in science, as logic appeals to the Swords types. As counsellors or psychologists they are not the patient, compassionate types (as the Cups counsellors tend to be). Instead Swords counsellors seek to understand what incidents or patterns of behaviour are causing or contributing to current issues. Doctors, lawyers, mediators, negotiators, accountants, scientists, architects, computer scientists, IT professionals and many non-fiction writers are Swords people. In sales, the pure types are so gifted with words that they can occasionally close a sale after dialling a wrong number.

When under great pressure Swords people can experience mental chaos which leaves them exhausted. The negative types can be incessant worriers and notoriously indecisive. Peace within results from mental discipline. If external pressures are unrelenting, Swords people can face mental collapse resulting from hyperactive thought processes.

Until they master mental discipline, these people attempt to meditate with one eye open, scanning the room for something interesting to focus on. In maturity, they often exhibit a calm, clear-minded energy. This type of mind is well suited to research or to courtroom interrogation, as it is not easily dissuaded from a purpose once engaged in the pursuit of the truth or an answer to a specific question.

The Swords person's strength often lies in organising others, especially in a group project. They are usually effective managers and good negotiators. They enjoy gathering knowledge through reading, studying and travelling. This knowledge can then be put to good use in planning an interesting, mentally stimulating life.

The lesson for Swords types includes being able to gather knowledge without losing sight of spiritual purpose. Eventually this translates as discovering, defining and being able to eloquently summarise their spiritual path to others. Perhaps it may involve teaching others of the benefits of mental discipline. There is an ancient spiritual group who believe that there are two paths to spiritual enlightenment, one through the head and the other through the heart. One of the texts they have left behind shows the process of guiding the advanced student.

> We initially explained to you that there are two paths to enlightenment, through the head and through the heart. In fact there is only one path, though the heart, but we had to answer all of your questions first. Are you ready for this path now?

With the great advances in science and knowledge generally, the lesson for Swords people is to gain understanding without losing faith. This often occurs when they realise that the more they understand, the more they discover how much there is yet to be understood. As their knowledge grows, so does their understanding that we are all minute in the infinite scope of life.

Be aware of

- indecision and the need to continuously seek out more alternatives before making a decision
- the tendency to rationalise your actions
- a need to ask the advice of others when you cannot decide for yourself
- any desire for the company of others to avoid being alone and facing yourself and your life
- when you are asking questions as part of natural conversation and when you are prying into the lives of others
- a tendency to skim over the surface of life without feeling it deeply.

The opposite to the Swords (thought) energy is the Cups energy, so try to cultivate some of the Cups compassion and sensitivity to the feelings of others for a more balanced approach to life.

Try to cultivate

- a combination of compassion and clarity of thought for balanced decisions
- patience with others when they don't want to share their thoughts and feelings with you
- respect for the privacy of others
- the ability to sit with your feelings without having to understand them or rationalise them to yourself
- an awareness of the value of the mind in making life more enjoyable
- patience for those around you who cannot express themselves as easily as you do.

Taking the Swords path

If you are taking the Swords path through life, you might benefit from developing an awareness of the following suggestions.

- Take some time away from thinking. This gives your mind and your body a chance to relax and unwind. Try regular massage, meditating or walking so you can draw your energy away from your mind and back to your physical body.
- If you can read one non-fiction book every month or two, you will discipline your mind. This can be done in bed at night for 15 minutes before you fall asleep.
- Be aware that when you have an idea, it can come out of your mouth or your hands. If it is talked about too much the energy is usually dissipated before you achieve your goal. If it comes out of your hands, others can discuss it with you when it is real and tangible.
- Some of life's bigger questions cannot be easily answered with words. Sometimes the search for spiritual meaning is answered in a way which goes beyond words.
- Deep and lasting stillness and inner peace come from a disciplined, still mind.

The Pentacles path

Key: To enjoy life's abundance while recognising that you can leave this world a better place than you found it.

The Pentacles path involves harnessing your God-given gifts, accepting your limitations and making a secure, comfortable life for yourself. The balance lies in being able to enjoy a comfortable life while realising that one day you will have to release it all gracefully. It involves being able to understand what is necessary for current circumstances.

For Pentacles people a few simple truths seem obvious. If you accept gravity, linear time, keep your body fed and watered and keep it within a certain temperature range, you increase your chances of survival immensely. While Wands people can be prone to chills because the weather suddenly turns cold, Pentacles people think ahead and bring a coat in case of such an eventuality. Pentacles people are long-term planners. They plan a career twenty years ahead, and even when contemplating a day trip they ensure they are prepared for changes in circumstances.

Pentacles types usually understand the importance of money in helping your life to run smoothly. While the other types may argue that this is not very spiritual, Pentacles people understand that with a little money and some organisation, a village in the third world can sink a well, irrigate local farms and feed everyone. With the aid of carefully spent money, the village can thrive. Pentacles people realise that when your immediate physical needs are met, you have choices about how you live your life. If you spend most of every day scrounging for food, a whole life can be spent focused on an empty stomach.

For the Pentacles types, human existence isn't hell and suffering in order to prepare for an afterlife. They realise that we can make our existence here heaven on earth with careful planning, hard work and group effort. They understand that 55 people rowing a boat can be much more effective than one or two, so they form groups, communities and eventually corporations. While many corporations exist as big dysfunctional families, there are some which achieve great goals while honouring the needs of their employees and their customers.

When a Queen of Pentacles builds a financial fortune, she can ensure the stability of her descendants through the right education (school, university and business education). Stability and structure provide an internal sense of security for Pentacles people. They are usually prepared to work hard to establish stability and a structured life. They recognise that once the basic needs have been met (food, water, shelter, clothing) they are free to concentrate on more important issues. A part of this structure involves spending some time each week or month tending to spiritual needs.

With their innate connection to nature, Pentacles people can derive a great deal of happiness from tending a garden. From a simple plot of earth providing a small kitchen garden of herbs, spices and vegetables, to a vineyard planted across undulating hills, Pentacles people love to watch plants grow. They feel a sense of abundance, when ensuring their plants thrive.

Pentacles types usually feel a sense of pride from a job well done. If they begin a business, customers can expect consistent and good quality products or services. Being a reliable supplier ensures that the lives of your customers are not inconvenienced by your actions. Because they are usually long-term thinkers and planners, these people go into business with the expectation of being in business for years to come. They act with awareness that reputation is slowly built and easily destroyed.

While many Wands people perceive happiness as being out of immediate reach, Pentacle types live more in the present. They are capable of planning for an improved future, but recognise that we need to make the most of current circumstances. This is why Pentacles people surround themselves with comfortable environments. Both at work and at home, they ensure that the chairs they sit on, the sofa and the view are usually conducive to relaxation. They believe that work brings rewards and that it is important to appreciate the rewards of their efforts.

The Pentacles path is often a business path. The responsibilities can be daunting for the other types, but a stable longstanding business provides goods or services, and employment to its staff which benefits their families. The influence of the Pentacles person can reach deep into the community in positive ways. From a home-based business to the large corporation, Pentacles people manage those enterprises that provide the rest of us with food, accommodation, travel, fuel, clothes and entertainment.

Whereas Wands people have an innate sense of urgency, Pentacles types possess a deep patience with life. Their slow, steady approach proves successful long term. While the Wands people sometimes attempt a project or a business and give up, abandoning it for another, more promising goal, this provides an opportunity for Pentacles people to purchase cheaply and make the business into the success it was meant to be.

Be aware of

- a need for routine stifling your personal growth
- any tendency to control circumstances financially
- remaining in a situation you don't like with the rationale that it is better the devil you know than the one you don't
- a tendency to work when you actually want to play
- the habit of putting off opportunities for joy in your life until retirement.

The opposite to the Pentacles energy is the Wands energy. This means that the opposite to routine is spontaneity and passion. For a more balanced approach to life you might consider embracing some of the Wands qualities.

Try to cultivate

- the ability to occasionally act on your spontaneous urges
- an openness to new places, people and ideas
- a sense of adventure with life's journey
- a few goals in your life which are just for fun and not work related
- an ability to speak your mind when others have unrealistic expectations of you
- an awareness of how tackling issues today can resolve them before they grow
- an appreciation of how often life supports you with its abundance.

Taking the Pentacles path

If you are taking the Pentacles path through life, you might benefit from developing an awareness of the following suggestions:

- It is important to step away from your comfortable routines occasionally, if only to discover some new, more rewarding routines. Routine can become stifling, even in paradise.
- Be aware of how your financial stability can assist those around you without making them dependent on you. Through offering scholarships, tools of the trade or employing an inexperienced junior, you can make a positive difference in the lives of others.
- Pace yourself through life with regular holidays. Resist the urge to work hard until retirement before relaxing. A long retirement is promised to no one, and those you love may not be there to share it with you. Take time throughout life to share special times with your friends and family.
- If you fall into the trap of comparing yourself with those around you who are more successful, make sure that you also compare yourself with those around you who are less successful and whose burdens are greater than your own.

Chapter 11

THE FOUR SUITS IN BUSINESS

Each of the four suits represents a personality type and a unique approach to life. People of each suit prefer different careers or to work in different parts of a large organisation.

The Wands

Wands people usually have a forthright approach and a passion for goals and challenges. Consequently they are well suited to sales and marketing. They love the freedom that being a sales representative offers them and they thrive on setting and meeting sales targets. Given a car, a notebook computer and a phone, they quickly vacate the office. Although unseen by those at head office, the results of their activities confirm that they are out in the world moving and shaking.

An unfortunate pattern for Wands people is that as they mature they are often promoted into managerial roles. While this is appealing in theory, they find themselves chained to a desk and swamped with paperwork. Soon they watch with envy as their sales team drives off into the distance for what is perceived as a day of freedom.

Wands people love the outdoors, and they are most successful if they can do the talking and close the sale while a Swords person back in the office completes the paperwork which Wands people generally find tedious and time consuming. They prefer to keep information in their memory rather than on a computer.

The Cups

With their soft approach and well-developed compassion, Cups people are best suited to customer service and the human resources department of a large organisation. They are often patient with customers who are experiencing difficulties and, with their strong instincts, excel when selecting the right people to join the company.

Cups people are also suited to being the company psychologist where they might help members of their 'corporate family' integrate more easily.

Graphic design, marketing design and support roles also suit Cups types, who thrive where they can make a difference emotionally and socially. They prefer to avoid competition but they can become skilled researchers and negotiators, especially when discretion is required. Cups people are sometimes found in the security departments of large corporations.

Preferring to avoid the limelight, Cups types thrive where they can support others or work in a team, sharing the responsibilities and receiving support when they need it. Sometimes Cups employees end up in the accounts department but, if they do, they are often found dreaming of earning a living through creative means.

The Swords

Possessing an appreciation of order and pride in the smooth running of any environment, the Swords people are well suited to administration. When given free reign they put effective systems in place to ensure a well-run organisation. Swords people are at home writing company objectives and job descriptions, planning for emergencies and in the legal department. They make excellent personal assistants, being efficient with paperwork. They are systematic, methodical and businesslike.

Swords people are also effective in sales, marketing and accounts, although they need plenty of people contact to be at their best. Those who belong to this suit are proficient all-rounders in business. Natural communicators, these people are clever negotiators. If you need to hire a venue or purchase some office equipment, ask a Swords person to source some quotes. They are at ease with email and the telephone, scanning the Internet while phoning suppliers for quotes.

During restructuring it can benefit the company to send a Swords person from department to department asking those 'at the coal face' how productivity might be inexpensively improved. Swords people are usually adept at writing up a list, a questionnaire or an assessment form. They are well suited to writing the company newsletter or redesigning company forms.

The Pentacles

Pentacles people possess an appreciation of order and routine, making them suited to the accounts department. The are effective financial controllers, able to carefully plan a yearly or quarterly budget and stick to it. Pentacles people usually feel uncomfortable without strong boundaries and systems, so they enjoy a position which has clearly defined limitations and responsibilities.

Traditionally Pentacles people struggle with Wands employees because they have opposing points of view regarding money. Wands people usually believe that you have to spend money to make money, whereas the Pentacles types have their attention on conserving money. This can result in conflict when the Wands sales manager demands more money so his sales force can reach their targets, while the Pentacles accounts manager considers this a waste of money. The Pentacles person continually reminds his Wands counterpart that he has a responsibility to the shareholders, while the Wands person argues that the competition may steal their customers unless more money is forthcoming.

A well-balanced business has a Wands sales force, a Swords administration team, Cups people in human resources and customer service and Pentacles people in the accounts department. Pentacles people keep a close eye on the bottom line, realising that if spending exceeds income for too long, no one gets paid. Their steady, determined manner makes them a sound choice as guardians of the company finances.

It pays for a company to consider the right mix of people in the right positions otherwise, as many of us have experienced, it can become like a large, dysfunctional family.

Starting a new business

Any of the four types can establish a new business but they will each have uniquely different reasons for doing so. The Wands types love the promise of freedom that working for themselves offers, so they will venture out on their own in order to be their own boss.

Cups types usually begin a new business in order to work at their own pace, in a beautiful and nurturing environment. They soon build a long list of customers if they are in a service-oriented business because they take time to ensure the customer is familiar with their product or service and they usually listen when customers have a complaint or are experiencing difficulties.

Swords people find the idea of a well-run business appealing. They put efficient systems in place so that anyone can run the business. Swords types prefer to write everything down, so that when it comes time to sell, they can offer the new owners a complete handbook on how to run the business.

Pentacles people usually go into business for themselves planning to make more money than they did when working for an employer. Careful to research the business and the competition, they are slow to commence trading as they want to become familiar with each area of the business first. Pentacles types prefer to save enough money to see them through the initial start-up phase. Even before starting these people have an eye firmly on the desired turnover, income and eventual sale price. Their business plan will include dates as to when they expect the business to reach particular targets.

As a sole trader you need elements of the four suits. If you do not, you can still succeed by engaging the services of professionals such as an accountant, a lawyer, a business adviser, a marketing person or a publicist. Select your advisers from the appropriate suit so that you thrive.

I recall one book publicity tour where the publicist accompanying me to radio stations and bookstores was painfully shy. She barely maintained eye contact with me or with those people we met during the tour and mumbled when speaking to anyone new. These days I employ a Swords person to manage publicity. Swords people are naturally curious, talkative, and at ease when meeting or telephoning strangers. For one book tour, my Queen of Swords publicist donned a telephone headset and made 14 calls in a row, typing details into the computer as she spoke. When she phoned a radio station which had a strictly music format, I was about to tell her so when she said, 'Thursday afternoon is fine, and we'll get there a little early in case you want Paul to look at your palms regarding that relationship.'

Chapter 12

UNDERSTANDING THE COURT CARDS AND THE CLIENT

Many tarot students and professional readers experience difficulty determining when a court card represents a person known or yet to be known by the client, an aspect of the client or a situation. The King of Wands can represent a mature, forthright passionate man, an Aries person (man or woman), or success through self-discipline (the Aries lesson). Reversed it can mean an undisciplined or immature man (having only the maturity of the Knight of Wands), an Aries person or a lack of success due to a lack of self-discipline.

When in doubt, many readers simply add a card to the court card to help them to refine the meaning.

- If the additional card is another court card, it confirms that the first card is referring to a person.
- If the extra card is a Major Arcana card it can suggest a spiritual lesson.
- If the card added is a Minor Arcana card it can give more detail to the person described by the king.

Looking at the above cards, the reversed Ten of Wands has been turned up next to the upright King of Wands. This might describe a man who is burdened by his activities. Perhaps he has his own business which is presently weighing him down, or he is treating his job as if he owned the business. Maybe he is working more than 40 hours per week, often into the evenings and throughout the weekends.

If the reversed Page of Swords is added to the upright King of Wands as shown above, this might suggest there is a talkative child near this person. Following a different train of thought, this layout might describe this king as a man who is filled with ideas and concepts he cannot seem to bring into reality. In this version of events, the King of Wands is made less practical by the reversed Page of Swords. A third possibility is that this man is impatiently awaiting news which is delayed. The pages represent news and a reversed page can suggest that the awaited news is delayed.

As the reader, it is up to you to decide if a particular court card represents a person or a situation. You can do this by trusting your instincts when reading or taking a moment to sense which meaning feels the most appropriate. Some readers avoid this by giving every possible meaning to each card on the table. This makes for a confusing reading as your client has to pick out the relevant pieces of the reading from all the information given to them. Your goal as a reader is to clarify the client's situation, so reducing the possible meanings for each card on the table is a part of this process.

If after a general reading the client's first question is around love relationships, then the reader's job is to ensure that they ask the question which will give the most clarity in this area. When Brooke explained that she had recently separated from Gary and that she was concluding a short relationship with Brett, it was clear that she was still grieving for both men. Before giving her clear information about a possible future partner, it was necessary to ask her to retrace her steps and examine what had occurred in these two relationships.

Gary appeared as the reversed Knight of Pentacles. He was described as a man who rarely let his guard down, remained aloof and sought control over most situations. Brooke was asked if she felt stifled at the end of that relationship and she agreed that she had but said that she missed the safety that arose from the routines which surrounded Gary. Pentacles people thrive on routine and when reversed they often cling to routines because of the inner chaos. Brett, her more recent partner, appeared as the reversed King of Wands. He was described as passionate, impulsive, hot-headed and commitment resistant. The reversed Wands court cards describe people who keep one eye on the *Exit* sign, in case a quick getaway is required. On request Brooke added the reversed World card to the King of Wands, which prompted the question if Brett was currently or about to travel overseas. Brooke confirmed that Brett had been living in Europe for six years and he was planning to return to Australia to live. The reversed World card can suggest that someone has travelled halfway around the world, and is perhaps due to complete the journey.

Brooke had moved from a restrictive, controlling partner to one who possessed limited self-control. Perhaps it was time for Brooke to find a man who was in between the two extremes shown in her reading. It's not unusual for someone to pick a partner who is completely different from the previous partner when they leave a long-term relationship. If she didn't want to find a partner who was in between the qualities of Brett and Gary, then she had to find an upright Knight of Pentacles or King of Wands.

When describing a person represented in an upright court card, it sometimes helps to include some of the qualities of the reversed card to sharpen the description. In a recent description of the King of Cups to a woman, it was mentioned that he might sulk when things don't go his way. She laughed and nodded, recognising her husband at once. 'He's as moody as an artist but with nothing to frame at the end of it.'

The court cards as aspects of the client

Just as each court card can represent a person, it can also represent an aspect of the client regardless of whether the court card describes your client or not. When a Knight of Pentacles appears in a layout for a 51-year-old Queen of Cups, you need to decide if the Knight represents a person (such as young man or an immature partner), a Capricorn person (male or female) or an aspect of the client. As a reader, it is up to you to decide which meaning applies to a court card at the time of the reading. The Court Cards as Aspects of the Client chart (see colour charts section of the book) lists the aspects of clients represented in the court cards.

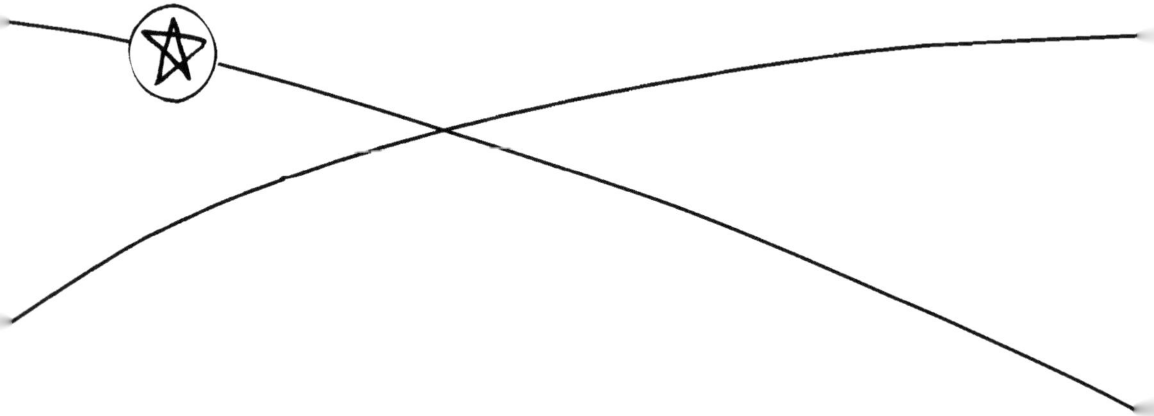

PART III

The Major Arcana and the meaning of our lives

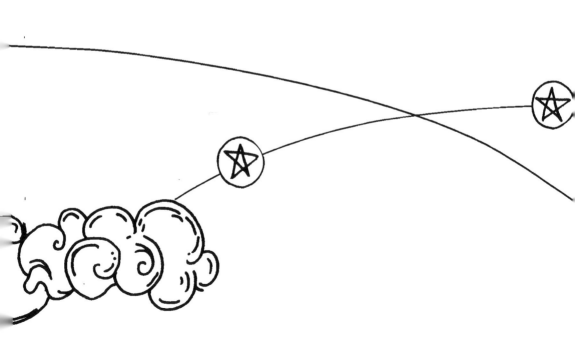

Chapter 13

THE MAJOR ARCANA

0 The Fool

General meaning

Against a sunny backdrop, a person pauses on a precipice. With a white rose in the left hand and a staff in the right, he ignores the white dog at his heels, as he stares into the sky imagining life's possibilities. Attached to the staff is a satchel containing personal belongings. The red feather symbolises passion, the yellow background represents intellect while the white rose suggests purity of motive. Yellow boots indicate that he understands life in theory, but is yet to test the theories in reality.

This is a card for seeing life's opportunities in an uncomplicated manner. When the Fool appears upright in a spread it can suggest that you instinctively know where your opportunities lie at this time. It can also suggest that you are leaping into something new without any prior experience.

Reversed

The Fool reversed represents a disconnection from instinct. This can result in having to ask others for advice and becoming confused with the myriad directions that they suggest you take. In some cases the Fool reversed can indicate that although you seek freedom from responsibilities and obligations, you are duty bound to finish what you have begun. Now is not the time to ignore responsibilities in the pursuit of freedom. This card reversed also can describe either clinging to a particular direction long after it has served its purpose or changing direction after encountering a small obstacle.

Finances

In a financial layout the Fool can describe taking a leap of faith and acting on your inspiration. This impulse may be opening a new business, leaving your job without another job to go to, or investing in a venture in an area where you have no experience. Inwardly you sense that the timing is right for a successful venture.

Reversed

The Fool highlights the foolishness of your current plans. Impulsive, unplanned actions may result in financial loss at this point. The reversed Fool can also represent the need to reconnect with those parts of yourself that can best advise you about the course of your life. It is possible that you are acting impulsively because you feel trapped in your life.

Health

The Fool is a positive card when it appears upright in a health reading. You have plenty of energy, enthusiasm and passion for life now, as well as faith that life will offer support in your pursuits. Although you may feel restless when this card appears, health is usually balanced.

Reversed

The Fool reversed can suggest a foolish disregard for commonsense behaviour that results in health complications. Christopher, whose severe diabetes did not prevent him from consuming a bottle of wine with dinner each evening, personified the Fool reversed. 'I have to die of something,' he declared. Despite the concern of others and the Fool reversed appearing in his layout he remained unperturbed. As his health deteriorated, Christopher had to give up work and outdoor pursuits, and was eventually confined to bed for most of the day. Rather than 'dying of something' his greatly reduced quality of life was the consequence of his short-term view regarding his diet.

Spiritual meaning

The Fool represents the ability to perceive windows of opportunity and invisible universal support for your endeavours. Sometimes childlike trust is required to take that first step on the road to happiness. Armed more with faith than a practical plan, you embark on a journey through life.

I The Magician

General meaning

A bright yellow backdrop contrasts with the figure's deep red robe and his white tunic. Pointing his magician's wand to the heavens with his right hand, he directs the energy received out of his left hand into the earth. The Magician represents the act of taking an idea or inspiration and turning it into something tangible. As musicians and artists create seemingly out of the air, each of us uses our energy, inspiration and philosophy to shape our lives.

To aid him in this process the Magician has a wand, cup, sword and pentacle, which represent the combination of passion, inspiration, planning and practical application he uses to make his ideas real. The infinity symbol suggests that he has done this before; he has only to remember the process rather than relearn it.

Reversed

The Magician reversed can suggest that you are not grounded or that you lack continuity of purpose to realise present goals. When representing someone around you, this person is likely to be wilful, controlling and unpredictable, making them a formidable adversary. In most cases the reversed Magician suggests that you need to become more grounded in reality through walking, other exercise or through focusing your thoughts and attention on the physical world.

Finances

This is a powerful card for financial success as it combines the right opportunity, motive, passion and application to make even seemingly impossible goals achievable. With careful focus on financial goals, you can realise your plans when the Magician appears upright.

Reversed

Financial success is unlikely until you can set and maintain a comfortable pace in the pursuit of your goals. When reversed, it is as though you are sprinting when you are better off pacing yourself for a marathon. Perhaps unrealistic goals are being pursued now. It may be time to be aware of limitations and realistic possibilities when setting and pursuing goals.

Health

Balanced health is indicated by the upright Magician. Energy flows easily spiritually, mentally, emotionally and physically resulting in good health and fitness. It is likely that you are aware of what is required for good health, including a sensible diet, exercise and uplifting surroundings.

Reversed

The Magician reversed can suggest fluctuating energy levels resulting in an unbalanced life. Psychological problems such as depression, mood swings and, in severe cases, psychotic episodes can be shown with this card reversed. Usually the reversed Magician simply suggests the need for more exercise to improve and maintain the physical body.

Spiritual meaning

The Magician describes the act of recognising how to make the most of your talents and skills to seize an opportunity when life presents it. Action now can make possibilities a reality. You recognise that ideas alone are valueless, and that success comes from practical application of your plans to make your ideas tangible.

II The High Priestess

General meaning

A woman sits calmly, clad in blue robes and holding a scroll (the Torah). Twin pillars stand behind her, between which is draped a colourful cloth. Water can be glimpsed in the background. A crescent moon lies at her feet. The crescent moon indicates that this is a time to think about and clarify plans. The posture of the High Priestess suggests that she is passive but still mentally alert.

This is a positive card for psychic and spiritual development. In everyday terms, it suggests a time to reflect upon plans while waiting for seeds to germinate. As the moon waxes from a new moon to a full moon, it is a suitable time to plant seeds, start new projects and act on your plans. The High Priestess describes a chance to retreat from life so you can clarify your goals. In meditation it is possible to discover those parts within us which may not be fulfilled by current pursuits. Time spent in reflection may offer viable alternatives.

Reversed

This card reversed represents the need to act on your plans. It offers a chance to return to the upright Magician card to focus on your goals and to act with conviction in the pursuit of those goals. The High Priestess reversed can symbolise the process of returning to life socially after a period of isolation or contemplation. It can also indicate a new circle of friends after a period of social stagnation.

Using your intellect to solve problems is another possible meaning of the reversed High Priestess, along with signifying a Piscean person. After a period of thinking about a desired goal, you are ready to act in order to make that goal a reality. This may require assistance from those around you, along with a precise and realistic approach (a return to the upright Magician).

Finances

This is a time to ask yourself if the pursuit of financial goals conflicts with your spiritual purpose at this point. The High Priestess offers the chance to align your spiritual and financial goals by contemplating the bigger picture of your whole life and beyond. In a financial question this card can suggest that you have planted seeds in your mind for financial goals, and that these seeds take time to produce tangible results. The High Priestess can also suggest the opportunity to earn an income through using your intuition, either as a reader or through investments based on intuitive information gleaned through meditation or dreams at night.

Reversed

The High Priestess reversed can indicate that a new circle of contacts is required in order to make current financial goals a reality. It can also describe meeting new people after a period of isolation. Perhaps you are changing jobs and meeting a new group of people (and financial opportunities) through your new position. It can also suggest increased opportunities available to you through your social network.

Health

The High Priestess indicates that meditation or contemplation are likely to benefit physical health at this time. By stilling the conscious mind, you may be able to access the subconscious mind through dreams (the moon at her feet) or through intuition, represented by the dark pillar (some things are not visible to the naked eye) and the pool of water behind her. The feet and the glands of the body are also represented by this card.

Reversed

The High Priestess reversed represents a return to life after a period of rest or even after ill health. You have sufficient energy now to actively pursue your goals. A return to the upright Magician offers the chance to become more grounded in reality, and focused on your physical health. Perhaps you have recently experienced problems with your feet or the glands of your body.

Spiritual meaning

The High Priestess offers an opportunity to go within to nourish yourself emotionally and spiritually. In the stillness of sleep or meditation, your soul has a chance to be heard. If you acknowledge its needs now, you will experience joy. If you feel spiritually impoverished, regular meditation can still your mind, allowing your spirit to communicate with your conscious mind.

III The Empress

General meaning

Holding a sceptre a woman sits on several cushions in a natural setting under bright skies. Ripe wheat at her feet symbolises fertility. She wears a triple crown containing 12 jewels. The glyph for Venus appears beneath her and water flows steadily in a nearby stream.

The Empress can represent pregnancy, progression with your plans in life or making a harmonious home for yourself. It can also describe an earthy, sensual woman with a rounded figure and a pragmatic approach to life. This is the woman who understands that although presently you may be hurt or grieving, you still have to eat. While she listens to friends declare what ails them, she prepares a small feast, understanding that companions are less likely to feel upset with a full stomach.

Reversed

The Empress reversed describes domestic disharmony. It often appears when you are in the middle of home renovations, or you don't have a permanent home. It also appears when you live in an environment that doesn't suit you. The reversed Empress can suggest that your plans are not progressing at this stage, and it can describe a troubled pregnancy. It can also indicate the need to return to the upright High Priestess card in order to re-examine your spiritual direction or to find stillness within to counteract the chaos in your home environment.

Finances

The Empress in a financial layout often describes someone who works from home. Progression with your plans is likely when the Empress appears in a financial question. This card also suggests finances linked with the home, such as a home loan or taking a second mortgage on the home to raise money for another financial goal. Financial progress is suggested with the Empress upright in a financial layout.

Reversed

The Empress reversed can indicate a home which feels less home-like because it is strewn with papers, files and office equipment. Sometimes it can suggest that your home environment is eating up all available finances. This can also occur during extended renovations. Perhaps chaos at home is affecting your career or financial opportunities.

Health

The Empress represents the sign of Libra, and the area of concern for Libra is the kidneys. Sometimes the appearance of this card can suggest bloating in the belly area soon after eating foods which disagree with you. This usually settles down in a few hours. Generally the upright Empress signifies good health.

Reversed

The Empress reversed can signify kidney troubles. It can also indicate that your present home environment is adversely affecting your health. Tracey was stressed and this was affecting her health. In a reading about her health the Empress appeared reversed, indicating her home environment was causing the problem. Tracey said she felt restricted at home and she and her mother argued constantly. Tracey was 28 and it was probably time to find herself her own home.

Spiritual meaning

The Empress represents a time to appreciate life's abundance, especially physically. From a warm caress to a hearty meal, life supports us in many ways. It is also a time to share your abundance with others, especially those at home.

IV The Emperor

General meaning

A mature man with a serious expression is seated on a stone throne, holding an orb in his left hand and a sceptre in his right. This sceptre is shaped as an ankh, the ancient Egyptian symbol of the life of the soul after physical death. It represents the union of the male and female energies and is one of the most powerful Egyptian symbols.

Rams-head carvings, which represent the sign of Aries, appear above his head and beneath his hands. The lesson for Aries people is self-discipline and the Emperor symbolises a man who possesses this quality. He is usually practical, straightforward and unemotional when problems arise, thus he makes a sound business leader, military commander or a strict father figure. He learns by doing and has limited patience for elaborate theories.

The Emperor indicates success through self-control. The predominant colours in this card are red and orange, symbolising a passionate, enthusiastic approach to living, however, the Emperor also understands that freedom comes from discipline. Those in society who lack self-discipline are often disciplined by others.

Reversed

The Emperor reversed can signify failure with your plans due to lack of self-discipline. Although plans are commenced with passion and enthusiasm, they eventually falter due to insufficient interest in longer term goals. By returning to the upright Empress you can allow others to support you. When ready, the innate desire to support yourself and to make your mark in the world will once again propel you forward to master the lesson of the upright Emperor. When difficult short-

Chart of the Minor Arcana

	Wands	Cups	Swords	Pentacles
Ace Beginnings	a physical beginning	an emotional beginning	planning a beginning	a financial beginning
Two Decisions	a decision regarding location	a shared emotional decision	an intellectual decision	a financial decision
Three Progress	travel, progress with plans	a shared celebration	a painful realisation	financial progress
Four Consolidation	a stable environment	emotional consolidation	reflection and realisation	saving money or conserving energy
Five Change	physical change and struggle	emotional change or loss	forced change of attitude through arguments	financial change or loss
Six Stability	success with physical goals	emotional stability	return of mental stability	financial stability
Seven Don't give up	success if you persist with goals	time to pursue deeper emotional goals	search for more alternatives	strong financial growth possible
Eight Strength	enjoy life's summer now	leave behind unfavourable circumstances	strength exists in choices	commitment brings rewards
Nine Reflection	time to review past pursuits	reflect on your sources of joy	examine choices for preferred consequences	reflect on practical efforts and rewards
Ten Completion	ease your burden through delegation	shared happiness with others	your beliefs are weighing you down	solid financial success is assured

The Court Cards as People

	Wands	Cups	Swords	Pentacles
Page	A passionate, enthusiastic and independent young person 	A creative, sensitive and sentimental young person 	A curious, talkative and sociable young person 	A serious, conservative and practical young person 
Knight	An enthusiastic, energetic and impatient young man 	A romantic, sentimental and creative young man 	An intellectual, talkative and curious young man 	A practical, conservative and responsible young man 
Queen	A passionate, forthright and enthusiastic woman 	A sensitive, nurturing, compassionate yet private woman 	A talkative, sociable, mentally adaptable, quick-minded woman 	A practical, conservative, steadfast and responsible woman 
King	A disciplined, enthusiastic and passionate man 	A creative, sentimental and compassionate man 	A clear-thinking, quick-minded, sociable and talkative man 	A practical, conservative and realistic man 

Compatibility Chart for the Four Suits

	Wands	Cups	Swords	Pentacles
Wands 	Easy compatibility as they share a life viewpoint. Both can be enthusiastic and impatient.	Cups people can find the Wands types too direct. Wands people sometimes find Cups types too dreamy.	A compatible pairing as Swords people generate ideas which Wands people act on enthusiastically.	Wands people live in the future whereas Pentacles people prefer to live in the present. This pairing requires a sense of patience.
Cups 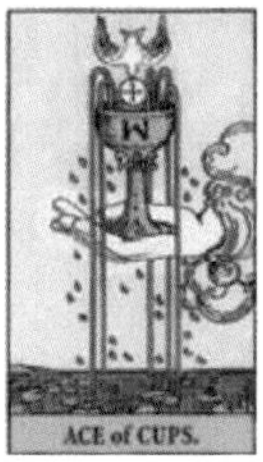		Perfect compatibility as both people perceive life as creative and romantic. Both are patient and sentimental.	Swords people love a good conversation whereas Cups people enjoy a companionable silence. This pairing can bring loneliness for the Cups person and boredom for the Swords type.	An easy partnership as Cups people provide the nurturing while Pentacles people pursue financial security.
Swords 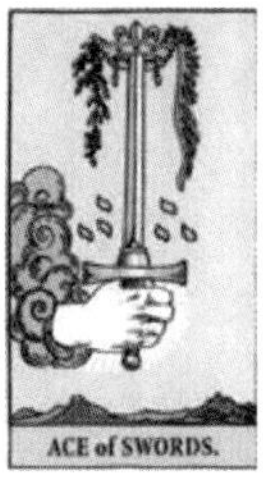			A companionable partnership as both people are curious, sociable and enjoy good conversation.	Swords people can jump from one idea to the next, whereas Pentacles people prefer to stick with one concept for years at a time. This pairing requires tolerance to work.
Pentacles 				A harmonious partnership with both people prepared to work steadily to achieve practical plans. Financial security is essential. An excellent business partnership.

The Court Cards as Aspects of the Client

	Wands	Cups	Swords	Pentacles
Page	An independent and passionate start to a project 	Dreaming of an emotional or spiritual goal 	Planning and discussing a desired project 	Study as a preparation for a long-term goal 
Knight	Seeking out opportunities through travel and movement 	Combining inspiration and passion in the realisation of goals 	Recognising and seizing opportunities before others 	Contemplating the best approach for long-term success 
Queen	Success through self-confidence and inner strength 	Success through trusting intuition and nurturing your plans 	Success through careful planning and negotiation with others 	Success through tenacity and hard work 
King	Success through self-discipline and focus on important goals 	Success through creative discipline 	Success through mental discipline 	Success through practical application to the goals at hand 

The Court Cards as Combinations of the Elements

	Wands - *Fire*	Cups - *Water*	Swords - *Air*	Pentacles - *Earth*
Page - *Air* *They exhibit the natural curiosity which is associated with the Air signs*	The airy part of fire. Intellect combined with enthusiasm 	The airy part of water. Compassion combined with intellect 	The airy part of air. Intellect combined with curiosity 	The airy part of earth. Practicality combined with intellect 
Knight - *Fire* *They display the abundant enthusiasm of Fire*	The fiery part of fire. Passion combined with enthusiasm 	The fiery part of water. Compassion combined with enthusiasm 	The fiery part of air. Intellect combined with enthusiasm 	The fiery part of earth. Practicality combined with enthusiasm 
Queen - *Water* *They are receptive, intuitive and adapt to their surroundings like Water*	The watery part of fire. Compassion combined with enthusiasm 	The watery part of water. Compassion combined with creativity 	The watery part of air. Compassion combined with curiosity and intellect 	The watery part of earth. Compassion combined with practicality 
King - *Earth* *They are relatively steadfast and practical in their approach to life*	The earthy part of fire. Practicality combined with enthusiasm 	The earthy part of water. Compassion combined with practicality 	The earthy part of air. Intellect combined with practicality 	The earthy part of earth. Practicality combined with a conservative approach 

Major Arcana Cards Representing Men

	The Magician	The Emperor	The Hierophant	The Chariot
Upright	An effective, powerful man with a strong focus upon goals. He makes plans and then fulfils them.	A disciplined, successful and sometimes dogmatic man. He believes what he can see or prove.	A conservative, patient man who appreciates stability and tradition. He is quietly persevering.	A man who combines imagination with mental discipline and tenacity. He displays natural leadership abilities.

Reversed	An ungrounded, mentally scattered man with no fixed purpose. He frequently changes his plans, his mind and his goals.	An undisciplined man who needs a partner with courage to help him succeed. He often shrinks from difficult life decisions.	A philosophically and spiritually broad-minded man who is curious about different life paths. A natural teacher, he enjoys studying spirituality.	An indecisive man overcome by his emotions or unresolved emotional issues. Alternatively cruel and then compassionate, he abandons his goals too soon.

Major Arcana Cards Representing Women

<table>
<tr><th></th><th>The High Priestess</th><th>The Empress</th><th>Strength</th><th>The Star</th></tr>
<tr><td>Upright</td><td>A private, intuitive and spiritual woman with hidden depths and a deep compassion for others.</td><td>A sensual, practical woman who appreciates good food and a simple life. She is nurturing and generous.</td><td>A woman who has discovered her strength and who is prepared to expand her life with quiet courage and self-confidence.</td><td>A woman who is connected to her source of creativity. She can see beyond the roles we play in life to who we truly are.</td></tr>
<tr><td></td><td>
</td><td>
</td><td>
</td><td>
</td></tr>
<tr><td>Reversed</td><td>A busy, active woman who doesn't have time to be still and to reflect upon life. She exhibits a sense of urgency to achieve her goals.</td><td>A woman whose spiritual hunger manifests as an incessant appetite for food and sensual fulfilment. She lacks generosity and she is often unfulfilled within.</td><td>A woman who seeks to control others because she has limited control over herself. Insecure and dominating, she is afraid of her shadow side.</td><td>A lack of faith in life's possibilities leaves this woman insecure or worried about the need for more structure in her life. Recreation may give her a rest from routines and restore her faith.</td></tr>
</table>

Cards for Health

ARIES – The head
The Emperor • King of Wands

TAURUS – The throat, neck and shoulders
The Hierophant • King of Pentacles • Four of Pentacles

GEMINI – The lungs and arms
The Lovers • Knight of Swords

CANCER – The breasts, the stomach and the lymphatic system
The Chariot • The Moon

LEO – The heart and the spine
Strength • The Sun • Queen of Wands

VIRGO – The pancreas and the intestines
The Hermit • Queen of Swords

LIBRA – The kidneys, digestive system (bloating of the belly after eating)
The Empress • Justice • Queen of Pentacles

SCORPIO – The nose, bladder, bowel and reproductive organs
Death • King of Cups

SAGITTARIUS – The hips and thighs
Temperance • Knight of Wands

CAPRICORN – Knees, skin allergies (including dry and flaky skin) and teeth
The Devil • Knight of Pentacles

AQUARIUS – The ankles, shins, retina, nervous system
The Star • King of Swords

PISCES – The feet and glands
The High Priestess • Page of Cups

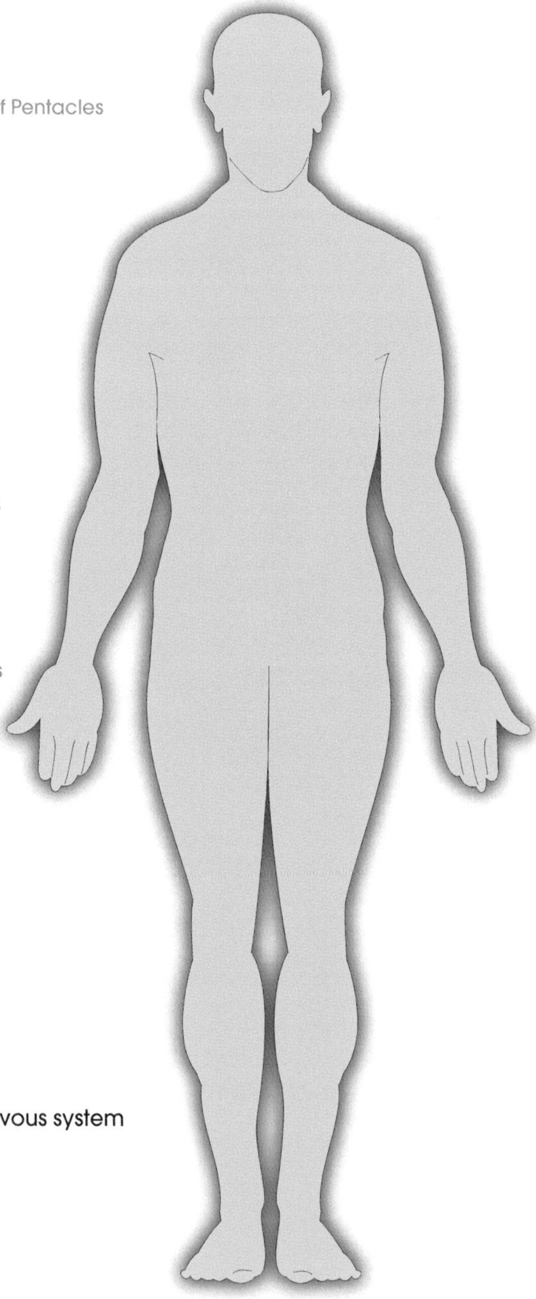

The Major Arcana
I–X Simple Card Meanings

I The Magician

An effective commencement of a project which is grounded in reality.

II The High Priestess

Decision-making with an awareness of the hidden and the visible aspects of the situation.

III The Empress

Progress with your plans. Pregnancy, a harmonious home environment.

IV The Emperor

A man who is keen to make his ideas and plans solid and tangible.

V The Hierophant

A chance to examine spirituality as a means for understanding life's changes (birth, death, loss).

VI The Lovers

Relationship decisions resulting in stability.

VII The Chariot

Represents the determination not to give up when emotional issues threaten your stability gained in the six.

VIII Strength

An awareness of your capabilities, your strengths and your weaknesses.

IX The Hermit

A time to reflect, in order to reassess your direction and your commitments.

X Wheel of Fortune

A chance to step back from circumstances in order to notice life's seasons. In doing this, you will know when to plant seeds and when to harvest.

The Karma Reading

This is not a predictive reading. It reveals your current strengths, weaknesses and highlights what you can do to spiritually re-balance yourself. The karma reading provides insight into where your energy is currently being directed. With this knowledge you can use your strengths to overcome your weaknesses.

1. Separate the Major and Minor arcana cards.
2. Remove the Seven of Cups from the pack—this card is central to the reading.
3. Shuffle the Minor Arcana cards, reversing some in the process.
4. Place the cards—one at a time—into three piles on the table to give them a perfect shuffle and to ensure that you touch every card.
5. Place the three piles into a single stack and slide them across the table in a line facing down.
6. Using your non-writing hand, select seven cards, one at a time, with your eyes closed.
7. Place each card in the position indicated above, with the Seven of Cups in the centre of the layout.

Briefly glance at the seven cards selected and notice which cards show an easy flow of energy. Take note of which cards reveal blocked or stagnant energies and remember that you can use your strengths to overcome your weaker areas. This is a layout you can use for yourself once a year, to gauge your spiritual progress in life.

Card 1

This relates to the face in the Seven of Cups. It describes the face you show to the world, your persona or how others perceive you to be.

Card 7

This corresponds to the shrouded figure and reveals where you are spiritually at present. The figure beneath this shroud reveals who we are spiritually.

Card 6

Corresponding to the cup containing the snake, it reveals your sexual and creative energies or unresolved sexual issues. A court card can describe your current sexual partner.

Card 2

Relating to the cup containing the castle, this describes your attitude to your home which is often established in childhood. It is rarely reviewed or updated.

Card 3

This corresponds to the cup containing jewellery and refers to your material power. This is your ability to attract or repel material success.

Card 4

Corresponding to the cup containing the wreath, it describes your personal power. It reveals your current ability to determine your life direction.

Card 5

This corresponds to the cup containing the demon and describes your current connection with your subconscious mind. Dreams, intuition and your deeper needs and desires are shown here.

Intuition Development Layout

Many clients ask tarot readers how to develop or improve their intuition, figuring that those people who use intuition in their daily work are most likely to know how to develop and strengthen it.

This layout is for those clients who want to know the best avenue to develop a reliable intuition. As we all have natural abilities in one or two particular areas, it is best to develop these areas rather than concentrate our efforts where they are less likely to be rewarded.

The client selects six cards one at a time, thinking about each area. As the reader you are advised to phrase each question before the client selects each card. The questions are best phrased as follows:

1. Can I effectively develop my intuition based on my feelings (Clairsentience)?
2. Can I effectively develop my intuition through auditory means (Clairaudience)?
3. Can I effectively develop my intuition visually (Clairvoyance)?
4. Can I effectively develop my intuition through contacting spirit guides?
5. Can I effectively develop my intuition through dreams at night?
6. Can I effectively develop my intuition through meditation?

Card 1	Card 2	Card 3	Card 4	Card 5	Card 6
Feelings	Sound	Visual	Spirit Guides	Dreams	Meditation

There may be several positive upright cards in the layout, suggesting that the client has more than one path to develop a reliable and accurate intuition. The most positive card (an upright positive Major Arcana card outranks a Minor Arcana card) points to the best avenue for intuitive development.

Detail each card, explaining why each area is worth pursuing or not worth the effort. You may have the client add a card to any position which needs clarification. Try not to add more than three or four cards, or you risk ending up with 15 cards for a six card layout.

In Sandy's reading the upright Judgement card appeared in position 1, indicating that she'd find success through developing her intuition through feelings. The only other positive upright card was the Eight of Wands in position 3. Sandy asked how she might best develop her visual skills.

I had her add one card for each of the following:

A. Developing her visual skills through taking time to 'see' at the end of each tarot reading.

B. Practising telepathy on the phone each night with a girlfriend.

C. Visualisation exercises.

The upright Queen of Wands in the A position suggested that Sandy needed to take some time to 'see' at the end of each tarot reading. This involves asking the client to give you a few moments to see if you can pick up any further information for him or her.

You can break any area into sub-headings as long as they relate to the area concerned. The meditation area can then be broken down into specific types of meditation or particular meditation courses offered locally.

Basic Questions

The questions below may help you to ask the most appropriate questions for your particular situation. These are not the only questions you can ask, but they may help you to clarify your issues.

Personal relationships

What does the future hold for me in personal relationships generally?
What does the future hold for my current relationship?
What can I do to improve our relationship?
Is it wise for me to pursue this relationship?
Is it wise for me to pursue a relationship with …?
What is the underlying lesson for me in this relationship?
What is the gift for me in this relationship?

Finances

What does the future hold for me financially?
What can I do to ensure financial success for myself?
What am I currently doing to prevent myself from becoming financially secure?
Is it wise for me to sell my shares in (x number of) months?
Is it wise for me to invest …?
What behaviour patterns do I need to change to ensure financial stability for myself?

Career

What does the future hold for me in my career generally?
What does the future hold for me in my current career?
Is it wise for me to continue in this particular career?
Will I still be in this job in (x number of) months?
Am I suited to a career in (alternative occupation)?
What is the underlying lesson for me in my current career?

Family

What does the future hold for my mother/father?
What does the future hold for my brother/sister in their business?
Is it wise for my mother/father to purchase the house at (address)?
What does the future hold for my mother's/father's health?
What can my family teach me this year?

Happiness

Will pursuing my current path in life lead me to long-term happiness?
What can I do to increase my happiness?
What do I need to resolve to enjoy a deeper sense of happiness?

Health

What does the future hold for my health?

What does my physical health currently reveal about my attitudes to life?

What do I need to resolve to enjoy an improved vitality?

Is it wise to have a surgical operation?

Is there a viable alternative to a surgical operation at this stage?

Will osteopathy/chiropractic/massage/yoga/meditation etc. resolve my current spinal problems?

How can I best maintain and improve my physical health?

Note: Unless you are a trained medical practitioner, do not diagnose. It is recommended that clients seek confirmation by a qualified medical or alternative practitioner regarding any health information given during a reading.

Spirituality

What is my current spiritual lesson?

What are my current spiritual strengths?

What do I need to learn in order to fulfil my life's purpose?

What do I need to resolve from my past in order to pursue my life's purpose?

How can I confirm that I am on my correct path spiritually?

How can I contact and communicate with my higher, or spiritually evolved, self?

What does the future hold for my relationship with God?

Children

What does the future hold for (the child's name)?

Is it wise to encourage my child in the study of music/science etc.?

What is the underlying cause of my child's nail biting/nightmares etc.?

What do I need to concentrate on developing in my child?

What can I do to help my child to be happy?

What is my child here to teach me spiritually?

Travel

What does the future hold for me regarding travel?

Will I travel overseas in the next 24 months?

Is it wise/safe for me to travel to … this year as planned?

Will I have enough money to travel to … this year as planned?

Will I be able to earn an income as I travel?

What will I learn from this travelling?

What is my underlying lesson in my forthcoming travel to …?

The Seven Card Layout

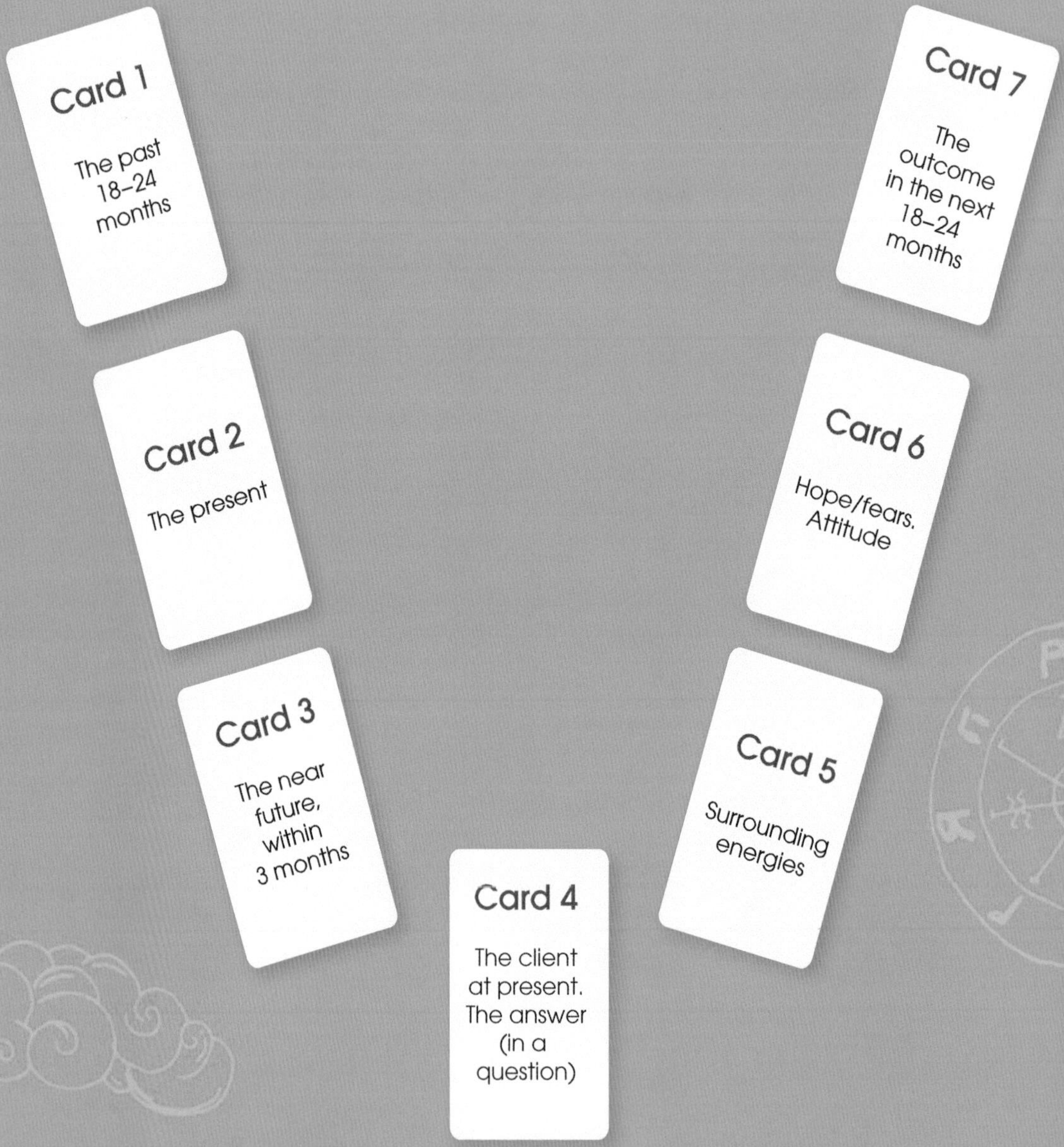

This is a simple layout which is is useful for general readings and for questions.

In a general reading the fourth card represents the client at present.

In a question, the fourth card represents the answer to the question.

term decisions are required to ensure long-term happiness, the reversed Emperor can suggest you lack the courage or self-control to make such decisions.

Finances

Success is assured when the Emperor appears upright in a financial spread. It signifies having sufficient discipline to see your goals through to conclusion. When this card appears in a layout for a young man, he may have been, or is about to be taken under the wing of someone in management. It can also indicate a father figure seeking to share his experience with a younger man, whom he recognises has the passion and determination to succeed.

This card can describe being disciplined with your time and your financial resources in order to progress with your career. Perhaps you are working full time and studying with a view to improving your career. Financial stability arising from discipline and control over your spending is signified by the appearance of the Emperor card.

Reversed

A lack of self-control in financial matters. The reversed Emperor is someone who prefers to borrow a huge sum of money to launch a new business instead of saving enough to begin on a smaller scale and build the business steadily. If a client lives a financial life as the reversed Emperor, they can expect to be declared bankrupt eventually. It describes beginning financial projects with a passion and commitment that soon dissipates.

Health

Headaches or accidents involving the head are the health areas to watch when the Emperor card is chosen in a health reading. When upright, this card describes a person who chooses a competitive, sometimes punishing exercise routine so they can eat whatever they like. Minor health ailments are often ignored by Emperor types.

Reversed

A lack of self-discipline can lead to health problems. Perhaps you have returned to the upright Empress to indulge your appetites for sensual pleasures or sweets.

Health issues arising from a lack of self-control are signified by the reversed Emperor. These include excessive intake of food, drugs or alcohol.

Spiritual meaning

Creative ideas require a practical structure before they can be realised, and the Emperor offers you the discipline and commitment to pursue your goals to fruition. It is a chance to take a spiritual concept or a creative idea into physical reality in an orderly, measured way.

V The Hierophant

General meaning

The Hierophant, or high priest, sits with his right hand raised to the heavens and his left clasping his staff which contains a triple cross. He wears a triple crown and three crosses appear down his tunic. Four more crosses are visible within circles on the floor. Two disciples wait at the Hierophant's feet, and a pair of grey stone pillars stand behind him, dwarfing him.

The Hierophant represents an acceptable code of conduct determined by those in authority. The disciples follow the Hierophant's directives and his example. In everyday terms this card can indicate that you are conforming to the expectations of others. This desire results in you modifying your behaviour in the pursuit of acceptance and understanding. The Hierophant is card number five, and upright fives suggest narrow-mindedness, so the upright Hierophant is limited in his outlook.

Reversed

The reversed Hierophant indicates a person who is aware of the most acceptable path yet who has a preference for the path less travelled. It is in seeking individual answers to life's questions that you can truly determine if and when the mainstream path is accurate. The Hierophant reversed indicates you are less likely to care about the opinions of others in the pursuit of truth and understanding. It can indicate a desire to have a lifestyle or a career out of the mainstream. Perhaps you seek self-employment or part-time work while you pursue creative or spiritual goals.

Finances

Taking a conservative, well-trodden path to financial stability is shown when the upright Hierophant appears in a financial layout. Success is likely. This is not a sudden, unexpected success, but the realisation of goals which occur at a moderate pace. Sometimes the upright Hierophant card can describe someone pressured by those around them to pursue an acceptable career or financial path.

Reversed

You may prefer an unusual approach to financial issues, which will require more discipline if you are to succeed. This necessitates a return to the upright Emperor in order to ensure sufficient discipline to complete financial plans. Often more self-discipline is required to work for yourself than to work for a corporation. Within the mainstream you can purchase computer software, hire consultants or attend classes to learn the systems that make a business thrive. More concentration is required to work outside the mainstream as you may find yourself having to make your own map.

Health

Neck, throat and shoulders are the areas signified by this card, either upright or reversed. Generally the upright card points to balanced health through a moderate lifestyle. Chronic health concerns rather than sudden issues are more likely with the upright Hierophant card. A conservative approach to health is shown by this card. If you ask what is the best approach to current health issues, the upright Hierophant suggests modern medicine rather than alternative healing.

Reversed

The Hierophant reversed suggests an unusual approach to your health is required to achieve the balance sought. Such approaches may include hypnosis, herbs, energetic healing or dietary restrictions. It may be time to consider the underlying spiritual lessons in current health issues. Tension in the neck and shoulders is shown with this card.

Spiritual meaning

Sometimes life's spiritual journey requires a guide, someone who has experience and who offers you practical guidance for your spiritual journey through life. The Hierophant is the recognition that although paths to the summit of life's mountains may diverge, they usually reach the same destination. You can choose to follow a path or to create your own path. Following an existing religious or spiritual path offers security and company for the journey. Going it alone offers a unique view but, when faced with overwhelming obstacles, it can be daunting.

VI The Lovers

General meaning

A couple stand naked before one another while an angel appears above them. The man looks to the woman for his fulfilment while the woman looks up to the angel for spiritual nourishment. The rich colours in this card offer yellow for intellectual understanding, purple for compassion, red for passion and orange for enthusiasm.

Replacing the pillars found in the High Priestess are the tree of life, which stands behind the man, and the tree of knowledge, which stands behind the woman. These represent the duality of life highlighting the lesson for Gemini: that is, to choose wisely between two alternatives.

Behind the pair of lovers is a mountain. This mountain represents the soul's ascent to God which can be achieved by taking the 'right spiritual path', which is different for every person. We briefly glimpse the mountain's summit when in love and during the ecstasy of lovemaking. This card reminds us that others (either physical or spiritual) must assist us in this journey, although each person's journey is unique.

The myth that there is one soul mate to share the entire journey with us pacifies our fears, especially when we realise that we have to face the challenges ahead, represented by the lion in Strength, our aloneness in the Hermit and the effects of our past decisions and actions in Justice. Later we will face loss in the Tower and Death, and our shadow side in the Moon before we can step from beneath heavy skies to glimpse the Sun directly. The Lovers also offers us a reminder that parts of each of us are pure when seen through the eyes of others.

The Lovers represents a decision between present circumstances and the path ahead. In love relationships it can symbolise the beginning of a new love relationship, or of a new stage in an existing one. When upright it is wise to move forward to the new opportunities awaiting you.

Reversed

A return to the upright five is likely (the Hierophant) where you may feel pressured by those around you to limit your choice to a more conservative or acceptable alternative. Perhaps you are not ready to pursue the path you have found, fulfilment may lie in remaining where you are.

In a general reading, the Lovers reversed indicates love relationship issues dominate your life at present, overshadowing other concerns, and demanding that a path be chosen before you can expect a return to inner peace. When reversed, the Lovers suggests that it is wise to remain where you are, despite the tempting opportunities awaiting you. In a love relationship question this card can describe a relationship which remains in the initial, romantic stage and is unlikely to deepen into a significant long-term relationship.

Finances

Financial decisions are shown when the Lovers appears in a financial spread. If the card is upright, you are ready to move forward to new alternatives. Sometimes the appearance of the Lovers in a financial layout can suggest a business partnership or financial dealings with a love relationship partner. Perhaps you are attempting to open a business with this partner.

Reversed

The Lovers reversed suggests that you are better to remain where you are presently, as you may not be properly prepared for current financial opportunities. A return to the upright Hierophant, where you can enjoy some of the unchanging financial routines it offers, is required at present. Indecision in financial matters is indicated by the reversed Lovers card. It can be due to relationship issues.

Health

A card for Gemini, the Lovers can suggest that you need to be aware of your arms, hands, shoulders and lungs. Depletion of nervous energy can sometimes be symbolised by this card.

Reversed

Indecision can be the root cause of health concerns at present. The Lovers reversed can also highlight current relationship issues affecting your health. It may be time to decide what to do about your relationship before it depletes your health. A return to the upright Hierophant provides stability and routines which may allow your health to stabilise.

Spiritual meaning

The Lovers represents the decision to pursue a fulfilling opportunity. Life presents a path which may lead to happiness, but this is only potential until you decide to take that first step. It is a time to commit yourself to the next part of your journey, usually with a partner. This love relationship or business partnership can be an opportunity for a creative association. The relationship offers a chance to reveal yourself to someone who recognises your unique qualities, and to share part of life's journey with another. It offers a temporary respite from existential aloneness as you journey through your physical life.

VII The Chariot

General meaning

A man stands with a fixed gaze beneath a star-covered canopy. His chariot rests at the edge of a river and a city stands behind him. A pair of sphinxes replace the pillars found in the High Priestess, reminding him of the duality of life. His fixed gaze conceals his inner struggle between his thoughts and his feelings. Examined logically, life appears to be simple and straightforward. Remaining balanced in your outlook becomes more complex and challenging when emotions are taken into account. The winged disc reminds him that his mind can allow him to soar above his emotions to glimpse life more objectively. His lesson is to combine his thoughts and feelings to arrive at a balanced view of life.

Being a number seven, the Chariot suggests that success awaits the person who does not give up. You are learning that courage is a combination of commitment and doubt. If courage only required commitment there would be no chance of failure but limited challenge. Life becomes merely routine. If you are consumed by doubts then you are unlikely to move forward to complete your desired plans. The Chariot depicts courage to pursue plans despite doubts. It resembles the Emperor, but with the awareness of the importance of your own feelings and the feelings of others which were discovered in the Lovers.

Reversed

When reversed, the Chariot symbolises heightened fears. Commitment is waning as you increasingly fear that the goals sought are impossible, or that you don't have sufficient courage or skills to fulfil your dreams. Do not hold on to these outmoded beliefs about yourself. Your future success does not necessarily depend on your past results. It may be argued that those who say that a man or woman cannot change are merely describing themselves.

The reversed Chariot can also indicate an increasing sense of frustration with current circumstances. Perhaps it's time to find a suitable emotional outlet for your frustration or anger, then you may be able to return to the upright six (the Lovers) to examine your choices. Emotions may need to be expressed before you can clearly assess your current circumstances and opportunities. When reversed the water in this card is above the figure, suggesting that emotions now dominate thinking. Holding on to emotions now may cloud your judgement.

Finances

The Chariot in a financial spread suggests that financial success is within your grasp if you keep your mind in control of your emotions. Success depends on remaining aware of your goals all the way to the finish line and beyond. Do not give up on your goals. The Chariot describes keeping a balance between financial goals and emotional needs, so pace yourself for the long road ahead. It often depicts someone who is already successful.

Reversed

Your emotions are clouding your thinking at the moment. The reversed Chariot indicates that financial success is impeded by unresolved feelings and beliefs. It is time to release old beliefs, habits and emotions so that you can move forward towards your financial goals. Once these emotions or outdated beliefs have been cleared away, you can return to the upright Lovers to make effective financial decisions.

Health

Being one of the cards for the sign of Cancer (the other being the Moon), the Chariot chiefly covers the health of the stomach, the lymphatic system and the breasts. Continual stress may lead to digestive disorders or problems with the upper digestive system. Upright this card usually describes balanced health.

Reversed

It is possible that unresolved emotional issues, such as unresolved grief, pain, anger or resentment, may be stressing your health. 'Don't hold on', are the watchwords for the reversed sevens. It is important to release unexpressed emotions lest they stress your physical health. When reversed, the Chariot suggests it may be time to express your pent up emotions to clear the way for you to return to the upright six (the Lovers), to review your choices in life. Physical health areas to watch are the same as the upright Chariot card.

Spiritual meaning

Life's demands are strong now. This means a tug of war between practical and emotional needs. While one part of you seeks to suppress your feelings in order to be more effective in practical terms, another part longs for the tender embrace of that someone special who was found in the Lovers. The Chariot calls for the acknowledgement of feelings and practical desires, and encourages people not to give up on long-term plans. This may require that you delay immediate gratification, through seeking long-term rewards which may arrive after consistent effort.

VIII Strength

General meaning

The duality of life presented in the High Priestess (the twin pillars), the Lovers (the two people) and the Chariot (the two sphinxes) continues in Strength, with the combination of mental and emotional courage. A woman soothes a lion using her mental courage, while the lion displays the emotional courage required to trust her. A wild animal trusting a predatory species is rare. The rich orange of the lion's coat represents passion and enthusiasm, qualities common to the sign of Leo, the astrological sign represented by this card.

This card is named Lust in the Thoth deck (by Aleister Crowley) because it represents the challenge of overcoming the lust for sensual pleasure, for gold, for fame and for recognition which the beast within us craves. This is the time when a young person recognises that feeding these lusts does not nourish the spirit, and that they must be cast aside if they are to reach the mountain top.

The white tunic the woman wears symbolises her pure motives in handling the lion. She is nervous but believes that if she acts with integrity in her dealings with the wild animal, he will respond. The infinity symbol above her hints that she knows from her experience gained in the previous cards that the lion will trust her. The bright yellow background suggests the power of thought.

This is the first of two cards for Leo (the other is the Sun). It involves learning to harness your passion and using your mind to direct your energy towards your creative goals. The lion of passion is often difficult to contain, as each time it is settled in a creative direction, a new idea presents itself.

The Strength card represents a person who possesses the courage to face life and displays the necessary self-confidence to reach for their desired goals. It describes having sufficient self-belief and self-worth to build the life you desire, knowing that you deserve the rewards of your efforts. This card is an eight and like all eights in the tarot, it signifies commitment and strength.

Reversed

When Strength is reversed, courage has receded, replaced by fear or doubt. This can result in the desire to control your environment, including everyone around you. We often seek to control that which we fear, caging the lion within. When passions are suppressed too long there is a risk that they will break free and wreak havoc. When this card is reversed the lion appears above the woman, showing passion dominating thinking, and animal desires overpowering pure motives.

When Rhianna asked about her husband Thomas at a reading, she was troubled. Thomas was signified in the layout by the reversed Magician with Strength reversed in the outcome position. Rhianna explained that Thomas was a strictly religious man most of the year, belittling those whom he deemed to be less devout than himself. Once each year, Thomas disappeared interstate without warning. Rhianna found out that on these trips he drank, gambled and paid for expensive prostitutes. Rhianna was shocked and confused by this behaviour. Upon his return from said trip, Thomas avoided answering her questions, and enraged her by saying 'God has already forgiven me'. Soon he would revert to being pious until the next time the lion escaped the cage.

Finances

The Strength card shows courage and strength of conviction financially, usually resulting from a period of financial success. In a financial reading this indicates you are fully aware of your financial worth, and have the confidence to pursue plans to ensure financial success. In a general reading strength can describe a period of financial growth and success.

Reversed

Emotional upheavals and doubts about current financial circumstances are signified when Strength is reversed in a financial reading. It is time for you to return to the upright Chariot card, in order to stabilise your emotions and set your mind to the immediate task of determining a fruitful financial path. Perhaps the animal desires (for fame, possessions or glory) are keeping you poor at this time.

Health

A card for the sign of Leo, Strength can indicate that the heart and the spine are areas of weakness when it appears in a health reading. Generally the upright Strength card represents sound physical health and the courage to face any present health issues with equanimity.

Reversed

Strength reversed suggests attention be paid to the health of the heart or the spine. It can also describe the lack of courage and inner strength necessary to build and maintain good health at this time. It can indicate you are exhausted due to an inability to set strong boundaries. This could be a result of taking on too many tasks at once. When this card is reversed the lion appears to dominate the woman (passion and desires dominating intellect). It is time to contain your passion or enthusiasm in order to channel this energy into worthwhile directions.

Spiritual meaning

Courage requires commitment despite inner doubts. An internal source of strength and confidence is needed when your path in life is steep and no one is available to support you on this part of your journey. Sometimes you will be called upon to give others courage, even when your own reserves are low. You have the necessary inner strength to face life's obstacles now, and current circumstances offer you the chance to prove yourself.

IX The Hermit

General meaning

Some clients perceive the Hermit as a period of loneliness when in fact the man in this card is at peace. Quiet reflection is necessary to deepen our understanding of life. Time spent alone can be rewarding as it provides the opportunity to sift through past actions and decisions, thus we learn from experience. The Hermit represents a period of deliberation, whether through meditation, consulting a counsellor, taking a walk amongst nature or keeping a diary.

The Hermit represents the recognition that action without reflection rarely deepens understanding. This card can represent time out for reflection either by choice or by circumstances. Often the Hermit describes a period where you are alone (not lonely) as you ponder your life circumstances.

Reversed

The Hermit reversed can highlight an underlying fear of being alone or loneliness that is masked by work addiction. You are too busy with engineered commitments to reflect on your life. Ongoing work commitments prevent you from addressing the underlying hunger or spiritual emptiness within. Sometimes the enormity of the realisation that we are alone and merely passing through this world can become overwhelming. Becoming focused on short-term goals and rewards can temporarily alleviate this insecurity.

It is time to return to the upright Strength card to find courage to face life. Time may be taken to reflect on what changes are necessary for a more fulfilling life. By immersing yourself in familiar and comforting circumstances, your inner strength can return, enabling you to gradually face your aloneness.

Finances

Reflection on past financial decisions and actions is shown by this card upright. It is time to think about what you want financially by examining past financial behaviour patterns. Taking time to do this can help you to change negative patterns, which will lead to a more rewarding financial future.

Reversed

You may be too busy with present commitments and obligations to take time to think about their financial future. Despite running her own business, Alice visited her aged mother several times each day to wash, dress and feed her. When I began to describe the reversed Hermit card Alice burst into tears asking, 'How can I take time to reflect? I don't have time to scratch myself.' The cards suggested that Alice's burdens were temporary, but the reversed Hermit card highlighted the need to reflect to become aware of this. With reflection Alice could realise that her mother needed professional help. This would give her time to salvage her business, which was close to collapse, and ensure a secure future for herself and her mother.

Health

Periods of reflection, stillness and contemplation are necessary for good health, yet this seems to be forgotten in the rush to work, earn and spend. The Hermit describes asking yourself simple, yet powerful questions such as, 'Am I happy? Do I like the life path I am currently taking?' and 'Will this project/job/move bring me more long-term fulfilment?'

Generally in a health reading the Hermit can represent the pancreas. As the answer to a question about health it suggests that meditation, counselling or a period of reflection may result in improved health. A weekend away in the country can sometimes be sufficient to release stress and to reflect on the situation.

Reversed

When the reversed Hermit appears in a reading it indicates that you may be too busy to stop and reflect on your life path, preferring instead to treat your physical health symptoms rather than search for underlying causes for health imbalances. If deeper needs are ignored for an extended period, the inner hunger that arises may lead to chronic depression.

It is time to return to the upright Strength card, to gather sufficient courage to make the changes necessary to bring fulfilment into your life. This process may be frightening, but fear can keep you sharp and remind you that you are alive. In the long term, avoiding those things which we fear doesn't usually make us any more secure. Instead we find new, smaller affairs to worry about.

Spiritual meaning

Your past courage and commitment has enabled you to reach a minor summit where you can reflect on your efforts so far. It is time to understand how you have reached this point on your spiritual journey, and to learn from past experience to quicken the journey ahead. Careful reflection upon past actions is rarely time wasted as it can help you to avoid repeating mistakes. Reflection may take the form of meditation, keeping a dream journal or consulting a counsellor to clarify your actions and motivations.

X The Wheel of Fortune

General meaning

The upright Wheel of Fortune indicates an improvement in circumstances after a period of few opportunities. The animals in the four corners of this card stand for the four paths taken in the Minor Arcana. They are yellow to show that although those four paths have been intellectually understood, they have not yet been applied to life.

The Wheel of Fortune represents a chance to observe where you are in life's seasons so that you may plant your seeds in spring for successful results in summer. It describes the departure of winter as spring approaches and advises you that it is time to dust off your plans and prepare for the work required to realise your desired rewards. Where you stand currently is the result of your previous decisions and your actions. Where you plan to go in the future depends on the decisions and actions you take now.

Reversed

When reversed, the Wheel of Fortune heralds the approach of winter, and a return to the Hermit card. This offers you a chance to retreat from outer concerns to rekindle a rich, rewarding inner life. Remember that the reversed Wheel of Fortune only has the appearance of ongoing limitations to those who do not understand the seasons. Those who remember past summers of opportunities and winters of scarcity know that the Wheel will turn and the seasons will change.

The reversed Wheel of Fortune indicates that the opportunities to pursue particular goals are thinning down now, and it may be advisable to seek alternative projects. This is a time to conserve your resources. Postpone plans for expansion when the Wheel of Fortune is reversed.

Finances

Improved financial circumstances are likely when the Wheel of Fortune is upright in a financial layout. Opportunities are increasing now, with several positive financial choices in the coming months. Being prepared and focused on your specific financial goals will prevent you from becoming confused or distracted from the path ahead when opportunities arrive.

Reversed

Financial opportunities are thinning now so it is wise to prepare for a financial winter. The reversed Wheel of Fortune indicates that preparation is required if you want to be financially comfortable in the coming months. Circumstances do not currently favour large investments or financial commitment to new ventures.

Health

Health is improving when this card is upright in a health layout. You are able to balance the four elements of fire (Wands), water (Cups), air (Swords) and earth (Pentacles) within yourself, resulting in good health. A period of low physical energy and vitality is behind you now with more positive times ahead.

Reversed

A gradual decline in health is indicated now which may be indicated by a steady decrease in energy. There is a need to return to the upright Hermit to reflect on your physical, emotional, mental and spiritual health in order to maintain genuine wellbeing. In most health readings however, the reversed Wheel of Fortune simply suggests a temporary personal winter. It is time to conserve your energy in anticipation of lower reserves of physical and emotional energy in the near future.

Spiritual meaning

From your vantage point this far on life's journey you can observe the seasons and cycles of life. You notice how some parts of the surrounding terrain are constantly shrouded in mist while other parts enjoy a more sunny aspect. By understanding that life changes as the seasons, you will be prepared to pursue ideas and plans when circumstances are favourable thus improving your chances of success. If one part of your life is contracting, look for the areas which are expanding.

XI Justice

General meaning

Justice is the second card that represents the sign of Libra and it indicates the act of making a decision and understanding the consequences. The upright sword with its double edge highlights the duality of life: one edge represents decisions and actions while the other represents consequences. The white shoe indicates purity of motive while the red gown represents passion. The blue square centred in the crown symbolises spiritual clarity, that is, an awareness of the spiritual consequences of your decisions. The scales suggest an attempt at fairness. These symbolise that balanced decisions require a combination of compassion, understanding, wisdom and practicality.

Justice can represent legal papers or documents being signed, such as when a house is bought or sold, a career contract is negotiated or a will is dispersed after the death of a loved one. Justice indicates that the paperwork progresses smoothly and that you are likely to be happy with the outcome.

Justice is also a card for taking responsibility for yourself. You are aware that your current circumstances are the result of past decisions and actions. This makes you more careful in making current decisions, when you realise that you will have to live with the consequences.

Reversed

When reversed, Justice indicates decisions or actions taken without thought of the consequences. Lacking full awareness of the facts, you have impulsively decided on a course of action which you now regret. The reversed Justice also indicates delayed paperwork or protracted negotiations. This card usually appears reversed when legal cases drag on without resolution.

Reversed Justice also implies a failure to take responsibility for your actions. It can describe seeking someone else to blame when your actions lead to upheaval or loss. It is time to return to the upright Wheel of Fortune in order to recognise how personal seasons are influencing your available opportunities. Instead of blaming others for your lack of success, you may realise that past choices or actions were not pursued in the right season for success. Perhaps during a financial winter you borrowed money to invest heavily and now you are burdened by debt.

Finances

Legal papers or documents surrounding finances are signified by the appearance of the Justice card in a financial layout. Perhaps you are in the process of borrowing a large sum of money, making a significant purchase or signing a contract regarding a new career position. Progress is unhindered when this card appears upright. You are taking personal responsibility for your actions, recognising that this is the most suitable time to proceed with current financial plans.

Reversed

Justice reversed can signify delayed documents, slow progress with financial negotiations, or legalities regarding finances. A reversed Justice in Alain's reading confirmed that he was about to lose his business and be declared bankrupt following a disastrous year during which his restaurant flooded twice during unseasonable storms.

This card reversed can signify long delays in the purchase of a home or a business due to extended legalities and sometimes due to inept legal support. This is especially so if the reversed King of Swords also appears in the layout.

Health

The health areas to watch when Justice is found in a health reading are the kidneys and the lower digestive system. This card indicates that you suffer from bloating in the abdomen after eating foods which disagree with you. This bloating is temporary and is helpful because it can show you which foods to avoid, reduce or not consume in combination with other foods.

The Justice card can signify that you are prepared to take responsibility for your health, recognising that current health issues may be the consequences of past decisions and actions. Perhaps a new diet or an exercise routine will provide an improvement in health when Justice is found in a health reading. Sometimes the upright Justice card can indicate a spiritual approach to physical health, when it is recognised that spiritual imbalances will eventually manifest themselves physically if not corrected. It can also describe legal proceedings related to health.

Reversed

Justice reversed in a health reading indicates that you blame others for personal health issues instead of taking responsibility for improving and maintaining good health for yourself. It may signify prolonged legalities surrounding health issues. A return to the upright Wheel of Fortune may assist in balancing the four elements (fire, water, air and earth) within, enabling a more even approach to health.

Spiritual meaning

Living an honourable life means taking responsibility for the consequences of your actions, both to yourself and to others. Justice offers the chance to recognise how your present life is the product of past actions and decisions. You can use the rewards of your present life as a reminder of your honourable actions, and the frustrations of your circumstances to guide you towards a more fulfilling life tomorrow.

XII The Hanged Man

General meaning

A man hangs inverted from a pole. He placidly surveys his surroundings, radiating a sense of inner peace and calm. The yellow aura surrounding his head implies that he is intellectually aware of the bigger picture, and is not worried by the restrictions of his present circumstances. He uses this opportunity to reflect on his life from the unusual perspective of his current position. The blue tunic represents spiritual awareness. The red tights suggest that passion and physical energy are available when required. Grey skies surround him but he is unconcerned, looking beyond the physical world towards spiritual realms.

The Hanged Man indicates that you have a choice either to struggle to pursue material goals or to accept current circumstances and the opportunities for self-discovery that lie beneath the physical conditions. It is another chance to reflect on the meaning of life. This is a deeper reflection than that offered in the High Priestess and the Hermit, for you have gained a wider understanding of life during your progress towards the Hanged Man.

Reversed

The Hanged Man reversed indicates struggling against the tide of life. It is a pointless struggle, for life is stronger than a single person. If this struggle continues, when you are released you will be too exhausted to pursue awaiting opportunities. You are likely to have missed an opportunity to deepen your understanding of life.

This card reversed is an opportunity to revisit the upright Justice card in order to judge with clarity how your past actions and decisions led to current circumstances. Then, armed with this understanding it is possible to take another, more rewarding path.

Finances

Be patient, is the message of the Hanged Man in a financial layout. Financial circumstances may be restrictive at present, however they will change of their own accord. Take this opportunity to examine what you have achieved financially and ask yourself if it was worth the effort. Ask too if your plans for your financial future will be worth the time and effort you may have to devote to realising them.

Reversed

The Hanged Man reversed is a reminder that this is time for surrender. Anything lost now was not meant for you anyway. The reversed Hanged Man offers the chance to return to the upright Justice lesson of personal responsibility. It is time to recognise how and when you sowed the seeds for the current circumstances and to gracefully accept the consequences of your actions.

In answer to a question about a financial project or investment, the reversed Hanged Man suggests this is a poor investment with minimal returns. If you doggedly pursue this financial direction you can expect to remain stuck or financially drained by circumstances.

Adriana complained at her reading that she had no financial choices. When the reversed Hanged Man appeared in the reading, she admitted to allowing her brother to talk her into placing all her savings, $250 000, into a clothing business against her better judgement. Now she had no choice but to accept the severe limitations this placed on her as she was unable to sell out of the business.

Returning to the upright Justice card offers a chance to recognise how difficult it can be to live with the consequences of hasty or poor decisions. While awaiting a change in circumstances, recognise how important it is to heed your intuition when important decisions are being made.

Health

Physical energy is low when The Hanged Man appears in a health layout. Take time now to read, to meditate and to rest. Pushing yourself physically may result in injury or a physical collapse. Taking time to reflect can help to restore equilibrium.

Reversed

The Hanged Man reversed indicates that you may be living with the physical health consequences of past actions. It is time to return to the upright Justice card to take more responsibility for your health and wellbeing or suffer even greater ill health. In Glen's health reading, the reversed Hanged Man appeared reversed and, he was reticent to accept that years of excessive alcohol and a poor diet might have contributed to his current health concerns. The appearance of the reversed Justice card also highlighted his kidney problems, which he confirmed began in his childhood. He confirmed that he knew alcohol was bad for his kidneys. 'Alcohol took to me. I didn't have much of a choice,' he said defensively.

Glen's refusal to make any real decisions to improve his circumstances is likely to see his health decline, until it is beyond repair.

Spiritual meaning

Knowing when to surrender to life is essential as you pursue your spiritual path. Inner growth is every bit as important as the outer conquests. The Hanged Man offers you the chance to see life differently from others and from your usual perspective so that you can release yourself from restrictive preconceptions. It is time to recognise that you are awake to your spiritual purpose, and that this awareness brings with it power and responsibilities.

XIII Death

General meaning

This is one of the most feared cards in the deck because most clients perceive it to mean a physical death. It usually means surrender, but clients' fears don't always subside. Surrendering to life, to a higher force or to a spiritual path can be one of the most difficult decisions to make because surrender often requires faith. If only we might borrow some of the faith offered in the Star, but it is not available to us yet until we accept the lesson of Death and surrender. When Death appears in a layout we may be forced back on to our own resources, and to trust that what life will eventually provide will equal that which it is presently taking from us.

The predominant colours in this card are white (purity of motive) and yellow (clarity of thought), two qualities that will enable us to make this transition more gracefully. The river in the background offers a reminder that we will all eventually pass from this life, as people and circumstances pass from our life.

A card for the sign of Scorpio, Death teaches us how to surrender gracefully to change, life's only certainty. When this card is selected you are likely to be completing a chapter or a cycle in your life, a change that is expected and necessary. Life is likely to replace what is being taken with something more appropriate.

Reversed

With Death reversed, you are likely to be resisting change, devoting all your resources towards preventing the inevitable. Remember that death of the old makes way for new, often more rewarding opportunities. You may be immersed in the past, distraught about the loss and unable to perceive that an ending usually precedes a beginning. You need to trust that sometimes life has a greater awareness of what is good for you than you have for yourself.

Finances

There is a death of a situation or a set of circumstances when Death is selected for a financial question. If you ask if a particular investment will be worthwhile long term, this card in the answer or outcome position gives a clear 'no'. The appearance of this card suggests that you may be completing an old financial chapter and beginning a new one.

Reversed

Death reversed describes resisting change which may bring new opportunities. Surrender now and allow life to take you forward to where you need to be. Faith is required to release the old when you cannot yet glimpse the new opportunities awaiting you.

Health

As this is a card for the sign of Scorpio, the appearance of Death in a health reading can indicate that the areas to watch are those for the sign of Scorpio, including the abdomen, bladder, bowel and reproductive organs. The nose is another health area signified by the Death card.

If the Death card appears with at least three of the following cards, it can signify a physical death: Ten of Swords, Six of Swords, Four of Swords, Three of Swords, the World, Judgement, the Tower or the blank card.

Reversed

When reversed, the same health areas are signified as with the upright card with the addition of depression, as you are devoting too much energy to maintaining a set of life circumstances which are fading. Resistance to change results in stagnation, as new opportunities cannot arrive until the old situation has been released.

Spiritual meaning

When Death appears it is time to gracefully release someone or a situation from your life. Inner peace comes from understanding that life will provide another, although different source of fulfilment in place of what it is taking away from you. In your heart you have room for both the old and the new however, at this point, try to remain aware of life's bigger purpose for you as this may give you the confidence to release the old from your life.

XIV Temperance

General meaning

A person stands at the water's edge, calmly pouring water from one cup to another. One foot stands on land while the other is immersed in the pool of water. This is the same pool which was glimpsed behind the veil in the High Priestess. The aura surrounding the head of this person is a reminder of the awareness of life's bigger picture gained in the Hanged Man. The wings show that Temperance is a blending of the human and the spiritual bodies. There is understanding that both bodies have distinct needs and it is in meeting these different needs adequately that makes for a balanced life.

This card represents a surrender of personal pride. In becoming aware of larger dimensions we can recognise how small we are in the scheme of things. When we lose a clear spiritual perspective it is easier to attach too much significance to our lives.

Temperance can signify travel, teaching, learning and taking a moderate path in life. It is a card for the sign of Sagittarius, as is the Knight of Wands. The path shown in this card leading towards the sun holds promise of learning while travelling and exploring the world. It represents the act of keeping longer term goals in mind while negotiating short-term obstacles.

Reversed

Your view of the path ahead is obscured by clutter. Perhaps it is time to return to the upright Death card to release those people, situations and possessions obstructing your path in life. If you don't clear the way to your destination, you risk being distracted from your life's purpose by something less meaningful.

Sometimes Temperance reversed can indicate the act of abandoning deeper goals in favour of short-term rewards. When reversed, Temperance reveals the shadow side of the Sagittarius character, which it represents. Negative Sagittarians can make running away from responsibilities appear like a quest. They may convince others that they have a new purpose, whereas they are actually distracting themselves from their true purpose because of their impatience.

Possibly you are ignoring either the spiritual or physical body in favour of the other. Prolonged avoidance of spiritual needs can lead to a barren life, whereas ignoring your physical needs can end in ill health or death. The reversed Temperance card is a necessary reminder that we are spiritual beings in physical bodies and that, although the physical body is important to us during our lives, only the spiritual body continues on the journey after death. 'You only live once', is the attitude displayed when Temperance appears reversed. With this philosophy, temporary rewards and the instant gratification of desires seem more appealing than the work required for spiritual growth.

Teaching, study and travel can also be signified by reversed Temperance. Look to the surrounding cards in the layout to confirm which meaning applies on the day.

Finances

Remaining aware of the ultimate financial purpose enables you to make short-term sacrifices without feeling deprived. Instead of needing an instant reward for efforts, you may delay a series of smaller rewards in favour of a greater achievement. This cannot be done effectively unless you are nourishing yourself spiritually. When your heart is full it is easier to forsake material or physical rewards.

Financial balance and moderation are evident when Temperance appears in a financial layout. You are acting with foresight, taking steps to ensure enduring success. There is an underlying sense that current sacrifices and choices are helping to fulfil long-term goals.

Reversed

Temperance reversed can signify financial recklessness, resulting in debt, risk taking and the desire for temporary solutions to entrenched problems. Instead of addressing the underlying issues, you want to win a lottery, secure a deal or interest an investor in order to stave off approaching creditors. It can also indicate taking on too many projects at once, draining financial reserves, or gambling under the guise of business. There is a sense of restlessness and ignorance of the financial dangers involved with such risk taking.

Health

The areas that correspond to Temperance (and Sagittarius) include the hips, thighs and the sciatic nerves. Accidents resulting from clumsiness or from competitive sports may also be shown with this card. When appearing in a health reading upright, Temperance suggests a balanced approach to physical and spiritual wellbeing and an ability to meet the needs of both.

Reversed

Temperance reversed in a health reading can signify intemperance. You are responding to an unquenchable desire for pleasure or fulfilment, resulting in an excessive intake of food, drugs or alcohol in the pursuit of sensual pleasure, and any other instant fulfilment. Without awareness of the spiritual purpose of life, you feed only the senses.

Spiritual meaning

Temperance offers a reminder of the need to take care of your physical and spiritual needs in life. A healthy life nourishes both the body and the soul, encouraging a harmony between the two as you pursue your spiritual purpose for this lifetime. Having positive spiritual goals and practical plans can increase your enthusiasm for life and your confidence that your goals will be realised. Temperance offers a glimpse of the bigger picture, lending a deeper sense of purpose to your life. The sun at the end of the path shown in this card is a promise that great joy lies ahead for you and this can revive your enthusiasm for life.

XV The Devil

General meaning

Orange and red are the predominant colours in this card, highlighting the passion and enthusiasm with which you pursue material goals. Chained together, the couple pictured are weighed down by their fears and desires. The fear of loss, poverty and of living in squalor, combined with the desire for a comfortable life confine them to a narrow path in life.

From the time you reach the Devil until you can move on to the Tower, it is as though you have forgotten the lessons learned in Temperance. You are ignoring spiritual needs in pursuit of material comfort, and there is a price to pay. The chains around the couple are loose. They can free themselves but the Devil represents the illusion that there is no choice but to accept the way life currently stands, and that life is composed only of what you can see, measure and prove.

This is the first time the five-pointed star is reversed in an upright card. It signifies that sensuality dominates spiritual needs.

This card indicates that you cannot see any viable alternatives to a current situation. Often you insist that the reading illuminates alternatives, however, each possibility offered is carefully discounted or routinely ignored. In many cases you feel disappointed at not being 'helped' with your burdens.

The Devil was selected in a layout for Shane, who asked if it was wise to sell his house. The moment he was told that it was unwise, Shane listed the reasons why he wanted to sell it, and how a previous clairvoyant stated that his worries would disappear if he sold up and moved away from the area. Shane's strained appearance and perpetually furrowed brow suggested a man who had worried for most of his life, and a move of house wasn't about to alter that. But

Shane seemed unable to take responsibility for his situation. He saw no viable alternative.

Overcoming avarice is the lesson of this card, as The Devil fills us with fear of poverty. Instead of pursuing happiness through spiritual nourishment, we seek more and more comfort for the physical journey. As life proceeds, we become weighed down by superfluous possessions which once promised us momentary pleasure. We risk forgetting about the journey as we pursue contentment and ease.

Reversed

The Devil is a more positive card reversed. It heralds a return to the upright Temperance card, and the awareness that life is a spiritual as well as a physical journey. It is easier to release your grip on material possessions, status and power when you remember that in 100 years few goals you currently have are likely to make any difference. When this card is reversed the five-pointed star is upright, suggesting that your mind has control over your physical desires.

When The Devil appears reversed we are recognising that the road to comfort leads us away from spiritual development. The dark background of the card forces our attention on the bodies of the couple in the card. When we tire of the momentary pleasures offered by the physical body the darkness surrounding us offers a chance to go within, and to remember our deeper spiritual purpose. Then we can cast away those possessions and material pleasures as we resume the pursuit of spiritual awakening. Returning to Temperance, we recall that we have spiritual needs as well as physical requirements. As a result we take only those material possessions that will assist us on our journey.

Finances

The Devil can be a powerful card for financial success. The tunnel vision indicated by this card means that you will not be distracted from the financial goals ahead. People who live for the realisation of their financial goals are more likely than most to achieve them, however, this card can suggest that you may not find this achievement fulfilling. You may believe that financial success cannot come from combined effort, and as a result you may persevere alone or seek control over your business dealings or financial partnerships.

Reversed

The Devil reversed indicates recognising other viable financial goals, and alternative ways to reach them. You are more broadminded in your approach and accept assistance and advice from those around you. A return to the upright Temperance card is necessary to release extraneous possessions and financial obligations. Once you have let go of this financial baggage you are less burdened for the journey ahead. Temperance offers an awareness of the need to travel lightly on life's journey, to be available for opportunities when they are presented to you.

Health

As a card for the sign of Capricorn, The Devil in a health reading suggests that you may be experiencing difficulties with the knees, the teeth or the bones. Sometimes skin allergies such as dry, flaking skin also occur with the Devil card. It can also suggest haemorrhoids. The upright Devil card can suggest career or financial stress is affecting your health at this time.

Perhaps it is time to seek viable alternatives to your current approach to health, to rebalance your health. You may cling to one method of redressing a health issue when another approach may be equally effective. When the Devil card appeared in Rosemary's layout it was reasonably certain that she was going to choose to undergo spinal surgery for her pain even though there was a possible alternative. A friend had mentioned that a combination of chiropractic care and yoga had cured her of a similar condition and suggested Rosemary postpone her operation for six months to test this possible, less drastic alternative solution. Thoughts of exercise and a stranger manipulating her back when she was embarrassed about her weight made this avenue seem impossible to Rosemary. Three operations later she is battling chronic back pain, a degenerating spine, and contemplating more surgery.

Reversed

The Devil reversed describes seeking several viable alternatives to build and maintain your health. An open-minded approach to maintaining health is evident now but this card can still herald the same physical problems as when upright. A return to the upright Temperance card might allow you to glimpse the bigger picture and release those burdens and responsibilities which stress your physical health. In this return to Temperance you may discover how your spiritual, mental and emotional health affect your physical health.

Spiritual meaning

Sometimes the joy of being in a physical body is the ability to collect possessions. A beautiful home, a tranquil holiday cottage by a river, an attractive partner, a collection of teapots or a shiny sports car can provide temporary joy as you move through life. The Devil reminds us not to become too attached to these possessions, lest they begin to possess us and seduce us from our chosen path. The Devil symbolises a long spiritual winter, during which you may feel deserted by God and lacking in spiritual direction. It is a chance to embrace materiality in order to discover that it can only offer fleeting rewards. The result of mastering this lesson is the realisation that although money cannot buy happiness, it can reduce hardship.

XVI The Tower

General meaning

Two people fall from a blazing tower which has been struck by lightning. A crown topples from the roof of the tower and one of those falling still wears a crown. The Tower shows life presenting you with sudden, unexpected change. This change occurs too rapidly for you to evaluate choice carefully, and reaction to circumstances is the best way of staying afloat. This change may not be bad and may take the form of an accident, a lottery win, an unexpected retrenchment from your work, or even falling in love when you had decided that your last opportunity for a fulfilling love relationship had already passed.

The clearest and most large-scale image of the Tower in recent memory was the destruction of the twin towers of the World Trade Center in New York in 2001. Events occurred too rapidly for many of those involved to carefully evaluate their alternatives. In such circumstances you do what you have to do to survive. The change brought about by this larger-than-life event echoed around the world.

By adding a card to the Tower you can clarify what form this sudden change may take for you. Adding the Seven of Swords means a theft; the Chariot a car accident; the Ace or upright Six of Pentacles, winning money; the reversed Six of Pentacles, retrenchment, loss of income; Justice, an unexpected law suit; the reversed Empress, unexpected termination of a pregnancy or sudden upheavals at home; or the reversed Eight of Wands, an accident while travelling.

When the Tower is placed in the outcome or answer position, add another card to enable you to conclude the reading on a positive note. Storms don't last forever, and you need to know what to expect after the storm has passed. The Tower is life's way of helping us to release those people, possessions and patterns of behaviour that hamper us in the pursuit of our particular spiritual path.

Reversed

The Tower reversed indicates sudden change that sweeps through your home or workplace but which leaves you standing. Perhaps you are one of those chosen by management not to be retrenched, or the day you are at home sick is the day the office burns down. Being the survivor of change is not always easy to bear. When the Tower appeared reversed for Jason he explained that most of his friends were HIV positive and several had already died from AIDS. The bolt of lightning had missed hitting him directly but this was small compensation for 35-year-old Jason who knew that he might bury most of his friends in the coming years. It was suggested that he discover why the disease had missed him and that perhaps he was here for a particular purpose.

The Tower reversed allows you to return to the lesson of the upright Devil, to prop yourself up with material possessions or safe routines until it occurs that the spirit also needs nourishment. A gradual release of material desires makes way for the pursuit of spiritual purpose. If material desires are not released, there is a risk that this will be done for you when you experience the upright Tower at some later date.

Finances

In a question about the wisdom of a financial investment, the Tower suggests that it is an unwise pursuit. Sudden changes in circumstances are likely to leave your investment decimated. This card is sometimes found in readings when the stock market is about to take a tumble; it was selected often in the late 1980s when the world economy entered recession.

Reversed

The Tower reversed implies that you may be able to avoid financial loss or ruin by acting swiftly and decisively when circumstances change. Unless you are confident and calm under pressure, you may prefer to avoid risky financial speculation.

Health

Sudden ill health is indicated by the appearance of the Tower in a health reading. Adding another card or scanning the other cards in the spread may give you an idea of the area of concern. Often the health issue occurs too rapidly to be avoided.

Reversed

Sudden illness or an unexpected health issue can be avoided through conscious actions or simply through unconscious decisions. Those passengers who failed to board the Titanic are examples of people who changed their circumstances before an unexpected accident, avoiding tragedy. Because the reversed Tower card suggests a return to the upright Devil card, you may experience a health issue represented by this card, such as problems with the knees, teeth, skin rashes or haemorrhoids.

Spiritual meaning

The Tower is a startling reminder that no amount of wealth can prevent life changes and recalls your attention to the path ahead. The Tower sits between the comfort of the Devil and the possible contentment of the Star. The choice is stark as you must either deny the spirit or face uncomfortable changes to reach deeper into yourself. The Tower reminds you that no amount of luxury can compensate for a deep spiritual unhappiness. Inner peace, however, can reduce the need for a comfortable life.

XVII The Star

General meaning

After the materialism of the Devil and the unexpected change of the Tower comes the uncomplicated, tranquil calm of the Star. Clear skies and natural surroundings allow for a connection to the earth and an appreciation of the elements. The Star can represent a holiday, a rest from the pressures of everyday life or simply a strong connection to your creative mind.

This card represents the sign of Aquarius, so the Star and/or The King of Swords in a layout can suggest an Aquarian person. The Aquarius lesson includes piercing the veil between the conscious and the unconscious, which in turn shatters the narrow-mindedness that exists between truth and tradition. The veil seen separating the High Priestess from the water behind her has been torn away now, revealing this clear pool. In this pool she can seek inspiration, intuition and a clear image of life. The act of pouring water onto land and back into the pool indicates an exchange of energy between the conscious and the unconscious mind. She remains centred in the present and so unlike Temperance there is no path leading on to the Sun. Happiness lies in the moment with this card.

Reversed

When reversed, the Star suggests a lack of faith that life is supporting you in your endeavours. It is time to return to the Tower, allowing life to remove unnecessary distractions which may be obscuring your view. When you have sufficient faith that life supports you, you are free to return to the upright Star to explore the freedom allowed by having fewer possessions and less structure.

You are not currently in touch with your unconscious mind, and may feel disconnected from your creativity, intuition and inspiration. You may feel as though you are bereft of purpose. To remember and then pursue this purpose you first need the faith offered by the Star. In a career or a travel question, the reversed Star card can suggest work-related travel, where you are not likely to rest and relax. Travelling with practical goals in mind is shown by the reversed Star.

Finances

Faith in life's possibilities and either a source of income from your creativity or creative solutions to financial issues are indicated by the Star in a financial layout. The Star can suggest that your needs are few and that life supports you in an uncomplicated way. It can represent a holiday or a time for recreation, suggesting that you can afford this now. The Star suggests that you have faith in future financial stability.

Reversed

You presently lack faith in financial circumstances and may seek to control those circumstances that threaten your financial stability. This card describes the annual holiday occupied by phone calls to the office sorting out urgent problems. You may be at the beach, but it might as well be raining because you are not relaxed enough to enjoy your financial circumstances.

The reversed Star is a message that if your work is a marathon, your holidays are the rest stops along the way. Perhaps you cannot glimpse the possibility of taking an overdue break, as financial commitments presently overwhelm you.

Health

The Star represents the sign of Aquarius and the health areas for Aquarius include the ankles, the shins and the nervous system of the body. The retina is also covered by this card, so it can relate to cataracts or eye surgery (including laser surgery) if it relates to the retina.

In general terms the Star is a positive card in a health reading, suggesting that you have a healthy, positive outlook on life. It can suggest that a holiday or a short break now may maintain your health.

Reversed

The Star reversed indicates a lack of faith that health will stabilise or improve, suggesting you should return to the Tower card and the changes offered there. Tania's allergies cleared up noticeably when she took a short break from her financial concerns and her pressured working life. She was so busy that it wasn't until she turned up the Star reversed that she made the connection between her skin flaring up and her work pressures. At a time when you most need faith, you are more likely to be pursuing control instead.

A lack of faith that life will support you and an overwhelming sense of duty to your work will stultify you, resulting in listlessness and frustration. The antidote to this is a restful holiday.

Spiritual meaning

The Star is a chance to stop on the path to your spiritual summit and renew your faith in your purpose in a crystal clear pool of spiritual refreshment. As you revive, you feel connected to the abundant life around you. Joy, happiness and creativity envelop you as you glimpse the summit without feeling a sense of urgency to arrive. You have faith that at the right time you will achieve what you have come into this life to accomplish.

XVIII The Moon

General meaning

Fears surface with the Moon card, as it lends an eerie light to surroundings. Animals gather at the water's edge, some from their hidden havens. A pair of towers stand mute, as the moon glides silently through the sky.

The Moon suggests that although emotional motivations are heightened now they are likely to be concealed, and while you may be able to recognise these hidden agendas, those around you may not wish to acknowledge them openly. The Moon can be a favourable card for writers, artists and those who channel their emotions into a practical form. It enables the creative writer or painter to visit those dark recesses of the mind, returning with raw emotions which can then be presented through a story, a screenplay or a painting.

The Moon can indicate strong dreams at night, disturbed sleep or insomnia, and a strong connection with your subconscious mind through dreams. The Moon is sometimes selected for a layout when you are experiencing prophetic dreams or dreaming viable solutions to current problems. Together with the Chariot, the Moon can represent a Cancerian person and the Cancerian lesson, which is to overcome your fears in order to transform creative ideas in tangible form. When upright, the Moon can depict a person whose mind governs their emotions.

Reversed

The Moon reversed suggests you may be currently overwhelmed by powerful dreams at night, and you may benefit from keeping a dream journal. Fear of the dark, disturbing fears and desires contained within your subconscious mind may drive you back to the upright Star to enjoy the lighter, less threatening aspect of your mind. The reversed Moon can suggest that you need a break from your routine to shake off any lingering fears or doubts about life circumstances. It is a time to re-create yourself through rest, relaxation and play.

Deceit, a lack of clear communication and a dread of confronting your fears are also signified by the reversed Moon. In a career layout it can suggest that those you work with avoid real communication in order to keep the peace. On the surface, the water is still, but underneath it is turbulent.

Finances

The Moon can suggest that you are earning your income from creative means. Perhaps too, it is time to read and acknowledge the undercurrents at work as appearances may conceal the true circumstances. In a career question the Moon sometimes appears when management is planning a restructure but has not yet told the workforce. On a deep level the workforce knows that changes are afoot, but fear may prevent workers from confronting a menacing practical problem. Working at night is also shown by the Moon appearing in a career or financial layout.

Reversed

The Moon reversed can indicate being in a state of denial around financial issues. The fear of squarely facing looming financial problems forces you into the temporary safety found in denial. When a client is preparing to invest in a financial enterprise, the reversed Moon card suggests that they need to look more closely at the stability of the enterprise. Perhaps funds are not being spent the way they seem to be.

Self-deceit or deceit in dealing with others is suggested by the reversed Moon. If you are inclined to self-deception, you may attempt a risky financial venture to settle outstanding debts. It is inadvisable to pursue a financial venture when the reversed Moon appears in the answer or the outcome position.

Health

As the Moon is a card for the sign of Cancer it can indicate health areas common to Cancerians. This card selected in a health layout is not a guarantee of health concerns, but rather an indication of areas to be monitored, especially the stomach, the breasts, the lymphatic system and sleeping patterns. Anyone who has experienced a period of ongoing disturbed sleep knows how it can sap you of concentration, vitality, good humour and emotional resilience.

A client was startled when it was suggested that she have a breast examination by a medical professional as the Moon had appeared in a health reading. She phoned two months later to say that the doctor had found a small lump in her left breast. It wasn't life threatening but nevertheless a shock for her.

Reversed

The Moon reversed can indicate a return to balanced health (a return to the upright Star) after a period of insomnia or disturbed sleep. This may occur when a new mother is once again able to sleep through the night as the baby matures. It sometimes describes denial of ongoing health issues when a client prefers to ignore a recurring problem with the hope that it might simply go away. Loss of sleep due to worry and stress can be indicated by this card in a health question. A return to the Star offers a holiday or a rest.

Spiritual meaning

At night in dreams old fears and insecurities surface and, like a dog barking in the night, they disturb your equilibrium. Fears, hopes, desires and romanticised ideals swirl around in your subconscious mind, seeking an outlet through dreams or through creative writing. This final test on the journey to the World card is an opportunity for you to acknowledge those doubtful, insecure parts of yourself. Great journeys sometimes encounter moments of mental or emotional frailty, but these moments need not prevent you from continuing in your life's purpose.

XIX The Sun

General meaning

After your darkest fears have been faced in dreams, creativity takes on a new form in the Sun. The Sun represents a playful time, a youthful carefree summer and plenty of opportunity. In this card a naked child rides a docile horse. Carrying a bright orange banner (the orange lion on the Strength card) and wearing a red feather (a reminder of the Fool), this young person holds no fear. This is the second Major Arcana card for the sign of Leo, and the once wild animal on the Strength card is now the banner. Passion (the orange) is channelled through the mind now, indicated by the predominance of yellow in this card.

The Sun heralds a time of creativity, playfulness and realisation of your goals. The sunflowers recall the enthusiasm of the Queen of Wands (the third card for Leo) and both the wall and the horse offer protection and stability. The Sun accompanies a time of inner peace, abundant creative opportunities and the joy of life. You have a deep awareness of the beauty of life, taking time to notice the seasons. You recognise that although challenges are sent to test you, ongoing happiness is a choice.

Reversed

When the Sun is reversed, competition is fierce for your desired goals. A creative lifestyle masks the determined efforts you have made to realise your dreams. Those around you may envy the way you live, unaware of the consistent efforts required to maintain your lifestyle. The reversed Sun indicates a time when achievements propel you into the public eye to compete with those who are already successful and perhaps more experienced than you in your field. This reversed Sun exemplifies a singer with a top 10 hit facing the pressure for a follow-up song to equal their current success.

A return to the upright Moon is necessary to overcome your fears. Perhaps your creativity is blocked, or you are now more aware of the competition than of the abundance of opportunities. More focus is being placed on the effort, the competition for opportunities and the need to be continuously creative than on the joys which being creative brings.

Without descent into the darkness of night, the light of day cannot be fully appreciated. In returning to the Moon and facing your deeper fears you will eventually be free to return to the upright Sun to experience innocence born of wisdom. Perhaps it is time to return to the other card for the sign of Leo, Strength. In drawing upon your inner strength you can move forward towards the World.

Finances

You are likely to be in a fiscal summer when the Sun is selected in a financial layout. Money flows easily to you now, although you are likely to be spending it as easily as it arrives. Creative projects provide a stable income, and new opportunities are readily available. The Sun is a card for being paid to do what you love to do.

Reversed

You are pushing for greater goals now, reinvesting your money and energy into building bigger opportunities for yourself. The reversed Sun shows a return to the unacknowledged fears of the Moon and these underlying fears motivate you to be more forceful in your pursuit of opportunities. Fear of poverty forces you to work through a glorious summer, and as a result you miss the rewards of the efforts you made in spring.

This card reversed often represents a client who works in sales. It shows a strongly competitive nature, which is the shadow side of Leo; there is an innate desire to be number one and be ever watchful of the competition. This card can indicate success in the sales field, even when reversed. Although financial success is usually confirmed by the reversed Sun card, it suggests that you may not enjoy this success because of the ongoing effort to maintain or expand this source of income. It is time to return to the upright Moon to reflect upon what motivates you to work so hard for recognition or the approval of others.

Health

Heart and spine are the health areas to watch when the Sun presents in a health reading. This can include angina, a heart murmur or simply a spine which requires regular adjustment from a chiropractor or an osteopath. Vitality and body heat are also areas signified by this card. Generally the upright Sun card suggests good health and vitality.

Reversed

The Sun reversed can suggest that for improved health you need to play more and compete less in life. This advice is likely to fall on deaf ears however, because competitive people tend to compete even when they play.

Health concerns are increased with the reversed Sun. The heart or spine may require close attention from a health professional now. An outlet for stress may restore harmony. Something creative (but not competitive) might prove worthwhile, such as painting, playing a musical instrument, writing, yoga or planting a garden.

Spiritual meaning

On this part of your spiritual journey you are filled with a sense of creativity and wonder. Life is gloriously abundant, and you feel like a child of the universe. Creative ideas flow easily as you approach life with a sense of joy, spontaneity and playfulness. If life is a game, you relish your chosen role. Like a child you adapt to circumstances easily, making the most of each day. The Sun offers a time to explore your creative opportunities and to share your understanding of life with others.

XX Judgement

General meaning

Judgement indicates the chance to review the steps on your path to determine if you have acted wisely or lost your way in the pursuit of your goals. In this card an angel calls the dead to arise for the last judgement. With spiritual clarity they can review their lives and judge whether they were worthwhile. This card represents clear judgement when it appears upright in a layout. It can signify the call within towards a life with a deeper spiritual significance, and it is up to you whether you heed this call.

The appearance of the Judgement card signals spiritual forces at work. We need stillness of mind and sureness of judgement to determine what significance to attach to our lives, and to the events unfolding within them.

Judgement is also a time to reap what you have sown. Only after the harvest can you know with any certainty if your path was worthwhile or fruitless, and it is only after you have reached the end do you know the true purpose of the journey. Good judgement is based on perspective. A bee collects nectar to make honey for survival but the greater effect of its travels is to pollinate the flowers, ensuring the survival of the plants. From a distance we can observe the greater purpose behind the goal of collecting nectar.

Reversed

Judgement reversed suggests clouded judgement. You may be acting rashly, taking into account neither the bigger picture nor the consequences of your actions. 'Act in haste; repent at leisure' applies here.

When Judgement is reversed it is time to return to the upright Sun to play. A great deal of our subconscious desires, fears and hopes experienced during the Moon are acted out in the Sun, which enables us to review, resolve and sometimes to release deeper issues. Returning to the Sun offers a chance to play before we are called again to review our actions.

Finances

The upright Judgement card in a question regarding finances usually indicates clarity of judgement regarding the question. Sometimes it can signify using sound judgement regarding the intended course of action. It offers a clear 'yes' to the question, 'Is it wise for me to invest in . . . ?' if the surrounding cards are also positive.

Judgement can also describe being aware of the spiritual consequences of how you earn your income. Earning your income ethically not only helps you to sleep better at night, but it makes sound financial sense for the success of long-term business ventures. Judgement can signify an understanding that in business reputation is slow to build but easily destroyed.

Reversed

Judgement is vague now. Perhaps you do not have all the facts and are unaware of the big picture, or the consequences of your actions. Judgement was reversed beside the Seven of Swords in Nigel's financial reading, confirming that he was ignoring his intuition or better judgement. Despite his own reservations, Nigel invested in a business owned by Conrad, a friend of his wife. Ten months later, Conrad declared bankruptcy and eloped with Nigel's wife, whom he had been having an affair with all along. As he sat reviewing his emotional and financial devastation, Nigel realised that he had acted without clarity of judgement and against his instincts.

Reversed Judgement suggests an unwise business venture or that your money is better off being invested elsewhere. Occasionally your judgement is so clouded that you spend the remainder of the reading arguing the benefits of the investment.

Health

On its own the Judgement card in a health layout is a positive sign. It can signify that you have balanced health due to balanced living in the past. It can also suggest spiritual healing may benefit you at this point. It can suggest physical death when found in combination with three of the following cards: the World, the blank card, Death and the Tower, the Ten of Swords, Six of Swords, Four of Swords or the Three of Swords.

More often than not, Judgement represents the process of having to live with the consequences of past actions. If you have consumed too much alcohol or physically punished your body over the years, you can expect to have worn it down. If you have maintained good health over the years, upright Judgement indicates continuing good health.

Reversed

Judgement reversed indicates that any ill health at this point is likely to be due to spiritual imbalance. The pursuit of a more spiritual life may redress this situation. Meditation, reading spiritually uplifting books or using your talents and skills for the benefit of others may bring health rewards.

In answer to the question 'Is it wise for me to pursue . . . for improved health?' the reversed Judgement card gives a clear 'no' answer. If a client sits opposite you, weak with cancer, it can be difficult telling that person 'no', but better to tell the truth than have clients pursue fruitless quests with the limited time and funds available to them. Remember too, that clients have free will to accept or reject all predictions.

Spiritual meaning

You are detached enough from life to see the spiritual path before and behind you, while recognising the powerful opportunity you have to experience life in a physical body. As a spiritual being with a physical body, you are aware of maintaining your body and your physical life while remembering your true spiritual purpose. It is time to reflect upon your life circumstances to see how you can enrich your soul, learn and perhaps teach others as you pass through this life. Recognising that we are all on paths to a deeper spiritual understanding can increase your tolerance for fellow travellers who are struggling or have lost their way in life. In simple terms, Judgement indicates that you currently remember your purpose in life.

XXI The World

General meaning

The World is the culmination of all those cards which preceded it. A woman is draped in a purple cloth (Justice). She holds two wands (the Magician and the Chariot) and is surrounded by a wreath in the shape of a zero (the Fool). A pair of infinity symbols are visible in red cloth above and beneath her (the Magician and Strength), and the four animals in the corners of the card (the Wheel of Fortune) are in full colour. The lessons from these cards have been mastered, bringing lasting success.

This card represents success, travel around the world or realising the major goals you have set for yourself. When the World appears in a layout it can represent reaching the pinnacle of your aspirations. You feel supported by life and by those around you. In a relationship question it indicates a lasting, fulfilling love relationship, and sometimes signals a partner from another part of the world. It can also suggest an initial meeting in another part of the world. It has appeared in readings where a relationship is the result of a meeting on the Internet. Despite both partners being at home, their meeting encompassed the world.

Reversed

Although you ascend the tallest mountain you can see, your arrival at the summit allows you to glimpse an even taller mountain. This taller mountain was obscured by the mountain you have conquered. This means that although you are successful, you will set even higher goals to reach. This success is neither your last nor your greatest success.

The World reversed also can mean it is time to return to the upright Judgement card, to clarify your judgement. Perhaps you have sought lesser objectives, without regard for longer term, spiritual goals. A lack of long-term fulfilment is the result of seeking transient rewards over more lasting spiritual objectives.

Finances

When appearing upright in a financial layout, the World foreshadows enduring financial success. Having balanced the four suits of the Minor Arcana, you have the passion (Wands), motivation (Cups), clarity of thought (Swords) and practical application of your plans (Pentacles) to ensure financial prosperity. If the World appears as the answer to a question about a financial investment, the investment is likely to be fruitful, depending on the surrounding cards.

Reversed

The World reversed in a financial spread suggests temporary financial success and that greater success can follow it. The World reversed can also indicate short-term success. This can still be rewarding, especially if you have parked money in a shares trading account, seeking to increase your reserves before pursuing a long-term goal.

The World can suggest that your financial path lies in another part of the world. In answer to a question about a business venture or a career path, it may be necessary to pursue this path in order to prepare yourself for a more extensive financial journey. Pentacles people tend to feel uncomfortable at this news, preferring to stick with one path, while Wands people find the possibility of a second opportunity a bonus.

Health

Good health is indicated by the World in a health layout. In a question about the outcome of an operation or a medical procedure, it indicates success when the surrounding cards are also positive.

Reversed

The appearance of the World reversed in a health layout signifies good health, but probably not with the energy levels you may have experienced in the past. Health may be tested occasionally in the future, yet this is still a positive card to have in a health reading. This is unlikely to be your last health issue.

Spiritual meaning

As you stand at your mountain's summit gazing out across the peaks and valleys, you are aware of your achievement. You realise that this is merely one of many mountains to climb, and that there is as much joy in the act of climbing as there is in the view. What others may perceive as luck, you know is the result of many days spent planning, climbing and persisting with your goals, to reach this peak. When the World appears in a spread you are enjoying the fruits of summer.

Chapter 14

CHARTS FOR THE MAJOR ARCANA

Major Arcana cards representing men

Easy reference charts

For twenty years I have resisted designing charts to simplify the tarot in case students rely too heavily upon the charts and don't seek deeper meanings to each card when giving readings. In early 2006, I designed a series of colour charts and produced a short print run of laminated A3-sized posters for my students.

During the first introductory tarot course students bought every chart available, and then two students requested smaller (A4) versions to take with them on overseas flights so that they might study the tarot at 33 000 feet. It was immediately apparent that instead of oversimplifying the tarot, the charts encouraged an easier access to card meanings.

In the following tarot course I noticed that students particularly liked the Minor Arcana 1–10 chart as they were able to hold it in one hand as a reference tool while giving practice readings in the class. The colour charts helped students to streamline their early practice readings, improving confidence and removing the need to constantly refer to the full card meanings in the book. These charts are not intended to replace the full card meanings listed elsewhere in this book, but to jog your memory as to the basic meaning of each card.

Aside from the kings of the Minor Arcana, there are four Major Arcana cards which represent men, and their descriptions are listed in the chart titled Major Arcana Cards Representing Men in the colour section of the book. These cards allow for greater accuracy when describing the personality traits of men represented in tarot layouts.

Major Arcana cards representing women

Aside from the queens of the Minor Arcana, there are four Major Arcana cards which represent women and their descriptions are listed in the chart titled Major Arcana Cards Representing Women in the colour section of the book. These cards allow for greater accuracy when describing the personality traits of women represented in tarot layouts.

Chapter 15

HEALTH MEANINGS FOR THE MAJOR ARCANA

Unless you are medically trained or a certified natural therapist, do not diagnose health issues when reading for other people. Even experienced doctors can misdiagnose as the human body is a complex set of systems. When clients ask about health the best you can give them is general information. If you suspect that they need help with health issues, recommend that they seek attention from a doctor or a qualified alternative health practitioner. Health questions may be harmless, as in 'What does the future hold for my health?' or they may have serious ramifications. Questions such as 'Do I have cancer?' require a medical doctor. Modern medicine can run tests which confirm or quash such fears.

When 48-year-old Tina asked about her health, the Four of Pentacles and the Hierophant suggested tension around the neck and throat, while the Chariot represented the stomach and the breasts. I suggested that she have a breast scan and she explained that she had recently had a benign lump removed from her left breast.

As a reader it is better to resist saying that someone has a life-threatening illness, but if it is believed that this is the case, strongly urge the client to undergo a complete medical check-up. If the client persists with difficult health questions recommend that they ask the more general question, 'What does the future hold for my health?'

In a general sense the different cards of the Major Arcana can represent parts of the body and health areas to watch. It will not shock your client if you mention that they may be experiencing back pain or stress at present, especially if they have recently paid for a series of osteopathic treatments or for a remedial massage. Linda called from Asia for a telephone reading. The Queen of Wands and the Sun appeared in a health reading, both of which are cards for the sign of Leo. This sign usually possesses a flexible spine but one that requires regular adjustment. Linda confirmed that her lower back had been giving her some pain recently.

In a health reading, the Major Arcana cards can reveal the physical, emotional, mental and spiritual state of the client's health according to the cards selected. Listed below are some Major Arcana cards where they confirm a particular health area.

It is important to remember that several cards confirming a particular body area strengthen the meaning in a health layout, including Minor Arcana cards. Simple health meanings for each card are listed below.

Card	Health area
The Fool	Upright—No particular area is associated with the Fool. This card suggests good health and vitality. Reversed—Being irresponsible or foolhardy with your health is suggested.
The Magician	Upright—Good health and balance physically, emotionally, mentally and spiritually. Reversed—Becoming ungrounded, confused and, in extreme cases, psychotic.
The High Priestess	Upright—The feet and the glands of the body. The Page of Cups confirms this. It can also suggest that meditation or time alone for contemplation may rebalance you. Reversed—The feet and the glands; but it sometimes suggests that it is time to meet new people as they will lead you to new approaches to health maintenance.

The Empress

Upright—The kidneys and the digestive system. This card can confirm bloating of the belly area directly after eating certain foods, which can last for several hours. The kidneys are confirmed as the health area if the Justice card appears also.

Reversed—Increases the upright meanings, suggesting chronic indigestion or kidney imbalance.

The Emperor

Upright—Headaches which are confirmed by the King of Wands in the spread.

Reversed—Dissipation of energy reserves through overcommittment. Headaches and bumps to the head are still confirmed when reversed.

The Hierophant

Upright—Ongoing tension in the neck or throat areas, and this is confirmed if either the King of Pentacles or the Four of Pentacles is also present in the layout.

Reversed—Similar to the upright card. Stress around a lack or a loss of money can also be shown by these cards reversed.

The Lovers

Upright—The lungs and the arms, along with the nervous system. These areas are confirmed by the appearance of the Knight of Swords in the layout.

Reversed—The meanings are the same as when upright, with the possibility of nervous exhaustion increased by the lack of routine and high stress levels.

The Chariot

Upright—Difficulties with the stomach, the breasts, arthritis, with water retention and with disturbed sleeping patterns. These meanings are strengthened by the Moon and/or the Queen of Cups. Disturbed sleep is confirmed by the Nine of Swords.

Reversed—The stomach tension is highlighted due to stress and the opposing needs the client is experiencing. It is possible that ten minutes of shouting might release some tension, but long-term stress management is required for good health.

Strength

Upright—The heart and the spine. This is confirmed by the Queen of Wands and/or the Sun. Generally the upright Strength card suggests good health.

Reversed—Continuous stress is affecting the heart or spine. This may manifest in angina, heart disease or back pain.

The Hermit

Upright—The pancreas, which affects blood sugar levels. Hypoglycemia or diabetes can be represented by this card. These health areas are confirmed by the Queen of Swords.

Reversed—The need for quiet contemplation. This is the time to spend a weekend alone in the country, to take an hour each day to write in your diary or to consult a counsellor. Action without reflection is suggested by the reversed Hermit.

The Wheel of Fortune

Upright—Health is improving. After a difficult health period you are recuperating.

Reversed—The need to maintain health now, as there are more difficult health issues ahead. Pacing yourself helps you to face the future with better reserves of energy.

Justice

Upright—Taking responsibility for your health. An awareness that what is done now for health will have positive repercussions in years to come. It can also suggest kidney difficulties, and allergies that cause bloating of the belly after consuming certain foods. This is especially so if the Empress card is also present.

Reversed—Blaming others for current health issues. It suggests a refusal to take responsibility for personal health. It can signify legalities such as a malpractice law suit following a botched health procedure. It still suggests the kidneys and bloating of the belly due to food allergies.

The Hanged Man

Upright—Depression, lack of vitality, perhaps resulting from chronic fatigue syndrome. In most cases, unless there are contradictory cards, rest is the answer.

Reversed—Energy levels are depleted and the client is ignoring the body's signals for the need to slow down and rest in order to recuperate. It is time to notice the body's warning signs and rest.

Death

Upright—The lower digestive system, the abdomen, bowel and the reproductive organs. The base of the spine is also represented by this card. The Death card might appear when a footballer has dislocated his coccyx or when a client suffers with chronic constipation. In more serious cases it can represent a hysterectomy or prostate troubles. The meanings are strengthened by the appearance of the King of Cups. It can also represent the nose, such as broken noses and nose operations.

Reversed—The meanings are similar, although the symptoms may have been ignored or they may be more subtle and less noticeable. This card only represents a physical death when it appears with at least *three* of the following cards, upright or reversed: the Ten of Swords, the Six of Swords, the Three of Swords, the Four of Swords, the World, the blank card, the Tower or Judgement.

Temperance

Upright—The hips and thighs, confirmed with the appearance of the Knight of Wands in the layout.

Reversed—The same meanings as the upright card, with the addition of recklessness or accidents due to clumsiness. Intemperance with food and drink are also shown here, which may affect weight and health or lead to gout.

The Devil

Upright—Problems with the knees, the teeth or the bones generally. Sometimes skin allergies are also associated with this card. These meanings are strengthened with the appearance of the Knight of Pentacles. Haemorrhoids are also represented by this card.

Reversed—The same as when upright, as well as the possibility the client sees new alternatives to stabilising their health.

The Tower

Upright—Sudden health issues requiring immediate attention. It is unlikely this health issue has been prepared for as the Tower describes sudden change.

Reversed—A warning of an impending major health issue. If the warning is heeded the health issues may pass.

The Star

Upright—A positive attitude regarding health. It also represents the retinas, the ankles and the nervous system. These meanings are strengthened by the appearance of the King of Swords.

Reversed—A lack of hope regarding health, along with the need for a break. A longer holiday may be necessary to allow time to reconnect with the creative self. It also represents the retinas, the ankles and the nervous system.

The Moon

Upright—Disturbed sleep. This meaning is confirmed by the appearance of the Nine of Swords in the layout. Other health areas to watch include the breasts, the stomach (ulcers in some cases), arthritis and water retention due to a slow lymphatic system. These meanings are strengthened by the appearance of the Chariot and/or the Queen of Cups.

Reversed—The same as when upright, and also disturbed sleep due to unacknowledged fears or emotional issues.

The Sun

Upright—Positivity and playfulness resulting from good health. It can also suggest health issues with the heart and the spine, especially if accompanied by the Queen of Wands or the Strength cards.

Reversed—The heart is an area to watch. It can signify angina; a heart attack if accompanied by the Three of Swords; or back difficulties if accompanied by the Ten of Swords. It is time to cease competing and begin playing when the Sun is reversed.

Judgement

Upright—Clear judgement concerning health at present. It can also represent important health decisions which may have lasting consequences.

Reversed—Failure to consider the consequences of lifestyle on long-term health. Perhaps a medical procedure or a course of action regarding health is ill advised at this time.

The World

Upright—Good health due to an ongoing balance physically, emotionally, mentally and spiritually.

Reversed—Health is fine at present but there will be a need to redress some issues regarding health in the future.

Often clients ask specific questions regarding impending medical procedures. These questions are easier to answer than general health questions because you can help the client to phrase the question clearly. It is essential to discuss the issue or the medical procedure in some cases because it helps you and the client to formulate the right question or questions to give the client the information sought.

Kyla was about to have an operation on her nose to straighten a deviated septum and hopefully to increase airflow. She wanted to ask if the operation would be successful but it was apparent that there were various levels of success possible with this procedure. After some discussion Kyla asked the following questions.

- Will my nose be straighter after the operation?
- Will I breathe more easily after this procedure?
- Will I be happy with my facial appearance after this operation?

From general health questions to specific issues, *always remind the client that you are not qualified to diagnose* and that it is up to the client to consult a qualified medical practitioner. See also the Cards for Health chart in the colour section of the book.

Chapter 16

A GLIMPSE OF THE MAJOR ARCANA

The following story illustrates stages of life. The major Arcana cards represent those stages. We experience these stages repeatedly throughout life in career, love relationships, raising a family and sometimes on extended travels overseas. The story is designed to help you to recognise how life issues and events are represented by tarot cards.

Sometimes in tarot classes students are given a life event and they are asked to name the card or cards which might best describe that event. As a story is told, students name the cards for each part of the story. Perhaps the story below will illuminate where you are presently in your life.

Soon after Julia was born she arrived home to a family of six elder brothers and sisters (the Fool). There was no money for a cot so she was carefully placed into an open suitcase which served as her new bed.

Inspired by her older sister Vanessa, Julia began to master her physical body in order to walk without the help of others (the Magician). At night Vanessa often snuggled up to her younger sister where they shared stories before falling asleep together (the High Priestess).

Julia's mother was busy working two jobs and organising the family so the task of raising Julia was left to her 11-year-old sister Renate. Renate rushed home from school each day to fuss over her new baby and Julia's face brightened at the sight of her elder sister, her source of love and gentle nurturing (the Empress).

As Julia grew her father encouraged her to work in the garden, planting and watering the herbs and vegetables with him. She enjoyed this as it gave her a chance to be alone with her dad (the Emperor). Together they patiently planned and shaped the garden which helped feed their growing family.

At school Julia thrived. She enjoyed the social activities and won prizes for her scholastic efforts. After school she taught the younger children to read, as her sister Renate had taught her when she was in primary school (the Hierophant).

At 13 years of age she discovered boys, falling in love with Trent. He was a kind, yet serious young man, 14 going on 45 (the Lovers). Being an only child without a father at home Trent considered himself the man of the house, suppressing his childlike urges in order to lighten the load for his mother (the Chariot).

Julia was unable to afford university fees and was fortunate to be awarded a scholarship to study psychology. She felt that she had found her passion through discovering her path in life (Strength). During her studies it was a requirement that each student undertake counselling sessions with a qualified counsellor. Julia used these sessions to heal her childhood issues around money or growing up without it (the Hermit).

After completing her studies Julia established a practice as a clinical psychologist. Her practice thrived (the Wheel of Fortune). Her increased income meant that she was able to support her ageing parents financially, repaying them for some of the sacrifices they had made when she was a small child. She was consciously shaping her life through her decisions and actions, including her marriage to Damian when she was in her late twenties. By carefully considering her choice of partner she felt she had ensured the best life possible (Justice).

When Julia was 33 her father became ill. Remembering all the cold mornings they had spent digging, weeding and watering the garden together, she felt it was important to spend some time with the man who taught her the value of hard work in realising her goals. She struggled financially through this period as she had to reduce her clinic hours, but realised that this may be the last chance to be with her father (the Hanged Man).

Despite realising that her father's death was inevitable, Julia was overwhelmed with grief and despair when he died. Facing her own mortality, she knew that her life would never be the same. Even when the grief subsided, a new chapter of Julia's life dawned (death).

Julia studied eastern philosophies and meditation in search of methods to nourish herself spiritually, feeling liberated by the results. Incorporating this new understanding into her practice, her business became more effective as she recognised her clients' spiritual and emotional issues (Temperance).

When her first child, Danielle, was born Julia found herself rushing between home, day care and her office as she struggled to balance her home and work needs. Gradually her meditation practice fell away as she grew weary with the daily grind. Without noticing it, Julia had become her mother; a busy woman who missed her children's early years due to work commitments. She was unable to see any choice but to increase her workload (the Devil).

Her mother's death the following year came as a complete shock. Julia felt overwhelmed and yet unable to pause amidst her busy life to sit with the grief. Retreating from Damian into herself, Julia's frantic pace masked her grief and kept her fears at bay. One evening Julia collapsed at work from exhaustion and ended up in hospital (the Tower).

During her brief stay in hospital Julia recognised how she had forgotten those practices which nourished her spiritually, including her meditation and her need to spend time in a garden to reconnect with nature. She spent a glorious week resting in the country away from work and family. Each day she sat on the verandah watching the gold and crimson autumn leaves form a multicoloured carpet across the fields nearby. Gradually her physical strength and her emotional confidence returned (the Star).

The grief Julia had suppressed for so long began to surface. Julia found her dreams at night becoming more and more powerful. It was as though her subconscious mind was demanding to be heard and acknowledged. Julia began keeping a dream journal which she shared with her counselling supervisor. Gradually as she addressed the issues brought up in dreams at night, her sleep became more tranquil (the Moon).

When she was in her early fifties and her daughter was at university, Julia decided to write a book about some of the paths to spiritual and emotional nourishment. Based on her work as a counsellor, she conducted some group workshops to test each chapter in her book before publication. In this way she was able to observe how different people responded to the various techniques she taught (the Sun).

In her early sixties Julia retired from her practice, moving to the country with her husband. She planted a kitchen garden based on her childhood garden and wrote articles for magazines. Careful to continue with her meditation and those practices which nourished her, she reflected on a worthwhile life (Judgement).

When her older sister Renate was diagnosed with a terminal disease, Julia took her to Europe for six months (the World). It was a small repayment for all the hours Renate had spent raising her as a child. When Renate explained that she felt guilty at the expense, Julia insisted that she come.

'I'm doing this for selfish reasons really. I want someone I trust to look after me on the other side when it's my turn to go, and if you're already over there I'm taken care of.'

'I'll save you the suitcase,' replied Renate.

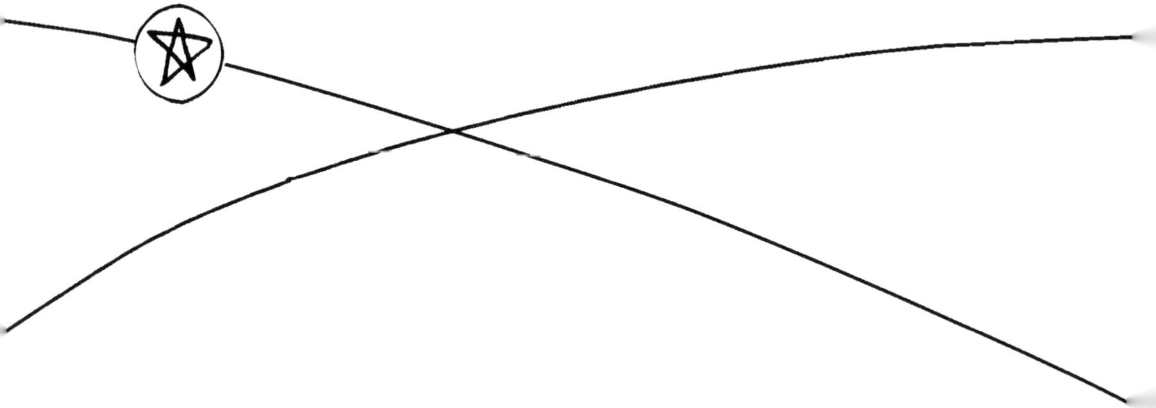

PART IV

Gaining experience

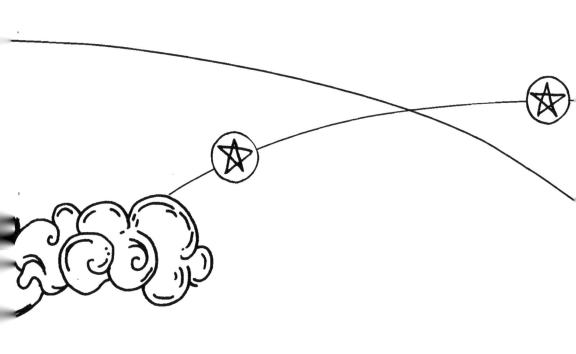

Chapter 17

UNDERSTANDING A LAYOUT/CARDS IN COMBINATION

Reading reversed cards

When the client shuffles the pack prior to the reading, they cut the pack at least three times, inverting cards and thus reversing some cards. Some of the cards in the deck are already reversed from the previous reading, and during this shuffling/reversing procedure these cards may end up upright. This shuffling and reversing process is done only once, at the beginning of the session with each new client.

Reading reversed cards is an integral part of tarot reading. If all cards are upright in the pack, your accuracy is limited when advising a client. Yes/no questions require clear unequivocal answers, especially when clients are making important life decisions based upon the information you are offering them. This is why clients are asked to reverse some cards when shuffling the pack. Remember also that not all upright cards are positive.

The client has the free will to accept or discard the information, however it is the reader's goal to offer clients the clearest information possible at any given time. Reading both upright and reversed cards in a pack helps you to do that. When you read with reversed cards you know with a degree of certainty that the answer to the question is a 'yes' when the answer and the outcome cards are positive upright cards.

Of course not all upright cards are positive. In a seven-card layout the answer is in the fourth card. The following cards in this position suggest a 'no' to the question: Five of Wands, The Hierophant, Cups, Swords and Pentacles, Ten, Nine and Four of Swords, The Tower, The Devil (in some cases).

It follows that cards that are negative when upright are more positive when reversed. All the above cards take on positive meanings when reversed. Two other cards, the Hierophant and the Eight of Swords, are also more positive when reversed.

When Tania asked about her health the Ten of Swords appearing in the position for past events described a previous low point with physical health. She confirmed that she had suffered a heart attack two years ago. The answer to her question, 'Will I have good health for the next two years?'was the upright Tower card. Although technically this upright card is a 'yes' answer, the card itself implies possible serious health issues approaching. To the Tower card Tania added the Strength and the Sun cards. Although these are positive cards, both are cards for the sign of Leo and the health areas for Leo are the heart and spine. The answer was that Tania would have health issues. She needed to ensure the health of her heart and take appropriate precautions to ensure her heart remained well.

Some students shy away from reversed cards, believing them to be more negative but this is not the case. As the list above shows, more than half the Swords suit is more positive when reversed, along with all of the fives, including the Hierophant, the Devil and the Tower cards. When the Tower appears reversed the sudden changes it announces are more likely to effect those around the client than themselves. Although many of the Wands cards suggest delays when reversed, this is not always detrimental. If you were delayed from boarding a flight which crashed, you are unlikely to consider this unfortunate.

Sometimes readers squirm when they have to deliver negative news to a client, but telling your client 'no' is part of being a reader. How do you know with certainty that the bad news you deliver today isn't actually good news in the long term?

The best approach is to tell the client the answer to their question *after* you have described all the other cards in the spread. This is because clients often tune out when their question has been answered. The client may become despondent when she hears, 'No. Barry is not coming back to you . . .' missing the more significant information 'because he is gay and he's eloped to Mexico to live with his new partner Alfredo. I see another man approaching and you are likely to be very happy together because you are a compatible couple.'

A reversed Seven of Wands signifies that the client needs to review the lesson of the upright Six of Wands. It is as though they have returned to a simpler lesson in order to master it, and to gain the necessary confidence to tackle the reversed card. The Chart of the Minor Arcana in the colour section of the book may assist in learning the order of the lessons of each card. Note that when an ace is reversed the client needs to master the lesson of the ten of the same suit, and when the Fool appears reversed it reverts back to the upright World. Reversed court cards

- can represent the shadow or negative qualities of the card
- reversed kings can describe the maturity of a knight
- reversed queens can suggest the maturity of a page
- reversed knights can suggest the maturity of the page
- reversed pages can suggest immaturity, unrealistic plans, delayed news.

To illustrate the reversed cards clearly, when a child learns to swim in the ocean he can become overwhelmed at not being able to feel the sand beneath his feet.

To redress these feelings of rising panic, he can return to the shore, feeling the sand beneath his feet once again. Reversed cards are similar to this. When overwhelmed by a lesson or a challenge it is natural to return to the safety of those lessons we have already mastered.

Linking the cards together

Helping a reading to flow usually depends on how well the reader has linked the individual cards together to form an accurate overall picture. The reader must see this picture clearly before they can explain it to the client. To ensure this happens take time to study the cards on the table.

Normally a client is happy to give you some more time if you request it, however clients receiving free readings (during your initial practice sessions, for example) are less likely to be patient, as they, unlike paying clients, have not had to invest time, effort or money to get the outcome. Do not let the client's impatience distract you as this initial learning phase is when you need to establish good habits when reading. There is no point in being quick if you lose accuracy.

Taking time to scan the layout can help you to determine what is actually going on for the client. It will help you to know where to begin and to recognise contradictory cards, allowing you to decide which meanings to attribute to each card. The things I look for when scanning the upright cards on the table before me include the following.

- *Are more than half the cards Major Arcana cards?* If so, add an additional card to each Major Arcana card to determine what is occurring in physical terms. Too many Major Arcana cards make for a deeply spiritual reading but don't necessarily offer the client information about life events.
- *Does any card number recur three or more times?* If you have three fives or four nines then there is an added significance. See the Chart of the Minor Arcana in the colour section of the book for basic card number meanings.
- *Do you have two or more cards confirming an astrological sign?* If you have the Moon and the Chariot then it's possible that a Cancerian person is involved in the question. With the Emperor and the King of Wands, it may be an Aries person.
- *Are all the cards reversed?* If so, then the client is facing more than usual obstacles in pursuit of their goals. The exceptions include all the fives, most of the Swords cards and the Devil, which are more positive when reversed.
- *Is any suit favoured?* If five of the seven cards before you are Pentacles cards, it is likely that the question is related to financial issues. If your client asks about her current relationship and most of the cards are Pentacles, she is likely to be asking about financial security. Perhaps a love relationship represents financial security to her. If most of the cards in a career question are Cups cards, the client may have a creative career, or a pressing relationship issue which demands an answer.
- *Request the client choose additional cards to clarify meanings* before any explanation is offered. This prevents complicated explanations, keeping the answer clear and concise.

With experience, you will begin to realise that adding the Six of Pentacles to the Chariot may mean the purchase of a new car, while adding the Tower to the Chariot may mean a car accident. Adding the Seven of Swords to the Chariot can mean car theft or deceit around the purchase or maintenance of a car. In one unusual reading the reversed Empress beside the Chariot represented the client who was living in his car. The Empress reversed represented an unsatisfactory home environment while the Chariot represented a car. This combination of cards can also indicate a child born in a car (perhaps on the way to hospital) if your client is pregnant.

To effectively link card meanings together you need to know thoroughly the meanings of each card in the pack. Although this can seem daunting initially, it becomes easier with practice.

When you know the client's question, you can limit the possible meanings of each card. A king appearing in a question about love relationships is more likely to mean a man than success through self-discipline (King of Wands), success through creative discipline (King of Cups), success through acting on a clear plan (King of Swords), or success through tenacity and hard work (King of Pentacles).

These same kings appearing in a question about health are more likely to represent areas of the body.

You can also eliminate many of the possible card meanings by the card position and the cards in combination. There will be exceptions to this naturally.

Although the reader begins the explanation with the first card (usually representing the past) and proceeds to the final card, there is no reason why the reader cannot ignore this process if it helps to clarify the reading for the client. If you find yourself jumping forward and then back again without good reason, chances are you are forming a bad habit.

The task of a tarot reader is to make sense of the current circumstances of each particular client. Sometimes clients don't want this, preferring straight fortune-telling instead. If you offer this you risk becoming an entertainer instead of a tarot reader.

Although clients usually arrive with a list of topics or questions, most clients actually have a primary issue. If you identify this issue early in the session and then help the client with this primary issue, you have done your job. Remember that you are spending between 30 and 90 minutes with your client and that life-altering change usually takes weeks, months or years, not minutes.

Interpretation limits

When you consider some of the bizarre meanings people ascribe to particular tarot cards, it is not surprising that some members of the public are wary of the tarot. Students occasionally ask me about 'the wish card', which is what some people call the Nine of Cups. Upright this card can be a card of fulfilment, but wishing is not the same as fulfilment. If you practise painting water colours until you are proficient, there is a strong chance that you will feel fulfilled when you paint. This fulfilment comes from work, not wishing. There is a risk that some tarot readers allow people to believe that if you wish hard enough or long enough, all of your wishes will come true. Wishing or identifying your goals in life is only the first step to achieving them.

Finding the right interpretation

Labelling a card with a single word is a lazy way to work. It limits your understanding of the cards and can prevent you from glimpsing deeper meanings of cards in combination in a layout. Be aware not to go to the other extreme and see meanings where they don't exist.

It is important to take note of the warning signs we are given. Ignoring symptoms of ill health can lead to hospitalisation. Finding the right balance between over-interpreting signs and ignoring signs takes time and practice.

Chapter 18

TAROT LAYOUTS

The client's initial contact with the cards

The client shuffles the cards, cutting the pack and inverting some of the cards from time to time. Usually three times is sufficient. This ensures that some cards are reversed. Because the client may be handling the pack directly after a previous client, some cards will already be reversed. In this case reversing some of the pack may ensure that these cards become upright. The client then places the cards, one at a time, into three piles on the table as shown below.

This means there will be three piles of 26 cards or two stacks of 26 cards and one of 27 cards if you have a blank card in your pack. The purpose for this is to ensure that no two cards remain together from the previous reading and that the client touches every card in the pack. In this way the client leaves a trace of their energy in the pack so that the reader can form a psychic link to the client more easily.

The reader then puts the three stacks of cards together into one pack and slides the cards across the table in a line. If the client is right-handed, slide the cards from right to left across the table. If the client is left-handed slide the cards from left to right across the table.

With their eyes closed the client then selects the number of cards according to the layout using their non-writing hand. If it is a general reading they select with a clear mind. For the Swords types who find it difficult to clear the mind, suggest they think of the card numbers, that is, one to seven if selecting seven cards.

If the client is asking a question, they concentrate on that question as they select the cards required. If their concentration lapses or they become distracted, it is best not to select any more cards until they are again centred and concentrating on the question. If you require additional cards to clarify the reading, the client closes their eyes, concentrates on the question and selects with their non-writing hand. When the layout has concluded the reader then gives the pack a brief shuffle (being aware not to reverse any cards) before the next question.

The seven card layout

The seven card layout (see the Seven Card Layout chart in the colour chart section of the book) is an effective layout for both general readings and specific questions. During a one-hour session you might use this layout five or six times, firstly as a general reading and then as the client asks specific questions. Some readers prefer complicated layouts involving up to 36 cards in a spread. This may impress the client but it is also likely to confuse the reader and it doesn't necessarily clarify the client's issues. It takes intelligence, experience and concentration to make this process seem simple and to ensure that the client departs with clarity.

The one-card cut

One-card cuts are useful for simple, clear questions and basic yes/no questions, but are limited in the information they provide as the answers offered are sometimes simplistic. If your client has an important issue it usually requires a more in-depth layout such as the seven card layout.

Step 1 Shuffle the pack as you think about the question. Keep it simple.

Step 2 Place the pack face down onto the table.

Step 3 Using their non-writing hand, the client cuts the pack, turning the top half sideways and, without disturbing or reversing the top card, place them face upwards.

Step 4 Take a moment to study the top card. This is the answer to the client's question.

The significance layout

This layout is useful if the client seeks to know what significance a particular person or situation has to play in their life.

Step 1 Identify the client's question, for example, what is the significance of Harry in my life? Ask the client to shuffle the pack.

Step 2 With their non-writing hand and with their eyes closed while concentrating on the question, the client selects four cards from the pack which is face down.

Step 3 The cards are placed in position as shown below with each card indicating the significance of that aspect shown.

	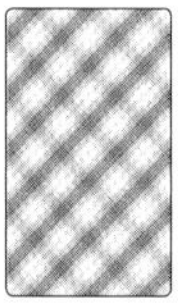		
Card 1	**Card 2**	**Card 3**	**Card 4**
Physical	Emotional	Mental	Spiritual

When Janette asked what significance her husband Lewis played in her life she selected the following cards.

Card 1	**Card 2**	**Card 3**	**Card 4**
7 of Wands reversed	Page of Wands	5 of Swords reversed	2 of Wands reversed

Interpretation

The first card (physical significance) suggests that Lewis is a physical obstacle to Janette's plans or perhaps to her desired lifestyle. In order to master the lesson of the reversed Seven of Wands, Janette needs to return to the upright Six of Wands. She needs to step back from Lewis and focus on those activities which she enjoys and which have previously been successful. Her self-confidence is then likely to return, enabling her to pursue her own plans despite opposition from Lewis.

The second card (emotional significance) suggests that Lewis may encourage Janette to pursue her plans, or that his influence makes her eager to act on her ideas. This suggests a positive emotional influence. It is possible that Janette and Lewis share a common emotional goal, and that both parties feel inexperienced (the Page) in the pursuit of that goal.

The third card (mental significance) indicates continual intellectual disagreements due to opposing ideas and attitudes to life. Negotiations are required to enable the energy to flow more smoothly in this relationship. Note that three of the four cards are from the suit of Wands. This suggests that one partner may be a Wands person or that both partners possess a wands approach of voicing their differences without regard to the other person's feelings.

The fourth card (spiritual significance) indicates that Lewis may be making Janette hesitate regarding a decision which may affect her spiritual direction in life. It is possible that one partner wants to leave the relationship or their physical (home or work) environment. The reversed Two of Wands suggests indecision, hesitation and a need to return to the Ace to act on a single, clear and urgent desire.

In summary, the least blocked area of this relationship is the emotional energy, so Janette can use this strength to redress the other areas.

When selecting one card for a clear, simple yes/no question remember that *one-card cuts are limited in the information they offer*. If your client is asking an important question, give it the attention it deserves and have the client select a series of cards for a more in-depth layout. Seven cards for a seven card spread is more appropriate for important questions.

If your client has four or five alternatives from which to choose and you have him or her select one card for each alternative, it can be confusing if several upright cards give a 'yes' to the question. When Cain wanted to decide between four university offers and the cards said 'yes' to three of those universities, I had to determine which card outranked the others.

Cain selects one card for each university while asking would he be offered a place at each of the four universities. The following cards appeared.

Colorado
Two of Pentacles

Los Angeles
Judgement

Washington
Eight of Pentacles

New York
The Star

First card, the Two of Pentacles, suggested that Cain would be offered a place, but it was outranked by the upright Eight of Pentacles. As this two was reversed it suggested that Cain might not accept the offer from the university in Colorado for financial reasons. He later confirmed that this university only offered a half scholarship while Washington and New York universities were likely to offer him a full scholarship.

Second card, the reversed Judgement card, is a firm no, implying that pursuing the Los Angeles university was likely to be unrewarding for Cain.

Third card, the Eight of Pentacles, is a positive card, which also indicates commitment to studies. This is a firm 'yes', suggesting that a place offered by the university in Washington might be worth pursuing.

Fourth card, the upright Star, is also a firm 'yes' for New York university. Being the only upright Major Arcana card in this layout it outranks the other cards.

Overall this layout suggests that Cain might be offered places in three universities. The most rewarding offers are likely to be with the university in New York, and secondly with the university in Washington.

The five alternatives layout

This layout is useful when the client has several possible alternatives from which to choose, such as four or five possible career choices, courses to enrol in or suitable home locations. The client can then ask a more specific question about the best alternative after this layout.

Step 1 List the four or five alternatives. If the client only has four possible alternatives the fifth card can represent 'other' (an as yet unknown alternative).

Step 2 After the client has shuffled the cards, spread the pack across the table to enable the client to select five cards.

Step 3 The client thinks about each specific alternative as they select one card. 'Is it wise to move to London to live? Is it wise to move to Paris to live?'

Step 4 Place each card in the order below as it is selected.

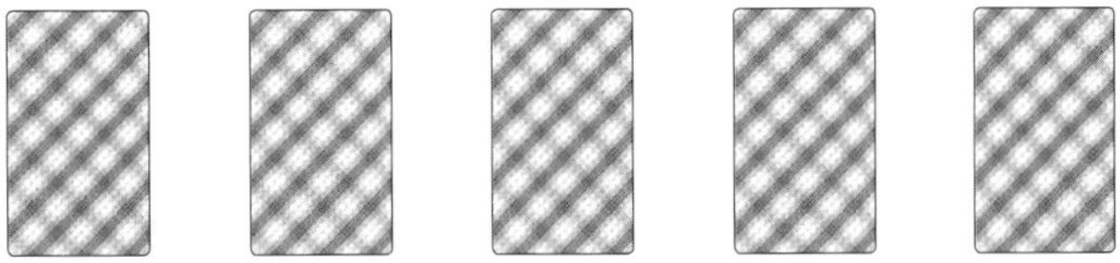

Card 1 **Card 2** **Card 3** **Card 4** **Card 5**

Step 5 Explain each card according to the alternative it represents.

You may ask the client to add an extra card to any alternative if you or the client seek more clarity. Resist the urge to add two or three cards to every position.

When selecting one card for each of up to five possible paths or choices, it is important to remember that this is similar to a one-card cut. *It is not the most accurate reading.* In a question on a career in complementary medicine, if the client receives a 'yes' to one or two alternatives, you might suggest that they follow with a seven card layout. Then they can ask directly, 'Is it wise for me to pursue a career in herbalism?' This will give you more information to work with and clarify what the client can expect when pursuing this path.

Consequences of actions layout

This layout is useful if you want to know the consequences of possible decisions or actions.

Step 1 Identify the client's question.

Step 2 The client shuffles the cards.

Step 3 With her non-writing hand and with her eyes closed while concentrating on this question, the client selects six cards from the pack which is face down and places them in the 'V' shape shown below.

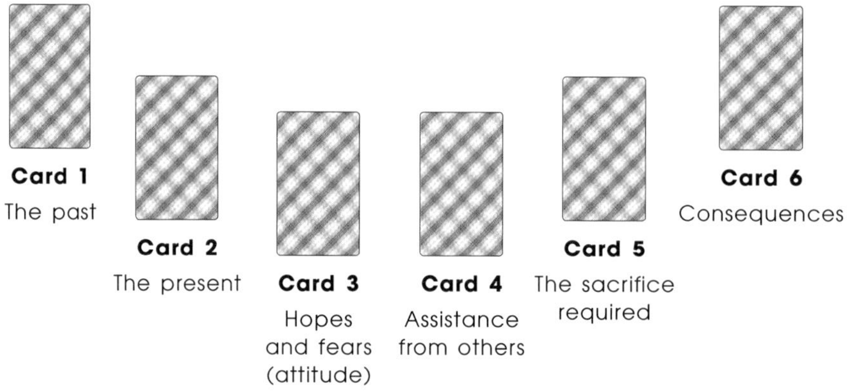

Step 4 Explain the cards meanings to the client and then summarise the layout.

When Stella arrived for her reading she was contemplating a separation from her husband of 22 years. This was made more complex because they shared a suburban medical practice together. 'What are the likely consequences of my intended relationship separation?' was her question.

Interpretation

Card one (the past). In Stella's case the Ten of Swords reversed suggests that circumstances reached a low point some time ago and that stagnation was the result. It is important to outline the past first, because current circumstance's are often the consequences of past decisions and actions.

Card two (the present) suggests that Stella is reluctant to face reality and to try new approaches to current circumstances. The reversed Seven of Swords can also suggest that someone is being secretive, perhaps having a love affair presently.

Card three (attitude). Stella is hopeful that life will improve if she leaves her husband. The reversed World card suggests high hopes, however there is an underlying fear that success will not be permanent because the card is reversed and that she will have to face subsequent challenges alone.

Card four (assistance from others) indicates that any assistance Stella receives from others will have to be paid for, as the reversed Six of Pentacles suggests money being spent in the pursuit of assistance or support from others. This means that Stella may have to hire a lawyer, a counsellor or even a furniture removalist to initiate her plans.

Card five (the sacrifice required) suggests the sacrifice required of Stella is that she remains committed to her purpose and constant in her plans. The Page of Pentacles is a card of learning, commitment and a practical approach to plans.

Card six (the consequences) indicates that the longer term consequences are positive for Stella as she is likely to be surrounded by like-minded friends. The Ten of Cups also suggests another stable love relationship lies ahead.

Areas to strengthen layout

When a client has a clear goal but is experiencing delays or frustrations in the pursuit of that goal this layout may be of significant benefit. This question can be asked in a seven card layout, but the areas to strengthen layout offer more in-depth analysis.

The question is, 'What areas do I need to strengthen to realise my goal?' Each separate goal requires another layout as qualities considered strengths in the pursuit of one goal may well be weaknesses in the pursuit of another.

Step 1 After shuffling the cards while concentrating on the question, the client selects nine cards from the pack, using their non-writing hand and with their eyes closed.

Step 2 The reader places the cards into positions, which have the meaning as shown.

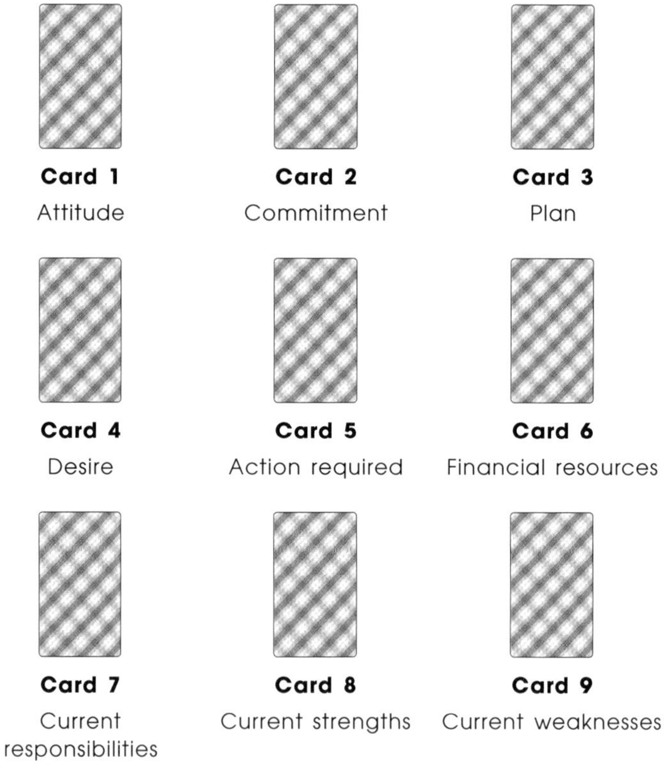

When Brendan asked about releasing his band's music CD the cards he selected for the goal of an internationally successful CD were as follows.

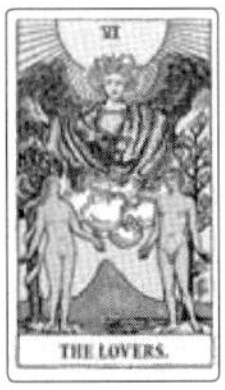

Card 1
The Lovers

Card 2
Four of Cups reversed

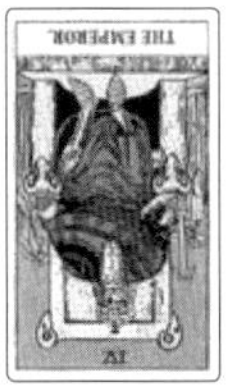

Card 3
The Emperor reversed

Card 4
Two of Swords

Card 5
Nine of Pentacles

Card 6
Four of Pentacles reversed

Card 7
Blank card

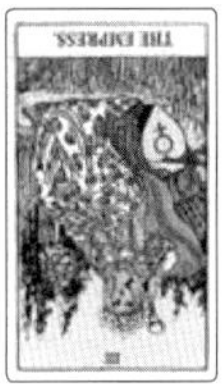

Card 8
The Empress reversed

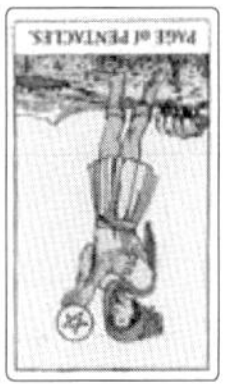

Card 9
Page of Pentacles reversed

Interpretation

Card one (attitude). The Lovers confirms that Brendan has decided to pursue this project to its conclusion. His attitude is positive and he is decisive about the project.

Card two (commitment). The reversed Four of Cups suggests that Brendan is no longer filled with joy regarding this project. Perhaps it is time for him to spend time amongst like-minded people who love his work or who are pursuing their own creative projects.

Card three (the plan). With the reversed Emperor card it appears that Brendan is undisciplined or has not yet made practical, realistic plans with an awareness of what the industry supports or what the CD buying public demands.

Card four (desire). With the Two of Swords in this position, Brendan is undecided about how much energy to devote to this project, and possibly torn between two projects.

Card five (action required). The action required at present as signified by the Nine of Pentacles is for Brendan to earn a solid income to support himself and his plans. He will require money to fund this project before a record company is prepared to sign him to a contract.

Card six (financial resources). With the reversed Four of Pentacles money is presently slipping through Brendan's fingers. He does not have sufficient money set aside to fund his CD. This may slow his progress.

Card seven (current responsibilities). With the blank card appearing in this position, it is likely that Brendan's current responsibilities soon may change unexpectedly. His attention may be demanded for another goal.

Card eight (current strength). The reversed Empress as his greatest strength suggests Brendan can return to the upright High Priestess to meditate on his goal and to plant a clear idea in his mind as to the desired outcome. The reversed Empress can also suggest that his frustrating home environment may help Brendan to be more active in the pursuit of his goal.

Card nine (current weakness). The reversed Page of Pentacles suggests that a lack of commitment to the process is Brendan's current greatest weakness. This page reversed describes intermittent commitment and a reluctance to apply yourself in a steady, practical manner to your goals.

In summary the suit most represented is Pentacles, suggesting that Brendan needs to be more realistic about financial issues while pursuing his goal. Note the three reversed fours (including the Emperor), which suggests that his plan is not yet consolidated or made tangible.

Beliefs layout

The beliefs layout is designed to help the client to determine what (if any) beliefs are restricting them presently. This is a useful layout when your client is feeling frustrated by life, circumstances and perceives limited opportunities. Sometimes it isn't that there is a lack of opportunities but that there is a lack of awareness of opportunities. It can be used for general or specific questions. While thinking of the question the client selects six cards. You, the reader, place them in a row as shown below. Each card represents a belief.

Card 1	**Card 2**	**Card 3**	**Card 4**	**Card 5**	**Card 6**
Past restrictive beliefs	Past strengths beliefs	Present restrictive beliefs	Present strengths beliefs	Future restrictive beliefs	Future strengths beliefs

Interpretation

Carlos asked what beliefs restrict him most regarding finances. He chose the following cards.

Card 1	**Card 2**	**Card 3**	**Card 4**	**Card 5**	**Card 6**
4 of Cups reversed	Queen of Wands	The Fool reversed	The Emperor	Death	4 of Swords reversed

Card one (past restrictive beliefs). The Four of Cups reversed suggests that in the past Carlos has been seeking more fulfilment in the way he earns his income. He was disappointed to find out that instead of fun, earning an income was a chore.

Card two (past strengths). The Queen of Wands indicates that Carlos's strength was that he found a way to express himself. An independent woman may have helped him towards financial stability.

Card three (present restrictive beliefs). The Fool reversed suggests Carlos's current beliefs have him feeling fearful about taking risks, or taking steps towards his financial freedom. He seems to be afraid that if he takes a wrong step, he will pay for it dearly.

Card four (current strengths). The Emperor suggests that Carlos's current strength is his self-discipline. He is capable of working hard towards his financial goals and maintaining the pace he has set for himself. He appears to be more realistic about finances than he was previously (the Emperor in present, and Four of Cups reversed in the past).

Card five (future restrictive beliefs). The Death card indicates that Carlos seems to fear change in the future. The fear of a financial collapse may prevent him from taking the necessary risks to increase his current wealth. It is possible that Carlos's beliefs around finances will be transformed in the future.

Card six (future strengths). The Four of Swords reversed suggests Carlos's future strengths include being able to take risks at the appropriate time and being prepared to lose in order to win financially.

In summary it appears that Carlos has become more realistic about financial stability and less inclined to want to be paid to play and enjoy himself.

This layout can be used to answer the questions regarding restrictions in love relationships, health, career, friendships and creative pursuits.

While beliefs are not visible, the results of your beliefs can be seen in almost everything you say and do. Examining your restrictive beliefs may enable you to address these attitudes and to liberate yourself from outmoded ways of thinking. This layout is likely to appeal most to Swords people because they enjoy examining beliefs in a bid to deepen their understanding of life.

Intuition development layout

Many clients ask tarot readers how to develop or improve their intuition. This layout is for those clients who want to know the best avenue to develop a reliable intuition. As we all have natural abilities in one or two particular areas, it is best to develop these areas rather than concentrate our efforts where they are less likely to be rewarded.

The client selects six cards, one at a time, thinking about each area. As the reader you are advised to phrase each question before the client selects each card. The questions are best phrased as follows:

1. Can I effectively develop my intuition based on my feelings (clairsentience)?
2. Can I effectively develop my intuition through auditory means (clairaudience)?
3. Can I effectively develop my intuition visually (clairvoyance)?
4. Can I effectively develop my intuition through contacting spirit guides?
5. Can I effectively develop my intuition through dreams at night?
6. Can I effectively develop my intuition through meditation?

Card 1	**Card 2**	**Card 3**	**Card 4**	**Card 5**	**Card 6**
Feelings	Sound	Visually	Spirit guides	Dreams	Meditation

There may be several positive upright cards in the layout, suggesting that the client has more than one path in which to develop a reliable and accurate intuition. The most positive card (an upright positive Major Arcana card outranks a Minor Arcana card) points to the best avenue for intuitive development.

Detail each card, explaining why each area is worth pursuing or not worth the effort. You may have the client add a card to any position which needs clarification. Try not to add more than three or four cards or you risk ending up with 15 cards for a six card layout.

In Sandy's reading, the upright Judgement card appeared in position one, indicating that she would find success through developing her intuition through feelings. The only other positive upright card was the Eight of Wands in position three. Sandy asked how she might best develop her visual skills and one card was added for each of the following:

- Developing her visual skills through taking time to 'see' at the end of each tarot reading.
- Practising telepathy on the phone each night with a girlfriend.
- Visualisation exercises.

Any area can be broken into sub-headings as long as they relate to the area concerned. The meditation area can be broken down into specific types of meditation or particular meditation courses offered locally.

Chapter 19

CLARIFYING THE QUESTIONS

A question I hear occasionally during an initial telephone enquiry is, 'How accurate are you as a reader?' It is a valid question. I don't quote accuracy in percentage terms, yet I have seen irresponsible advertisements for telephone tarot services which assert that their readers are 97 per cent and 99 per cent accurate. The accuracy of the answers lies in the precision of the questions. A poorly worded question is likely to result in a vague answer. Sometimes an important issue requires a series of questions to establish the most rewarding actions to take.

Sophie arrived for a reading with one specific issue—her love relationship with Trevor. In order to give her the most accurate information, it was suggested that Sophie ask the following four questions.

- What does the future hold for my love relationship with Trevor?
- Is it wise to pursue this love relationship with Trevor?
- What can I do to improve this relationship?
- What does the future hold for me in love relationships generally?

If the first question gives your client the information they seek, there is no need to pursue the remaining questions. For questions where there are several alternatives, the five card alternatives spread in the previous chapter is the best approach.

Often the client has been thinking about an issue for days or even weeks. It is your role as the reader to simplify the issue and to gently guide the client towards the most accurate wording of questions. One of your goals as a tarot reader is to clarify the client's choices, highlighting the most rewarding alternative shown for them in the cards. If the client ignores your reading then you have done your best.

In some cases clients may return once a year for three years in a row before they have heard the message. In my younger, less tactful days I recall asking a client to replay her tape from a previous reading and save herself the reading fee. It is better to consider that perhaps there has been some subtle change in the client's situation, or they may be needing to hear the same information again in order to accept it.

At times clients don't realise that they are asking ambiguous questions or several questions at once. Adrian was keen to know about his investments and he asked, 'Will all of my investments be profitable this year?' Realising that such a broad question was likely to return a 'no' verdict, I probed to find out how diverse his investments were at the time. Adrian owned two rental properties, had a managed share portfolio and he was day-trading in stocks part-time. His question was broken down into several separate, more precise questions.

- Will my property investments be profitable this financial year?
- Will my managed share portfolio be profitable this year?
- Will I be successful overall with day-trading this financial year?
- Is it wise for me to hold on to the property at 53 Westleigh Street?

Although clarifying the client's questions can take up precious minutes of the reading time it often means the difference between fulfilment and frustration for the client. Clients usually prefer clarity. Helping the client to word a question needn't interrupt the conversation you are having, as the client looks to you to guide them. Your guidance is the difference between a novice and an experienced reader. Clients are prepared to pay more for the ten years you have spent refining your craft. Your craft is more than knowing the meanings of cards. It extends to:

- how you guide the client to word more accurate questions
- how you present the information you need to give to them
- how effectively you manage to end the session on a positive note.

Often clients arrive with questions which are in fact topics. 'I want to know about a singing competition,' Lesley asked during a recent reading. Having trained as a singer, Lesley wanted to enter a television singing competition, the first prize being a recording contract. Feeling Wands-like on the day I urged her to forget the cards and give it her best shot.

To my surprise the answer to Lesley's questions was a clear 'no'. It was time to help her form more questions in order to discover why it was not wise to enter this competition. The questions offered to Lesley are listed below.

- Is it better for me to concentrate on my university course and my voice training this year?
- What is the likely outcome for me if I enter this singing competition?
- Is there a more suitable singing competition for me to enter this year?
- Am I better suited to another part of the music industry rather than singing?

Although Lesley arrived with a question about a singing competition, she actually had several questions about the topic of her musical career direction. Had she been given a simple 'no', Lesley might have departed feeling lacklustre. Instead we were able to ascertain that she has a successful career ahead of her in the background of the music industry, after she completes her university studies.

When Nicola had questions about her health and what might improve her back pain, the seven card layout was used. Her health was discussed in order to word the best possible question for her needs. It turned out that her severe back pain had been ongoing for six weeks, during which time she had consulted over a dozen alternative practitioners, at a cost of more than $1500, unsuccessfully. I suggested that perhaps it was time to consult a medical doctor or a medical specialist.

Nicola's question was 'Is it wise for me to consult a medical doctor regarding my back pain?' The answer was a resounding 'yes'. She did so and two weeks after the reading Nicola phoned to say that she had been told by her doctor that she had bone cancer in her spine. Armed with this new information, Nicola had new choices to make concerning her long-term health.

I did not diagnose or suggest remedies, because I am not trained in medicine or anatomy and physiology. Nicola had already consulted with a variety of experienced practitioners so she had effectively eliminated many of the options we might have explored in tarot questions. By discussing the situation before giving the reading we were able to arrive at the best question for Nicola's particular needs.

Chapter 20

TRUSTING YOUR INTUITION

Although you can read the tarot with great accuracy without intuition, using your intuition can allow you to give your clients additional information.

If you want to choose a school for your child you might intuitively glimpse the school and decipher the name clairvoyantly. Alternately you might research local schools before cutting the cards once for each school using the five alternatives layout.

It doesn't matter how you reach your conclusion so long as the conclusion is accurate. If the question has great significance to you *it is advisable not to read for yourself* but instead seek an objective tarot reader. It is difficult to be impartial when reading for yourself.

Heeding your body

Your body is capable of becoming a valuable barometer in assisting you in decision making, if you pay enough attention to it. To achieve this you need to quieten the mind in order to listen to the body. This can take months or years to master. Meditation is one effective way to still your mind, a method made easier through the use of a guided meditation CD or tape. You may need to listen to the one CD 10 to 20 times before you experience results. Some people attain a similar state of mental stillness through hobbies as they allow the conscious mind to settle.

One of the benefits of listening to your body is that you are less likely to be deceived by people. For people to successfully deceive you, you need to be out of touch with or ignoring the signals your body is giving you. In simple terms, for others to deceive you, you must first deceive yourself.

Greed is often used to deceive. Promises of quick riches often has your body sending its message of distrust, but your mind is already planning how to spend the money. When you experience confusion between what your mind is telling you and what your body is feeling, then something is not right and needs closer attention. It might simply be that you are nervous about the possibilities, but often it is more.

In practice this translates into more effective readings for your clients. At the beginning of a session, as the client shuffles the cards, one way to trigger intuition is to say to yourself, '*The issue today is . . .*' The end of this sentence is often a single word, such as *when*, *where*, or *why*. Then check to see if you can glean anything further. If the word is *where*, then repeat it in your mind until you have another sentence. '*Where am I going with my career?*'

In most cases the issue you identified mentally in the first few minutes of the session surfaces in the general reading or in the first specific question. If it does not, say to the client, 'I'm confused. When you sat down I was aware that you are unsure about where you are going with your career, but this hasn't come up in the general reading or in your questions so far.' The client will either confirm or deny your instincts. In many cases the client confirms the issue, but explains that they want to clear away the less important issues first. *However, for several reasons it is best for the client to ask the most important question early in the reading.*

- The issue may require two or three questions to clarify it to the client's satisfaction.
- Time may run out before the client has asked about their most important question.
- The most important issue/question will surface in any other question asked until it has been answered. If the most important question has been asked but not fully answered, you can expect to see the cards from that layout

appearing repeatedly in the layouts for other questions. This is a hint that you need to return to the primary issue/question and ensure that the client has all the information they need.

Developing intuition comes with practice and self-discipline. If you are a tarot reader, clients are effectively paying you to develop your intuition so take the opportunity.

While developing your intuition, try to determine your intuitive speciality. Are you gifted with

- locating lost objects
- glimpsing spiritual purpose
- clarifying underlying lessons
- financial market predictions
- psychically scanning animals for health readings
- giving house numbers for most likely future addresses
- locating hidden money
- contacting the deceased to clarify the intentions of a will.

A former student discovered that she was able to attune herself to the client's body in order to give accurate health readings. She found, however, that she developed their health symptoms, and although her accuracy was astounding she was left with their side effects, which sometimes lingered overnight. Not being a medical or alternative practitioner, she was also leaving herself open to law suits for unqualified health diagnoses. Taking on the feelings of the client is not recommended, as you leave yourself open to emotional and psychic exhaustion.

Body barometer exercise

This simple exercise may help you to develop your intuition. It is more than a psychic development exercise, it is a meditation—an opportunity to bring your awareness back to yourself. In the present is where all power in life exists. With repeated use, you may find yourself becoming more powerful and effective in your life without expending any additional effort to realise your desired results.

It is the power of simplicity. Five times each day ask yourself *How does my body feel about this?*

Spend at least three minutes answering this question. At first ask this question of yourself randomly, then try it every time you make a decision. Your body will tell you how it feels, even about small decisions. Acknowledging your physical body and your feelings is the first step to relying on the information it is conveying to you every day.

Chapter 21

CONFLICTING CARDS IN A READING

Sometimes when answering a specific question using a seven card layout, the answer (the fourth card) and the outcome (the seventh card) conflict. This makes it difficult to give a clear 'yes' or 'no' answer to the client's question.

Sometimes answer and outcome cards conflict because the most appropriate question has not been asked. When Benita asked if she would find a job which made her happy it was necessary to ascertain what she wanted in a job. This was more a topic than a single question.

Alexandra was considering whether to publish a book she had written and also which publishers might be interested in working with her. According to the cards there were three likely interested publishers. Alexandra then asked if it was wise to submit this book to each of those publishers.

The Magician appeared in the answer position (card 4 in a seven card layout). (The answer is usually withheld until the end of the layout.) The Magician suggests that Alexandra is grounded in reality, effective and that opportunities to publish the book are presently around her. If the outcome is ignored for the moment, then the appearance of the upright Magician in the answer position gives a solid 'yes' to Alexandra's question.

The reversed Page of Pentacles appeared in the outcome position (card 7), suggesting that Alexandra may lose her commitment to having the book published by an international publisher or that she may decide not to pursue an offer. The

Page of Pentacles is a card of commitment but when reversed it can describe a lack of commitment or a project abandoned.

With the answer card upright and the outcome card reversed we have conflict. If both of these cards were upright and compatible you might confidently state that it was wise for Alexandra to approach publishers with her new book. If both cards were reversed you would be assured that it was not wise to pursue a publisher at this point.

When one card is upright and the other reversed some readers become unsure, adding more cards until they feel confident or until they are completely confused. Since the answer card is upright and it is a powerful and positive Major Arcana card, this suggests that it is wise to pursue publishers at this stage. However, since the outcome card is reversed it suggests that Alexandra may decide not to pursue publishers at this stage. The answer is essentially that yes it is wise but no, you are not likely to pursue publishers at present. Alexandra later chose to self-publish her book.

When there is conflict between the answer and the outcome take a moment to study the cards carefully. Tell your client that you need a few moments to make sense of the spread. There is no point in answering your client's questions rapidly if you are wrong. The client is likely to remember your accuracy long after they have forgotten how long it took you to deliver your findings. With a reversed outcome card (card number 7) if the answer card is positive and upright then the possible meanings might be:

- yes, but not now
- yes, but with delays
- yes, but not in the way the client expects
- no, because both cards are negative (either upright or reversed) and because . . . (depending on the cards present).

If the answer card is negative or reversed while the outcome card is upright and positive, the answer might be:

- no, because another opportunity is approaching instead
- no, not at this stage
- no, because . . . (depending on the meaning of the upright outcome card).

If each card in the layout appears reversed to you the reader, then the answer is a resounding 'no'. Take time to explain the meaning of each card, as this may help the client grasp why the goal they seek is unlikely to be fulfilled.

If all the cards appear upright to you the reader then the answer is a resounding 'yes'. The exceptions are those cards which are more positive when reversed.

Focusing on answers to clear questions is often easier to decipher than the initial general layouts which begin a reading. This is because when the client asks a clear, unambiguous question, all the cards on the table relate to that question. This reduces your choices as a reader by eliminating many of the possible card readings.

Chapter 22

FATE AND FREE WILL

There are basically three schools of thought regarding fate.

- The first belief is that all things are fated, and that we have limited free will in our circumstances.
- The second is that we are free to determine our future, which results from the decisions we make and the actions we take now.
- The third belief is that we have free will, but that this free will is limited by our past actions and decisions. Current decisions and actions will further limit or enhance this free will.

Your approach to each client needs to be flexible to allow for their beliefs, while honouring your own beliefs.

A fated life

If your client believes strongly in fate, ensure that you speak positively about their future, without falsifying your reading. There is a risk that your client may seize upon one negative sentence and leave shattered by what they have heard. Clients who believe strongly in fate tend to put the tarot reader on a pedestal, and take what is being said literally.

The more positive of these clients tend to wait more patiently for opportunities to approach them, and their vigilance is often rewarded because they are usually more prepared when opportunities arrive. When they are feeling negative, fatalistic clients often resist taking responsibility for their past actions and their current circumstances.

Success equals luck for fatalistic people and this can diminish the effort they put into preparing for and maintaining a successful life. At our lowest ebbs in life, we might all appear to be unlucky, and at our highest points we might be considered to be extremely lucky.

Free will

Clients who believe in free will are more likely to push for change when they don't like current circumstances. They usually ask more practical questions of the tarot reader, seeking assistance in how to reach the goals they desire. Clients who believe in free will are less likely to consult a tarot reader, as they feel that practical decisions and actions build the future they desire.

When a free will-focused client does consult a reader, they are likely to have researched several possible paths carefully, before asking which path offers most fulfilment. These clients recognise that the reader is simply a consultant. They accept that the reader is only able to perceive the most likely future from current circumstances, and that through the use of free will, they can change any future predicted.

Fated by free will

A third approach includes clients who accept a combination of fate and free will. They believe in free will, but accept that present opportunities are limited by past actions and decisions. This makes sense if you compare the journey through life with a car journey. If you drive to work, each decision along the way brings you closer to or further away from your intended destination. It might appear that sometimes you were heading the wrong way because you were driving in the opposite direction to join a freeway. It is possible too, that at the last minute you decide to take a day off. Similarly, in life you can decide not to complete your intended journey, but to set a new goal for yourself.

If instead you set out to work in the opposite direction and continue in this direction, your chances of arriving at work on time diminish with each minute you spend driving. Your previous decisions are limiting your ability to realise your goal of arriving at work on time. The act of exercising your free will has fated you to achieve a different outcome from the one you initially pursued.

Clients sometimes arrive despondent or frustrated because they have set a goal that they seem to be heading away from. Their decisions and actions are not assisting them in the pursuit of their goals and, as a reader, your task may be to show them the consequences of their decisions and actions. You may then be able to show these clients which decisions or actions are more likely to result in the realisation of their desired goals.

Those who believe in fate and free will usually agree with the traditional concept that luck is where preparation meets opportunity. When a singer has diligently practised her craft for 10 to 15 years and then is 'discovered' overnight, is this simply a lucky set of circumstances? The same circumstances arriving for someone who is unprepared is unlikely to offer similar long-term rewards. A creative friend insists that it takes at least 10 years to be an overnight success in many endeavours.

Chapter 23

LEARNING THROUGH DIRECT EXPERIENCE

Many tarot readers have a few cards in the deck which they cannot fully understand. When these cards appear in a spread it is tempting to ask the client to add another card to accompany the card you do not comprehend. Although this helps the client during a reading it does not help you as a reader. Sometimes the only way to fully understand a card is to experience it directly. This may mean that you find yourself in circumstances which confuse or frustrate you. Every time you cut the cards asking, '*What is the lesson for me in this situation?*' you cut the pack to a card you do not understand.

Many years ago I found myself in despair at the loss of a love relationship. Each time I asked the tarot what the lesson was for me at that point, I cut the pack to the upright Chariot card, a card I had difficulty with. Inwardly I was torn apart and exhausted with a lack of sleep, yet I had to stand up and walk back into my life and my work.

'*How can I hope to read for clients when I feel this way inside?*' I asked myself.

Eventually I found I was able to keep my mind separated from my emotions and to recognise the opposing forces of thoughts and feelings. In allowing my thoughts and my feelings to be heard, I soon returned to a balanced state. My readings improved as I became more compassionate for those who consulted me when they also felt fragmented by life. This, I realised, was the lesson of the Chariot.

Learning each card through direct experience is the slowest way to master the tarot, but once you have you are unlikely to forget that card and the situation it represents. A card which springs to mind for me is the Three of Cups, when I first held my son, who was a few minutes old. He sighed quietly as his parents wept with joy.

If you can observe your friends and your clients closely, the meanings of each card will surface, especially if you continually ask yourself, '*Which card or cards might symbolise this situation?*' A friend recently described herself as being the only person in a large company without an office. She explained that her boss had left her on her own, out in a thoroughfare while three offices stood empty nearby. This situation was the Ten of Cups reversed, which describes feeling excluded from the group. She felt left out and eventually her co-workers treated her as a temporary worker, despite her four years with the company.

Chapter 24

IDENTIFY THE CARD EXERCISE

Now that you have a greater understanding of the cards, why not try this exercise? It can be completed alone or you can play it as a game with up to ten players. One person describes a situation while the others name cards which can depict that situation. Lay the whole tarot pack out before you in the order shown below. This will assist you to remember the card meanings to answer the questions below.

The Major Arcana from 0 to 21
The Suit of Wands Ace to King
The Suit of Cups Ace to King
The Suit of Swords Ace to King
The Suit of Pentacles Ace to King

Lay the cards horizontally across the table, using two or three rows for the Major Arcana.

List the card or series of cards that best describe the following situations:

1 You receive a promotion at work.
2 A child is hit by a train.
3 Your home loan is approved.

4 Your engagement ring is stolen by a family member.
5 Your shortness of breath is diagnosed as asthma.
6 You visit your grandmother in the old country.
7 The surgery is successful.
8 You start your own business with the payout from your retrenchment.
9 You are about to embark on a relaxing holiday.
10 Your undisciplined son is due for a court appearance.
11 You purchase a new car.
12 Your job is at risk due to a recession.
13 A child is born.
14 In attending a course you enlarge your circle of friends.
15 After a deep loss you are embracing life again.

Answers

1 Six of Wands (achieving a goal) and/or the Six of Pentacles (the work environment and securing a new job).
2 The Tower (an accident) and the Chariot (a car, truck or train) cards with a page card representing the child. The Five of Cups describes the emotional loss.
3 Ten of Pentacles (the bank or finance company) and the Six of Pentacles (receiving money from others).
4 The Seven of Swords (theft or deception), the Six of Pentacles reversed (financial loss) and the Six of Cups (family, home or someone from your past).
5 The King or Queen of Swords (the doctor) and the Eight of Swords (asthma).
6 The Ace or Eight of Wands (travel cards), the Page of Swords (a flight) and the Six of Cups (a place you have lived previously), and the World reversed (completing a journey you have begun some years ago).
7 King or Queen of Swords (the surgeon), the Ace of Swords (the surgeon's knife), and many upright cards for success, including the Six of Wands (victory), the Four of Swords (recuperation), the Four of Wands (a return to stability) the Six of Pentacles (a return to work).
8 The Ten of Pentacles reversed (a large business shrinking), the Six of Pentacles reversed (leaving your job), the Four of Pentacles (leaving your job with a lump

sum of money), the Ace of Pentacles (a new job or financial direction), the Page of Wands (pursuing a new goal) and the Eight of Pentacles (commitment to career goals).

9 The Ace, Three or Eight of Wands (travel), the Page of Swords (by air), the Chariot (by road or rail) and the Star (a relaxing break).

10 The Page or Knight of Wands reversed or the Knight of Swords reversed (the undisciplined son), the Emperor (the judge), the Six of Pentacles reversed (a fine), the Eight of Swords (imprisonment), the Nine of Swords (worry over the outcome and its consequences).

11 The Ten of Pentacles (the finance company if a loan is involved), the Six of Pentacles (the purchase), the Chariot (the car) and the Knight of Wands (you driving around), or the Knight of Wands reversed (you driving hastily and recklessly).

12 The Ten of Pentacles reversed (a large company shrinking or the economy shrinking) and the Six of Pentacles reversed (leaving a job).

13 The Empress (pregnancy), the Empress reversed (ending of a pregnancy), the Three of Cups (a celebration or an addition to the family), any of the four pages (describing the nature of the child) or the Six of Cups (a nurturing family life).

14 Temperance (study), the Three of Pentacles (study), the High Priestess reversed (widening your circle of friends after a period of solitude), the Three of Cups (enjoying social gatherings) or the Ten of Cups (like-minded people together).

15 The Three or the Ten of Swords (loss), Death (end of a situation), the Tower (sudden end to a situation), the blank card (unexpected end to a situation), the Five of Swords (argumentative end to a situation), the Five of Cups reversed (returning to life after a period of grief).

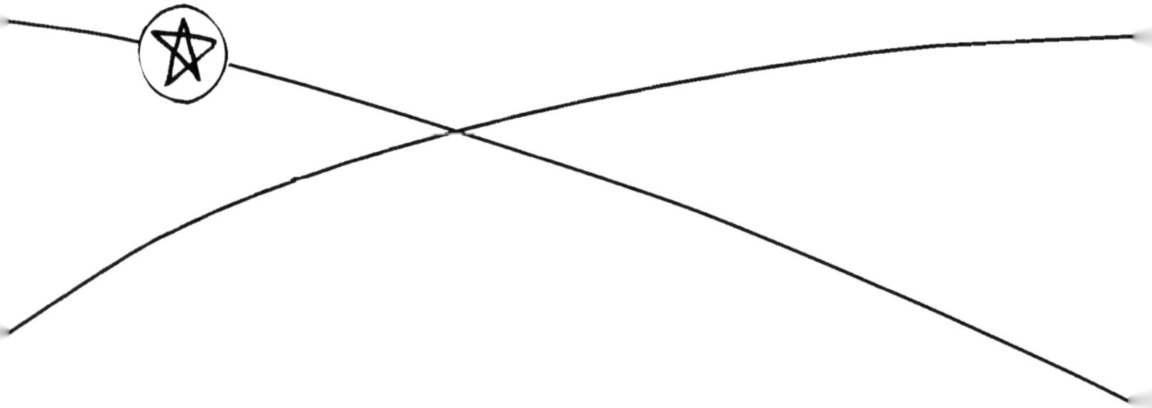

PART V

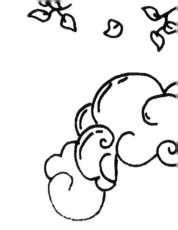

Becoming a professional reader

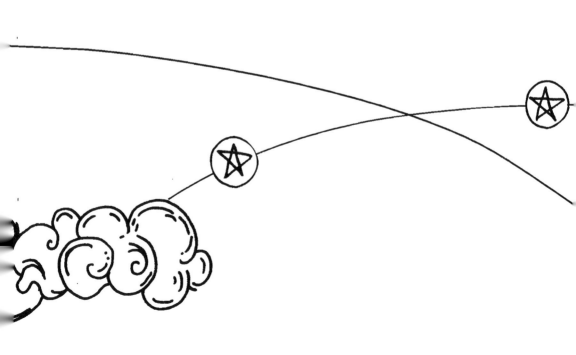

Chapter 25

PSYCHIC CLEANSING AND PROTECTION

As a tradesman regularly cleans and services his tools, so too must a tarot reader tend to his/her spiritual health. If you read for clients you will collect dross or negative energy. This is usually not noticed at first, but if you read long enough, it builds up layer by layer until you are less sensitive to your clients and more weighed down by the energy of past clients to read effectively.

If you do not release this energy for years at a time you risk ill health, psychic burnout or physical collapse under the burden of dross. It doesn't even require years at the trade. One desperate, emotionally distraught, scattered client can imbalance you as a reader for a week or longer.

It's not the client's fault. He or she has sought your services because you offer to clarify issues for those in crisis. As a result you have to expect to read for people who are angry, upset, grief-stricken or burdened by life circumstances, and they are often relieved at having an ear for their troubles. When clients tell their stories they can unconsciously release the negative energy of these incidents in your reading room. Then when the client departs, the energy remains.

In simple terms, if you smoked one cigarette during each reading you gave, without ever opening a window, how long do you think it might take for the windows to become grimy and the walls to yellow with smoke stains? How long before you and your clients were breathing air which was filled with stale smoke from a reading you gave last week?

Following are some simple cleansing techniques for you to choose from.

- **A lighted candle or an open fire.** This helps to raise the spiritual energy in the room and to dissipate the dross left behind. Ensure that the candle is in a bowl or on a plate for safety and that it is extinguished at the end of the day or when you leave the room for a lunch break.
- **Fresh air circulating** in the room between clients or even during the reading, depending on noise and the weather.
- **Washing the walls and windows** with a solution of cloudy ammonia and hot water once a year helps to maintain a balance in your reading room.
- **Burning incense** in the room once a week or once a month. Be sensitive to clients and other practitioners.
- **A bowl of water placed in the reading room** can help to absorb negative emotional energy. Change the water daily. Adding natural sea salt (available at most health food stores and some supermarkets) to the water increases its effectiveness.
- **Meditation**. Meditation using a whirlwind of white light can be employed to sweep the room, entrance hall or waiting room clean.

Having cleansed your working environment, it is important to cleanse yourself. If you become weighed down with dross you will be less effective with your clients. Signals that tell you that you are being drained include

- Sudden exhaustion or you feel scattered/not yourself.
- Sudden stomach bloating—you feel fine until your client arrives and within 15 minutes your stomach is bloated.
- Feeling ravenously hungry but food doesn't satisfy you, or constantly craving chocolate or sweets. You are in search of energy.

Simple yet effective methods for cleansing yourself include

- **Meditation**, every day or at least once a week.
- **Swimming** in the ocean or a pool.
- **Taking a bath** which contains a handful of natural sea salt.
- **Taking a walk.**

Many tarot readers believe that imagining your physical body surrounded by a protective white light which will prevent negative energy from reaching you is sufficient protection from dross. But I don't believe this is enough for the circumstances of tarot reading.

Penetrating someone's energy field, usually done unconsciously, occurs as a result of desire. The logic of the person desiring might be that my tarot reader or massage therapist seems to have it all. Happiness, inner peace and a rewarding job. This desire creates a psychic cord of energy between the client and the tarot reader and this cord can disturb the reader. If five clients a week form these cords to the reader it is not long before all the joy has gone out of helping clients.

It is important to clear away old or negative energy daily. For those readers motivated by financial success, if you don't cleanse regularly, you can expect your appointment diary to reflect your cleansing practices. If your reading room is full of the energy of previous clients, you effectively have no room for new clients. Consequently new clients stay away as a result. For the same reason it is advisable to replace your cards every 18 to 24 months, burning the old pack. Some readers become attached to their packs, forgetting that they are only printed paper and tools of the trade.

Chapter 26

ADDING COMPLEMENTARY SKILLS

Adding complementary skills to your repertoire is essential if you plan to be in business long term. Providing a variety of services allows for a varied working day and this helps to keep you fresh. The list of possible skills you might add is endless but some suggestions are.

- counselling skills
- astrology
- palmistry
- healing
- Reiki
- massage
- Bach flower remedies
- Australian bush flower essences
- hypnotherapy
- life coaching

Clients may initially seek a prediction or clarification regarding an important situation, but they may need more help than a single tarot reading can offer. Even if you don't want to use other modalities, having an understanding of them may enable you to recommend the most appropriate form of assistance for a client to make changes in their lives. Clara's reading revealed she was spiritually and emotionally exhausted after a failed relationship and she required rebalancing in order to make sound decisions. After five deep healing sessions with a local healer, Clara was ready to approach relationships with less suspicion and more generosity. The tarot reading indicated the changes required to find happiness, but Clara had to take the steps.

Adding complementary skills

If you feel you would like to go beyond predicting the change to facilitating the changes in clients' lives, then you will need more skills than tarot reading. Using Bach flower remedies can help clients settle and focus during the reading process. These subtle essences can offer clients support during the reading. They may even be taken by a client over a period of weeks after the reading, to assist them in making changes.

Counselling skills are an essential part of tarot reading, and taking even a short, basic counselling course is highly recommended. In many cases ongoing counselling may benefit a client.

Astrology charts offer a different perspective for clients, especially those who want a relationship compatibility chart. Palmistry offers a life reading for those seeking long-term information. You might also decide to offer your clients Reiki healing. Often clients arrive needing healing of some sort as they are usually stressed by their circumstances or by their decisions.

Hypnotherapy is useful for increasing a client's confidence (to get a better job or a more rewarding partnership), inner strength and self-worth. These qualities are lacking in many people, holding them back from being all that they can become. Confidence is one of the fundamental influences in success.

Some clients don't arrive for a tarot reading with pressing issues. Instead they seem to have lost their way in life generally. They may be successful, healthy, in a fulfilling love relationship, yet lack a sense of fulfilment. These clients might respond well to life coaching. From the client's viewpoint it offers the opportunity to have an independent observer examine your life and encourage you to pursue directions which may feed your spirit.

In considering adding complementary skills to your practice, the emphasis here is on *complementary*. Recently I was handed a business card which read

Healer
Actor
Gardener

This business card suggested that this person doesn't really know what business they are in. Complementary services for tarot reading probably do not include house painting, glass cutting, TV repairs or stock broking. Services such as psychic healing and cleansing, counselling and meditation classes are more appropriate. Selling incense, crystals or smudge sticks for home cleansing, and sales of books you believe will help your clients also may be a more workable mix in your business.

The more skills you offer a client the more likely they are to return and to refer friends to you. In the initial consultation experienced readers ask the client which service they seek, in order to determine which service suits the client's needs.

Chapter 27

MAKING THE TRANSITION FROM AMATEUR TO PROFESSIONAL

The process of making the transition from an experienced tarot reader to a professional reader can be difficult for many people. A former student and tarot graduate Jamie described it perfectly. 'I'm afraid that some of my former work colleagues will see me at a market giving a reading.' She explained that she might be embarrassed or feel like a fake before her former work colleagues. When asked how she might expect to feel in three years after she has given 1000 paid readings, she stated that they might still feel that she was a fake.

What many aspiring professional readers need to do is to compare where they might be in three years to where they are working now. Jamie might now commence her working day at noon, only work three days a week, with an income which has risen 45 per cent in five years. Jamie is likely to have no more job security than before, but chances are she will love her work, admire her boss (herself) and every Christmas she is likely to receive more than a dozen cards from grateful clients, as well as letters of thanks during the year. When she wants, Jamie might take the day off from her tarot business for a massage and an energy balance before her weekly piano or flying lesson. Some professional readers are already like this and with commitment and determination, Jamie might become one of them.

Many experienced and competent readers falter when attempting to make the transition from amateur to professional reader. For some it is because they are so familiar with giving free readings or swapping readings for dinners, clothes, shoes or favours, that they don't know how to ask for and accept a fee for their service. For others it is because they need guidance and support on practicalities such as setting an acceptable fee, recording the reading and keeping to the allotted time.

Some people are embarrassed to request assistance, however all of us receive assistance from time to time in our lives. We are helped and help others in return. There is nothing wrong with help in getting started because in the end we sink or swim on our own merits. Clients return because you give them something valuable. That may be compassion, clarity, motivation or simply hope. If you don't offer your clients something genuinely worthwhile, they are unlikely to consult you a second time.

To become a professional reader you need to start thinking like one. It may help to see some purchases you want to make in terms of how many clients you need to earn the money. Do not think this means you see your clients in only monetary terms, but if you are going to earn your living this way, it has to be part of your thinking. You support your clients through predictions, listening, advising or being empathetic or by suggesting helpful services. They in turn support you, by helping you to have a comfortable existence.

As a professional reader you can fill your appointment diary by focusing on the phone ringing and people booking for readings. If you focus on giving tarot readings that is what happens. Of course you also need to advertise, be skilled with the tarot and to be prepared for your clients when they phone. This means that you need to have a room to read in, a small table and two chairs and tape recording facilities.

Expect a slow period initially as you commence your tarot business, allowing time for the word to spread and clients to respond to your advertising. There are several ways to increase your appointments in those early months, to ensure your business thrives. These include

- reading one day a week at a market
- giving a free talk and demonstration of the tarot at your local club
- offering discounted readings for a month or two
- organising a feature story in a local newspaper.

Reading at a market gives you the chance to give a series of brief readings in a short period of time. Where you might give five readings a month from your home office initially, you might give 25 readings at a market in four weeks. Saturday and Sunday markets are easily found through market guides (available as a magazine in newsagents) or through driving around on weekends.

When you have located a number of markets, narrow down the possibilities by using the tarot. Ask the cards one or all of the following questions.

- Is it wise for me to read at . . . market?
- Is there a space for me as a tarot reader at . . . market?
- Is the . . . market suitable for me at this stage?

After attending a recent introductory tarot course Donna offered tarot readings at her son's annual school fete. With her rickety card table pressed up against the old sandstone hall she offered readings at $10 for 20 minutes. Late in the afternoon a man who had watched her reading for others strolled over and asked the price. Although he appeared to be able to afford the price he hesitated, so Donna made him an offer. He could have a 20-minute reading and at the end of it he was to pay her what he thought it was worth. Donna knew it was a risk, but she had no one waiting so he sat down and they began. Twenty minutes later he stood up, and smiling, handed her a $100 note saying, 'It was worth every cent.'

If you live in the country you may have to wait for annual fairs or spring carnivals to present your skills before a large crowd. Consider driving into a town or a city in search of a market because regular clients at a market will improve your practical tarot skills rapidly. Nothing can replace the confidence which stems from direct experience. When you have given hundreds of readings and clients have returned repeatedly because you have been accurate and helpful, you feel strong when a client disagrees with your interpretation of events. Instead of feeling deflated when challenged, you may take the time to re-explain yourself in terms the client can relate to more easily.

This occurred recently when a client selected the blank card for the past position. The blank card signified sudden changes in the past which led the client to unexpected changes in location. She insisted that nothing had changed in the past and that her life had been very ordinary. Giving the impression that she still lived three streets from where she was born she shook her head. I probed, to discover when questioned, it turned out that her childhood was spent in Ireland, South Africa and England before the family settled in Australia.

If you are unsure of yourself and do not probe in order to prove that an interpretation is accurate, the client may consider you to be a poor reader.

Offering your services as a guest speaker at your local club can be a powerful way to let the community know about your services. A free talk to the local Rotary club, business club or any local group can help to improve your profile. You need to offer one or two brief demonstration readings so the audience can see the process first-hand. This also arouses curiosity. A demonstration also helps to reduce any fears they might hold about the tarot reading process. When they see how simple and practical the process is, they are more likely to want to try it out for themselves. Bear in mind that free talks can be a hit or miss affair. Some may result in no readings or sales of any sort while others will provide clients, students and book sales.

The more talks you deliver the more you can improve your presentation skills, especially if you focus on improvement. The more experienced you become, the less likely you will be unnerved by the practical setbacks which occur on the talk circuit.

Advertising a discount is another way of increasing clients during the initial months of your practice. It might read **Tarot reader** Anthony Bolton is offering **half price readings** until 30 May.

Despite being a practical, accurate reader with a kind approach, Helen was stumped when clients asked, 'Are you clairvoyant?' When Helen replied that she was not they didn't book readings with her. Following are questions you may be asked and the suggestions for the answers.

Are you clairvoyant?

No, but an experienced tarot reader can give an accurate reading without clairvoyance if the client asks clearly worded questions. My job is to help you word your issues into concise questions so that you walk away with the clarity to help you make your important decisions.

Can you give me a brief demonstration on the phone before I book a session?
No. It is unprofessional to offer 'tempter' readings. Listen to your intuition for a moment and you will know if I'm the right reader for you.

When do you see people?
I read here on Mondays, Fridays and Saturdays by appointment, and my sessions last for an hour. My readings cover the past two years, the present and the next two years.

Can I bring my partner?
Yes. Your partner can sit in the waiting room. I don't like two people in the same reading as it can lead to confusion when questions are asked.

How much do you charge for a reading?
My fee for a reading is $XX and the session takes an hour. It includes a tape and during the session I'll give you a general reading and then you can ask up to five specific questions. Please bring some questions with you. I can help you word them for accuracy when I see you.

Many accurate but inexperienced tarot readers give up their dreams of becoming full-time professionals after stumbling during the first months. Lack of confidence in their abilities coupled with expensive advertising soon forces them into other employment, yet this need not be the case. Using the approach previously outlined, you can make it through that first year. It is possible to work full time and still attend markets on Saturdays or Sundays. You might choose to work three days a week in a 9 to 5 job and read in the evenings and at the weekends without exhausting yourself. The part-time or full-time job helps you reach that critical one-year milestone.

After the first year, you will have a small, or even large, client base. This means that you won't have to find as many new clients. In a few years you won't need to pretend to be confident as many of your callers will be regular clients.

The reading process

• *Introduction*	Introduce yourself and show the client to their seat or into the waiting room.
• *Instructions*	Show the client how to cut and shuffle the pack.
• *Reflection*	Take time to ask yourself these three questions. *'The client's issue today is'* *'The client's need today is'* *'The best way to present this information today is'*
• *Selection*	Have the client select cards for your preferred layout.
• *Silence*	Ask for a moment to make sense of the layout.
• *Explanation*	Detail the layout to the client.
• *Questions*	Follow the general reading with a layout for each question.
• *Reminder*	Preface the client's last question with a reminder that it will be their final chance to ask questions.
• *Last question*	Complete the final layout, finishing the reading on a positive note. Summarise the theme of the reading.
• *Tape/farewell*	Give the client the tape and a business card. Accept your fee. Recommend that they replay the tape in the next few days.
• *Cleanse*	Step outside and cleanse yourself before your next client. Wash your hands and face if necessary.

Chapter 28

YOUR READING STYLE

Your personal reading style determines your clientele. It not only influences the number of people who consult you, but what they want when they arrive at your door. When you have discovered your personal style, you have found your market. Do not expect everyone who consults you to be pleased with your reading, as their preferences may differ from your reading style. Reading styles vary greatly, and they include the following.

The mystical reader

This reader offers the full mystical experience, including incense, a crystal ball, candles burning on ledges and perhaps a poster or a photograph of a spiritual master hanging on a nearby wall. They often display several packs of cards, from mainstream tarot packs to gypsy cards. Sometimes they ask the client to select the pack they prefer for their reading.

The mystical reader speaks in metaphors, rarely referring to any issue directly. Instead of saying that the client feels trapped in their life by debts, routines and responsibilities, this reader might say, 'You travel a long path with a burden. I see a weight on your shoulders. You carry this weight alone. Sit with me awhile and lay down this weight for a moment.'

The mystical reader is preferred by clients who enjoy a quest. These clients usually replay the tape of the reading later and reinterpret the reading in different ways. This reader's strength is that they remind us that life is more than we can see and touch. The mystical reader often appears like a tarot reader portrayed in films.

Mystical readers can inspire their clients and reawaken within them a desire to nourish the spirit and to pursue the magical aspects of life. This type of reader often perceives life as a journey for which we have been given keys and need to find the corresponding locks. These keys may open hearts, houses, career opportunities or the gates of understanding. The mystical reader reminds us to use those keys lest they rust. Mystical readers are children of the universe who resist the seriousness of adulthood, preferring instead the joys of exploring the spiritual realms. In an introductory tarot course I noticed a mystical type was very focused on taking notes. Upon closer scrutiny she was drawing a cluster of toadstools at the foot of a tall tree. Soon she had drawn a forest, filled with the nervous eyes of unseen creatures while I described the suit of Cups.

The nurturing reader

The nurturing tarot reader is often the big-breasted mother figure who offers the client a cup of tea and some cake she baked that morning. She is often ready with a comforting arm and reassures the client that everything is going to be okay. The nurturing reader might ask the client to phone back with a report on proceedings in a week as they genuinely understand the value of support and love, which can be scarce in the modern world.

The nurturing reader is the person to consult when you're licking the wounds resulting from rushing blindly into life. This reader doesn't lecture or moralise, but offers compassion and understanding. She reminds you that although circumstances may be difficult presently, your courage will eventually be rewarded. Often even such momentary kindness is sufficient to rekindle hope and confidence in life's possibilities.

The nurturing reader might send you home with a gift: a crystal, a bottle of essential oil to help you in the coming weeks or some flowers from her garden.

At the very least she will hug you as you depart. You will usually leave with memories of her kindness and emotional generosity.

The life patterns reader

The life patterns reader is more concerned with the part you are acting in the play of life. This reader is inclined to highlight how your life attitudes or beliefs have led you to your present circumstances. Asking pointed questions about your parents, your siblings and your life so far, this reader is concerned with your life as a puzzle and the picture they can see forming.

The life patterns reader feels a sense of duty in steering you away from the rocks in life and towards a more satisfying, fulfilling life. As a result, this type of reader appears less sympathetic than the nurturing reader, and more direct in presenting their perceptions than the mystical reader. This is the reader to consult when you are ready to surrender some of your negative or unrewarding behaviour patterns in order to build a different life for yourself. Avoid this reader if you want someone to sympathise with you because the life patterns reader observes your agendas, both overt and hidden, as you sit down.

Clients often receive homework from patterns readers, the reader having determined which traits the client may benefit from eliminating or strengthening. Patterns readers are more interested in what motivates people than predicting the future. Typically they understand that it is what you do now that shapes what you will become in the future. They are keen to assist you in the pursuit of your life dreams if you are prepared to do the work necessary to get yourself there.

The life patterns reader usually begins the session by stating to themselves '*The issue today is . . .*' in order to recognise the immediate issues facing the client. This type of reader scans the issues and then observes the clients' blind spots. In doing this the reader knows how to tell clients what they need to hear in a way that clients can accept. Instead of saying, 'You know what your problem is . . .' it may be couched as a question. 'Do you think it's possible that the way your father ignored you as a child is being replicated in the way you approach your staff at work?' In this way the client does not feel threatened and is encouraged to voice their opinion regarding the life patterns that may be occurring.

Life patterns readers usually believe that the client already knows what is going on, and that as readers they have the task of voicing the client's fears and hopes. Being reminded of summer approaching when you are knee deep in the coldest emotional blizzard can be a gift. It doesn't shorten the winter but it can warm your heart and strengthen your resolve when you need it most.

The direct approach reader

Another group of readers offer a direct approach. Stating what they see immediately, before they have time to edit it mentally. This can result in startling accuracy but it can also leave the client emotionally bruised. This matter-of-fact approach is best suited to clients who want honesty instead of tact.

After a reading from a tarot reader with the direct approach you know exactly where you stand in your life circumstances. This is the reader who tells you directly that pursuing your love relationship is futile and will waste another three years of your life. They then explain that someone new will arrive in two years if you are prepared to leave your current relationship and find a counsellor to examine and to change your relationship patterns. This type of reader is likely to belong to the Wands suit.

You'll be able to recognise your reading style by closely examining your clients. If they are practical people who arrive well prepared with a list of questions you probably have the direct approach. If most of your clients arrive in tears and are unable to release you from your welcome hug, you're probably a nurturing reader. Clients find the right reader for themselves instinctively.

No particular type of reader is better or more accurate than another. Readers of different styles find clients who appreciate that reader's approach. When friends tell you that they received a reading 'but she wasn't very good', in some cases it may be due to conflicting personal style. Those who enjoy mystical metaphors are often disappointed by readers with the direct approach. Likewise those who want the undiluted facts soon become irritated by mystical readers.

When clients telephone to book a tarot reading your conversation is likely to reveal your reading style.

Identifying your particular reading style is simple when you can answer the following two questions.

- What type of reading style do you prefer when consulting a tarot reader?
- What physical, emotional, mental or spiritual mountains have you climbed in your life which have strengthened you?

What you bring to the reading table

Many tarot readers bring a wealth of experience to the table when they settle down to give a reading. Life struggles, past accomplishments and even cultural perceptions can contribute to the rich tapestry weaving throughout the conversation which is a reading. If you have singlehandedly raised a child, built a business, overcome physical or emotional obstacles or gained deeper insight into life through suffering, then these qualities can be brought to the table when you give a tarot reading.

Lucy explained how her son had been born with a physical deformity which required a series of hospital visits in his first two years of life. Lucy was initially worn down by the continual demands placed upon her, without any guarantee that her son would eventually be healthy. Thrown back onto her own spiritual and emotional resources Lucy eventually developed a profound faith that her son would be healthy and happy. Five years later he still suffers with restricted mobility but he is happy. Lucy brings her *faith* to her readings, inspiring her clients to believe in life's possibilities, even when they cannot glimpse possible solutions from where they stand.

Maya moved from one country to another and was initially very lonely and isolated. After three years Maya learned *how to be alone without being lonely*. She brings this to her readings by explaining to clients who are considering leaving a love relationship that it is possible to be fulfilled without a partner beside you.

Gunther explained that for many years he wrestled with a deep spiritual hunger. He enrolled in courses, self-development workshops and read many books, but this deep hunger persisted. It occurred to Gunther one day that there was not one simple answer to his yearning. He found that meditation nourished him spiritually and as a result during his readings he searches for those *activities which might nurture his clients spiritually.* Gunther believes that if more people attended to their spiritual needs tarot readers might have less demand for readings.

April spent many years searching for what she had come into this life to accomplish. She had no real direction for 35 years until she discovered the joy of teaching. Now April makes a point of using her tarot readings to *clarify each client's life purpose*.

Chapter 29

THE JOURNEY TO BECOMING A READER

Many people feel daunted when it is time to begin life as a professional tarot reader, especially if they don't have a mentor or a supportive friend to assist them through those early months. There are several ways to start your journey as a reader.

Reading at markets

Reading at markets is a well-trodden path for those seeking plenty of experience giving short, low-cost readings. Many beginners feel that they are not giving good value for the client's money so they extend the reading time or even refuse to accept payment. The best ways to combat feelings of inadequacy include giving many readings to increase your direct experience and to consult other readers in order to see what they offer for their fees.

Experience usually builds confidence, especially if the experience is positive. If you read for 15 clients over a three-month period who are being retrenched, you will probably feel competent to deal with the next client who is being retrenched.

A run of difficult readings can discourage beginners from wanting to be a tarot reader but difficult readings also stretch you and expand your skills as a reader. When you have difficult sessions have the courage to stay with them. Ask yourself what they are teaching you. One disruptive student taught me how to be a much more assertive presenter.

It is almost impossible to know with certainty what you have said to a client that is meaningful to them. You imagine you have given your best reading ever and the client throws the tape away while you congratulate yourself. You may walk away from a reading depressed at your lack of ability yet the client has heard the one sentence they needed to hear that day.

Reading at home

If you cannot work at a local market, you have exhausted your friends and you are not ready to work in an alternative healing centre, set up a room at home for readings. A home office need not take up much room, and can be assembled and dismantled quickly. It requires a small table, a neutral coloured cloth, two chairs, a tape recorder with a microphone (to record the session for the client), a blank C60 tape, a small candle (placed on a dish for safety) and a tarot pack. If the room is used for another purpose you may need to tidy up beforehand so that it is not too crowded or messy when your client arrives. A neat, simply furnished room is less likely to distract the client from the reading process.

Consider what might distract or unnerve a client arriving for a tarot reading at your home office. Being met at the door by a half-dressed reader, two crying children, a ferocious dog or glimpsing books such as 'Witchcraft for Beginners' is likely to do the trick. Strong incense is offensive to sensitive clients.

If you do read from an office at home, remember to look after your personal safety. Reading for clients late at night is not recommended, nor is visiting clients to give readings unless you are accompanied by a friend. If you have doubts about a client during the intitial phone call, refuse to book them or pass them on to another reader. You might tell them that you are booked out for nine months or that another particular reader might suit them better. As a reader, you are within your rights to refuse to read for any person, but it is best if you handle refusals delicately to avoid offending people. It is better to refuse to read for someone if you feel that they have a hidden agenda.

If you visit friends or acquaintances to give readings, ensure you leave your phone switched on (in silent mode) so that you can make an emergency call if required. Some female readers prefer to work from a healing centre or a bookshop where there is always someone on the premises. Carol, an experienced tarot reader, only reads for male clients when her husband is home. In reality, most clients, male or female, are so immersed in their issues that they don't notice the reader.

Trading services

When starting out, and even later on, trading readings for services is a viable option. You gain experience and have people who give word-of-mouth referrals. A friend recently traded a tarot reading with a woman whose husband installed the reader's air conditioner in return. It is not unusual to swap a reading for a dinner. You will no doubt receive dinner invitations with the tag line, 'Oh, and don't forget to bring your cards'.

Although the end goal is to trade tarot readings for useable currency, reading for a hairdresser in return for a haircut can be a wise trade. Hairdressers talk to a great number of people in the course of a week. If they receive a good reading they will probably tell 40 or 50 people about your services in the following month. This is much more effective than newspaper advertising. It is likely that at least 50 per cent of your clients will hear of your services through friends and acquaintances.

In the first 24 months you might trade a reading for goods or services regularly. Trading one reading with a client may be enough, but to establish a habit it often requires two or three readings. By the third traded reading you have become their preferred reader. Later when you are enjoying a busy tarot practice, these early clients will expect preferential service, reasoning that they are your original clients and that they helped you to become established. Treat them with respect and your practice will thrive.

As a tarot reader it is best not to read for clients who are in the eye of an emotional storm. When your practice is busy, you might allow two free appointment times each week for original clients or for those who are only in town for a few days.

Business cards

Even when trading a reading for a pair of jeans, a haircut or a ride into town, ensure you have a business card to give to your client. It is difficult to recommend you if they do not have your phone number. More than 90 per cent of all recommendations will be lost if your client leaves without your phone number, so print your cards first.

Handling the phone

If there are several people living in your house it is probably better to list your mobile telephone number so that potential clients can get through when they phone. Bizarre outgoing messages on the answering machine can be off-putting to first-time callers.

It may sound obvious but don't allow too much time to lapse between the client's first phone call to you and your return call or you will lose bookings. Potential clients may phone a list of readers and they will book with the first person to answer the phone or to return their call. If you cannot return a client's phone call within 24 hours it is best to begin your conversation with them by apologising for taking so long to get back to them. Twenty-four hours can seem like an eternity to a client in distress.

When phoning a potential client back, offer them two appointment times. If you give a client too many alternatives, they may become confused. It is useful to ask if the person prefers a daytime, an evening or a weekend appointment, provided you work these times. Sometimes a client prefers to visit you during a weekday so that their partner will not know that they have had a reading.

Telephone readings

Clients may be on a visit from overseas or have to move overseas or interstate. If clients like your reading style they will prefer to phone you rather than find another reader, and recommend you to their friends in Boston, Paris or Hong

Kong. If at a later date you decide to visit these places, you may have clients wanting a reading with you. These clients may recommend their friends see you during your visit and you may end up with a full calendar of readings.

It is best to offer a set time and fee for telephone readings, to reduce the pressure of having to keep the client on the phone if they are paying by the minute. If you know that you have 30 minutes, you can work within that time frame to deliver an effective reading. It is possible to give a general reading and three questions in 30 minutes. Although face-to-face readings usually last 60 minutes, telephone readings often last only 30 to 45 minutes for the same cost. This is because it requires more effort on the reader's part to give a telephone reading because you don't have the clients' facial expressions to tell you when you are on the right track. If the client is taking notes during the reading, there is often an eerie silence when you conclude your explanation of each layout, as the client writes down what has been said.

Telephone reading procedure. The client usually phones for a telephone reading paying via credit card at the time of booking. The reading may take place several days or weeks later. You will need merchant service facilities to process the credit card payment. If you cannot arrange merchant service facilities with your bank you could consider the following options for payment.

- Direct deposit into your bank account through Internet banking. The client will then fax or email the Internet banking receipt to you before the reading commences.
- A cheque posted to you. This needs to arrive a week ahead of the reading so that the cheque will be cleared in your account before the reading commences.
- A money order posted to you. These are usually cashed at your local post office.

Be aware that clients may have every intention of paying you, but if payment has not reached you by the time you deliver your telephone reading, the urgency to pay you diminishes greatly after the reading. To avoid becoming resentful about non-payment for your services, ensure that you are paid in advance for telephone readings.

When the client phones for a reading, explain that you will begin with a general reading and then follow with specific questions. Ask the client to give you a few minutes to prepare the general reading. You then proceed as follows.

- Shuffle the cards, reversing some while mentally stating 'This is on behalf of . . .'
- Slide the cards across the table in a line and select seven cards one at a time, with your eyes closed and using your non-writing hand, while mentally asking 'What does the future hold for . . .?'

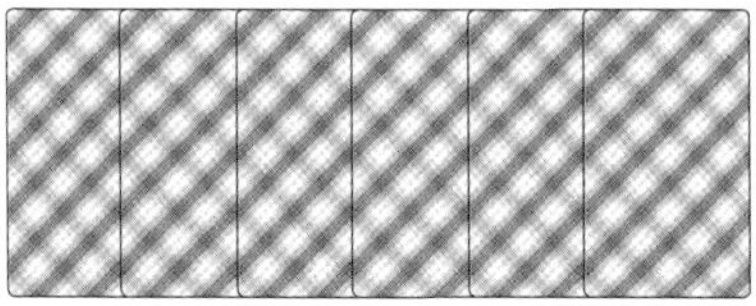

- Place these cards into a V shape in the usual manner, as if your client were sitting opposite you at the table.
- Take a moment to examine the cards before you.
- If you are recording the reading, begin recording by stating the date and explaining that the client has free will in all things predicted.
- Ask the client for their astrological sign. If you have a few astrological signs represented by cards on the table, the sign might be one of these.
- Explain each card in turn as you do in a face-to-face reading.
- Ask the client if it makes sense to them, or if they'd like you to clarify any part of the reading.
- Place these cards back into the deck and briefly shuffle it again.
- Repeat the above procedure with each question after you have clarified the question. In a question about a love relationship, you might select seven cards while mentally asking 'What does the future hold for Dianne's love relationship with Carlos?'
- Announce when she has arrived at her final question so that the client has the chance to decide which question is more important. You might say 'We are coming to the end of this reading soon, so you have time for one last question.'
- If you are recording the telephone reading you'll need a speaker phone so that both sides of the conversation are audible. If you have the software, you may record the reading on an MP3 recorder, transferring it to a CD via your computer before mailing the CD to your client.

Interstate or overseas

When you have gained confidence you may wish to expand your services interstate or even overseas. Prepare well, targeting venues for free talks and local radio stations that will give you airtime. It takes time and dedication but you can build up a client base interstate or in another location with patience.

Charging a suitable fee

Starting out as a reader usually means charging less than more experienced readers at first. Five to ten phone calls to other readers in your area will give you an idea of the average current reading fee and it is wise to place yourself in the lower realms of this fee. This fee will increase as your experience increases. Your aim is to offer a respectable service at a fair price. If you are in business to pay off your new home extension and not to provide a service to your clients, you probably will not have your clients for very long.

Think about offering your services free at least once a year as a guest speaker to small community groups or spiritual development groups. It will help hone your speaking skills and enable these groups to raise necessary funds to keep them going.

Publicising your tarot services

Paid advertising is only one way to reach the public. Guest speaking, radio, television appearances, newspaper articles and magazine stories all reach those people who may become your clients.

If you decide to pursue publicity on radio and television, consider taking a presentation skills course. Typically these courses give you tips of what not to wear for television (no stripes or complicated patterns), how to look down the camera as though speaking to a friend, and how to speak in clear, measured tones during your radio interview. A good course will repay your investment many times over.

In the early days when you have more free time than clients, design your business cards, plan the layout of a brochure or draw up advertisements for local newspapers and magazines. Free advertising can also be helpful. Placing a simple, well-presented poster on a local noticeboard can attract local clients. Many community centres, libraries and local shops allow you to put up cards or brochures on your services.

When advertising, it is more professional to use your full name as it is necessary always to present yourself as a rational businessperson. If you behave in a professional manner at all times, you appeal to those conservative people who may consider tarot readers as exotic and unreliable. At a recent corporate Christmas function five tarot readers were hired to spice up the party. Four readers dressed up as gypsies with shawls, hoop earrings etc. while the fifth reader didn't. At one point the fifth reader had a line of almost 20 people waiting for a reading while the 'gypsies' sat idle.

To summarise the basic points in this chapter, the following list details some practical tips on getting started as a professional tarot reader.

Starting out

- Offer short, inexpensive readings at local markets.
- Set up a home office as it will allow you to read after hours or on the weekends. Keep your home office simple and tidy.
- If you have any certificates related to the services you offer, if possible hang them where you read as these may inspire confidence in your clients.
- Be prepared initially to swap readings for goods or services to spread the word.
- Return all phone calls promptly and offer potential clients a choice of two or three possible reading times. Too many alternatives can confuse clients.
- Offer your services free as a guest speaker at a fundraising event (as a reader in the tarot tent) or even at your local school fete.
- Always carry business cards with you.
- Advertise your services in the local newspaper, on community notice boards in local community halls, and on the Internet via a website or advertisements on search engines such as Google.com.

- Remember that your friends probably will not refer too many people to you. Initially it is your colleagues and acquaintances who will recommend you to others, as they only know you in the role of the tarot reader.
- Start locally and gradually expand your advertising, emphasising how your service is unique.
- Ask each client how they heard about you, to know if your advertising is working. This way you will know how to advertise more cost effectively next year.
- Start as you mean to continue. A solid house begins with firm foundations, so too does a thriving tarot business.
- Use your full name in all your advertising as it is more professional.
- With access to a computer you can produce effective advertising posters for local notice boards. Starting your tarot business need not be costly.

Chapter 30

VALUING WHAT YOU OFFER TO CLIENTS

Many readers undervalue the service they offer clients. They charge less than they are worth, offering their clients a 90-minute session when they had previously explained it lasts one hour or wearing themselves out in order to please their clients.

Learning to value yourself and what you offer your clients is essential if you plan to be a tarot reader long term. Readers burn out for a variety of reasons including:

- lack of psychic protection
- lack of psychic cleansing
- poor working conditions
- seeing too many clients each week
- not taking care of their own health and wellbeing.

It is healthy to question your abilities periodically. Rather than believing you are the world's best tarot reader, having a few doubts about a particular reading or a week of readings is natural. Believing what you offer to clients is rarely good enough is entirely different.

After you have given 20 readings you are usually familiar with your preferred layout. After 40 readings you become acquainted with the presentation process, and by 50 readings you are generally better at tying the cards together to paint a picture of the client's life circumstances. By the time a reader has given 80 readings they are usually confident and less stressed during the reading process. Keeping a log of your readings is usually helpful.

If you are severely hampered by a lack of confidence after giving 80 readings then you may need assistance from a more experienced tarot reader. Having a tarot supervisor guide you for a period of time may be the answer. It is not uncommon for clinical psychologists and counsellors to seek the guidance of a more experienced practitioner for weekly supervision. Tarot readers can also benefit from regular supervision.

A tarot supervisor can ensure you are using effective psychic protection techniques and cleansing yourself regularly. Your supervisor can also discuss your more complicated readings. In some cases a more experienced tarot reader may be able to highlight what you are doing in your practice which is limiting your success.

Some readers stress themselves unnecessarily when reading for clients. They feel obliged to speak continuously for the allotted time and in doing so, don't allow the client to absorb what is being said. Do not try and squeeze an hour reading into 35 minutes if the client is late. Explain that you have to finish on time and that the fee for the session remains as agreed. You do not need to take responsibility for the client's lateness. They usually accept this arrangement as reasonable.

If you plan to be a professional tarot reader, you will need to budget for several support systems such as regular massage, an accountant or a life coach. These services will help you to remain balanced so that you can give the best possible service to your clients. Readers sometimes ignore their own health, while lecturing clients on what is required for good health and vitality. In the same way that well-maintained machinery runs longer without breaking down, you will also succeed longer in this field if you look after your number one asset—yourself.

It is also essential to know what makes you different from other tarot readers. Some readers think that price is the deciding factor but this is not so. Many clients happily pay more for a reader who offers them specific benefits. These could be anything from a handy location to a specialisation, such as investments.

Persisting with difficult readings

Early on in your reading career it is possible to be put off by difficult readings, even when clients don't have any ill intentions. In a recent introductory tarot assessment course the student had to give a 30-minute reading to a stranger. This included a general reading and two questions. Sandra, the 'client' (also a tarot reader) received a free reading.

Sandra disagreed with the reader's interpretations of particular cards throughout the reading, making it very difficult for the reader. I allowed this to occur because in real life I give almost ten readings each year in the same circumstances. It amazes me that a client will pay for a session, argue the possible meanings of certain cards with me, and then ask me to sign of copy of my tarot book; the same book the client used to learn the cards.

After the assessment, Sandra departed. The student reader declared that she felt that she wasn't very good, because even the client didn't agree with her. I pointed out that her client was bossy, single-minded and unable to hear what was being said, explaining that she is likely to realise it when she re-plays the tape of the reading. Tarot readers are usually difficult clients because they are not familiar with being clients.

The following day Sandra phoned to discuss the meaning of a card. She wanted me to agree with her about the meaning but I wasn't the reader that day, simply a witness. She argued that the World card reversed might signify a good relationship and I agreed with her, before pointing out that on the day the reader decided that it meant a partner from another part of the world. When questioned, Sandra confirmed that her partner was from another part of the world, validating the reader's initial assessment of the layout.

When asked if she felt that perhaps she tried to take over the reading process the previous day she faltered, admitting that on the tape she heard herself arguing for half the session. It was suggested that perhaps she was still arguing, and she laughed and accepted the reader's initial assessment of her situation.

Without an experienced reader to alert the student to the fact that reading for fellow tarot readers is usually a struggle, the student might have lost faith in herself and possibly even given up reading for others.

Try not to allow difficult readings to affect your self-confidence. In order to have a safety net in case you become overwhelmed by a series of difficult readings, keep a Positive Feedback file. In this put all the letters, postcards and emails from clients who have been satisfied with the readings they have received from you. Read it to restore your sense of balance after a difficult reading.

When you have given several hundred readings, you learn to persist when clients cannot relate to the information you are giving them. The client is not deliberately making the reading difficult for you. In many cases they do not recall the incident you are describing from the past.

Answering the sceptics

There will be times when you have to answer the sceptics, some of whom make some extreme claims about the validity of tarot readers. Sometimes you cannot blame them when you see advertisements making outrageous claims such as

- *never fails to reunite the separated*
- *causes speedy and happy marriages*
- *overcomes bad luck of all kinds*
- *curse removal*
- *lucky spells*

Sceptics sometimes claim that tarot readers plant seeds in the minds of their clients, and consciously or unconsciously those clients fulfil the predictions. Any clinical hypnotherapist is probably aware of how powerful suggestion can be, however there are flaws in this argument. When a reader outlines the client's past and present circumstances, how can the reader know this if they did not know the client prior to the reading? How could the reader plant the seeds or suggestions in the client's mind if they have not met one another? How do sceptics explain how an experienced tarot reader can describe surrounding people and situations when giving a telephone reading and the reader has never met the caller, and in many cases the reader has not even been to the city or the country where the caller resides?

A healthy degree of scepticism is useful to a client, especially in an industry where clients can have limited confirmation of the reader's accuracy until long after the reading took place. It is likely that the clients with the best intuition find the readers with the best intuition. This is because when they phone to inquire about prices they trust their instincts when talking to the reader. It is probably no surprise that even if sceptics decided to have tarot readings, without trusting their instincts, they are more likely to find someone who makes the wild claims listed above.

The best way to reduce the noise of sceptics is to resist the temptation to promise what you cannot deliver and to consistently present your readings in a professional manner. Fearful, conservative people are more likely to have a reading from someone who has a mainstream presentation, but if you prefer a different appearance and approach, you'll find diverse clients.

Chapter 31

BUILDING YOUR REPUTATION

As you establish yourself as a tarot reader, you gradually build a reputation. Think carefully about the reputation you would like for yourself, as once established, reputation can be a pair of wings or an anchor. Reputation is simply the general consensus of how others perceive you to be as a person, and as a tarot reader.

Why be concerned with building a reputation? As your reputation develops (assuming that you are building a positive reputation) you can reduce your advertising budget. Current clients tell their friends, who in turn have a reading and then tell their friends. As your reputation strengthens, resist the temptation to believe your own publicity. For every satisfied client you hear positive news from, there is likely to be another client who was not happy with your service. When clients are pleased with your service they will often tell you. When they are disappointed they are inclined to vote with their feet, consulting a different tarot reader when they want another reading. This means that you are less likely to receive negative feedback from clients than positive feedback.

From a business point of view, when clients complain to you about a product or a service, it is usually because they want to remain your client. If they have no expectation that you will do anything about their complaint or that you can offer them a better or more suitable service, they are inclined to quietly walk away. It has been said that a happy customer tells an average of ten people about your product or service while an unhappy customer tells an average of twenty people. Good news travels fast but bad news travels faster.

Sometimes you will build a clientele rapidly by reading for someone who is well connected. This is the client who speaks enthusiastically of your talents to a dozen people before sunset, six of whom are on the phone to you immediately. Although it can be flattering, living up to expectations can be an added pressure when you require objectivity during the reading process.

Building a solid and positive reputation is not easy, but if you plan to be in this business for a long time you might as well be respected by clients and colleagues alike for your efforts. As clients move away, fade away and pass away, you need new people to replace them. A good reputation makes it easier for you to find these new clients.

Chapter 32

THE TAROT AS A CAREER AND BUSINESS

If you want to be a professional tarot reader it may serve you well to begin by treating the tarot as a business.

Setting boundaries

As a tarot reader, you set the pace of the reading from the beginning. The client usually doesn't think of a reading as a process, because they are concerned about personal issues. Having firm boundaries around the reading process ensures that the reading runs smoothly and that your reading day runs according to plan.

When your client is impressed with your accuracy as a tarot reader, they sometimes believe that you know them very well. This is not so, for it is almost impossible to know someone after sitting with them for only 60 minutes. Sometimes when clients feel that you are the only person who understands them and the difficulties they face in life, they occasionally assume a friendship. If this occurs it is up to you the reader to gently but firmly re-establish boundaries between you both. If you do not do this early on, you risk painfully disillusioning the client later. Symptoms of a client's boundaries dissolving include clients who linger around after a reading, clients who phone you repeatedly in the days following a reading or ask you out to dinner, or clients who seek another appointment within days of the first reading, in a bid to be with someone they believe truly understands them.

You need to set boundaries around the following areas if you intend reading professionally. Some areas in which you need to set boundaries are listed below.

- The length of time each reading will take (you might offer 30- and 60-minute readings).
- Fees and means of payment.
- Reading for only one person at a time. Friends and partners can sit in the waiting room.
- Not reading for clients who are affected by drugs or alcohol.
- Not extending reading for clients who come late.
- Stick to the times for your first and last appointments.
- Avoid giving brief, free readings over the phone.

It is up to you to decide how you want to run your practice. Make sure the client is aware of this and be reasonably scrupulous about sticking to it. You cannot expect clients to have boundaries if you cannot maintain your own.

Further things to consider regarding boundaries can be found on the website www.paulfentonsmith.com.

Treating your tarot reading as a marketable skill and not a 'precious gift' is the first step towards a successful tarot practice. Giving a one-hour reading can be draining. Students find this hard to believe but it is not long before they discover how exhausted they feel. Some describe the pressure which comes from such a responsibility, knowing that another human being will probably be acting on the information you are giving them. By this point they understand that they are genuinely earning the money they will charge.

The pressure to be accurate, concise and helpful to your client does not diminish as you become more experienced. You merely find new ways to deal with it. If you don't like the pressure you feel when you sit down to commence a reading for a stranger, perhaps a career reading the tarot is not for you.

The following are some ways to take the pressure off at a reading.

- Explain to your client that you need a few minutes to examine the cards carefully, in order to be correct when you speak. Let the client know that you don't want to contradict yourself as this may be confusing. At this point the client is usually happy to give you a few minutes. If you simply scan the cards in silence, some clients will erroneously conclude that you have seen a disaster and are searching for a way to give them the bad news.

- Ask the client for an additional card or two if you are confused by the sequence of cards on the table before you.
- If you are confused by the general reading (or any other layout) explain this to the client. You might begin with 'I'm a bit confused here. This part of the reading suggests that you are happy with your surroundings whereas these cards describe a situation which has reached its lowest point. It's possible that both these things are occurring at once, in different areas of your life. I'll explain this step by step. Please let me know if anything doesn't make sense to you.' By saying this to your client you can uncover a more accurate glimpse of the future together.
- After you have detailed the past card, ask your client, 'Does this make sense to you?' If they say no, request another card to clarify the original card. Detail both cards in combination, that is, if the first card is the Ten of Swords and the additional card is the Ace of Pentacles, you might say that after things reached a very low point a new career or income stream offered your client a way forward in life.
- Speak slowly, calmly and in a reassuring manner. Give your client a sense of confidence in you through your professional approach.

Professionals in all fields make tasks appear simple, routine, even casual. This is why experienced readers usually charge more than beginners. With ten years' experience you learn how to deal with difficult clients, how to word complicated questions, where to refer clients who need further help and how to subtly adapt to each client as they sit down for their reading.

Chapter 33

YOUR CLIENTS' NEEDS

There are different types of clients, who consult readers for different reasons at various times in their lives.

Clients in transition

When Angela moved from Australia to Canada, she felt isolated at home and at work. Her social life was non-existent at first and so she phoned for three telephone readings in the first 12 months. As she settled into her new environment and completed her transition, Angela required fewer tarot readings.

When a client experiences a major transition such as a move from one location to another or a divorce, a supportive person such as a tarot reader or a counsellor can be of great assistance. When you read for such clients be aware that when the transition is complete you may not see that person again. When this happens do not take it personally. Who needs a tarot reading when you are having a good time?

Major upheavals

When tragedy strikes clients may be on the phone to you immediately, especially if you have supported them through previous difficulties. Reading for a client during such upheavals is difficult, because the client's hopes and fears cloud the issue and reduce accuracy. Encourage the client to have a distance reading rather than giving them an immediate response. Ask them to give you five questions which you will then ask on their behalf after the phone call. In this way you are able to concentrate on the questions without being scattered by the client's urgency.

Making sense of life

Sometimes a client will consult you when they are unable to make sense of their lives, especially after an unexpected death. Broad philosophic questions often accompany these types of readings, and initially it may help the client if you can pass a message on from the recently deceased loved one. If not, helping the client to word meaningful questions and then answering those questions can be of real benefit to that client.

Good and great readings

Noticing which type of person (Wands, Cups, Swords or Pentacles) is sitting before you allows you to adjust your reading style to accommodate the client. It makes sense that while Cups clients like time to reflect, Swords people think you have died if you don't speak for 20 seconds. While Wands people like a laugh, a challenge and prefer to hear the news without any spin, Pentacles people favour an ordered reading process. Pentacles people can become concerned that they might not be correctly following your card-shuffling instructions, so reassure them. When clients select their first seven cards from the downward facing pack with their eyes closed, say something like, 'That's right' when the first card is placed onto the table. This confirms to the client that they are doing exactly what has been requested.

Explain the reading procedure at the beginning to help clients to know what to expect. Swords people like to have the plan outlined. Pentacles people feel reassured by the structured format whereas Wands people sometimes feel that you are delaying the reading with unnecessary detail. Words of explanation will be lost on Cups people if they do not feel comfortable. Making a Cups person comfortable might require that you offer them a glass of water, a cup of tea, or simply that you have a warm and comfortable reading room.

In some cases your welcome sets the tone for the whole session. If you are off-hand or distant, your clients may not feel that they can discuss those issues which are troubling them. The client responds to your energy when they arrive, and you respond to theirs. The arrival of a brittle, aggressive client may distance you immediately, as you protect yourself from a possible (even unintentional) onslaught of words or energy. Noticing how you respond to each client as they arrive can help you to determine how you'd like the session to run.

A client's anger or aggression may not be related to you in any way. Perhaps they have wrestled with traffic or they may be concealing their terror at what you are about to tell them and by becoming angry and dismissive of you, they hope that bad news might be less painful this way.

Great readings result when you put the client at ease, remain non-judgemental, encourage them to ask questions and outline the process before you commence. A brief conversation as they shuffle the pack can help you to establish rapport (and a psychic cord to the client) to facilitate the unimpeded flow of psychic energy and information from the client to yourself.

Essentially you and the client have the same goal. Both of you want the reading to be good. Some negotiations may be necessary if your client has unreasonable expectations or too many questions.

Are they listening?

A regular source of disappointment and frustration occurs for some readers with clients who arrive for the session, ask their questions and fail to hear what is said. Sometimes a client doesn't hear the reader because they desperately want to believe that a particular outcome will occur. In other cases they seek a prediction, not a program for achieving a desired goal or lifestyle. This is not to suggest that a client should hang on every word, yet clients may return several times and still ignore what they are told.

During Miranda's second reading she asked about several possible love relationships and a new home. She sat seeking a brighter future. It was explained that she had the choice of waiting for Mr Right to rescue her from her dismal circumstances, or she could rescue herself. She was homeless at this stage, and each time it was suggested that she examine ways to earn sufficient income to survive in this city, she avoided examining the possibilities.

Miranda departed feeling disappointed, explaining that as a part-time tarot reader she understood how her clients felt when they left. When asked if many of her disappointed clients were prepared to help themselves, or if they were hoping for a wonderful future to materialise out of nowhere, she confirmed that disappointed clients were often unwilling to help themselves. She was asked if she was willing to help herself out of her difficult situation. She argued that she just wanted to hear good news. When given the choice of being told that good times are ahead or to having confirmed that your efforts are about to be rewarded she stated that she wanted both, eventually accepting that the latter option was more rewarding. At this point she was asked when she was prepared to make a start towards the life she desired.

Although many clients accept that tarot readers are consultants, to assist with decision-making, some put the reader on a pedestal. Some clients still believe implicitly in fate, and make no effort to shape their destinies. They seem to believe that if the tarot reader tells them that they will be successful, lucky, happy or fulfilled, then it will occur. They do not see that opportunities for success or fulfilment are within personal control.

There is a risk that what you tell clients might sound like platitudes, but fundamental themes occur in lives which may prevent us from realising our full potential. These include

- the need to recognise the value of what you bring to your friendships and relationships
- learning how to ask to have your needs met
- accepting that some people are unable to value you, and that being in a relationship with such people is wasting time and energy
- realising that you can learn new and more effective ways for living a fulfilling life
- understanding that you cannot change other people
- the importance of being heard and acknowledged by others.

Many of us have blind spots around certain parts of our lives. For some it is a financial blind spot, while for others they cannot see destructive emotional patterns. The tarot offers you a glimpse of life without your blind spots and take it from one who has secured a look, the view is amazing.

Chapter 34

FINDING HOPE

One of the tasks of a tarot reader in practice is to help clients to find hope in their lives. The search for genuine hope and not merely a creative fantasy can be challenging at times.

When Lorna arrived she was exhausted from worrying about her finances, and with good reason. A widow, Lorna relied on her son for financial guidance. Due to retire in three years, she had been working part-time managing the accounts for a small business. This was sufficient income as the family home had been paid off. Her son Thomas persuaded Lorna to mortgage her home to its full value so that he could persue a business venture. Eighteen months later Thomas had lost all of the money, been declared bankrupt and was serving time in prison. Lorna did not know what his crime was because Thomas refused to tell her.

She consulted me for financial guidance because Thomas was not due for releasse for several months. Lorna could not afford to keep up the mortgage payments. Lorna's security had been lost to a man whose ambitions were greater than his capabilities and yet she still awaited his release from prison so that she might ask him for more financial advice.

Lorna selected four cards for alternative solutions to her dilemma as part of an alternatives layout. It turned out Lorna had several options.

Card 1
Sell the house now

Card 2
Sell the house later

Card 3
Ask brother for help

Card 4
Other

The upright King of Pentacles described a brother who was a practical man, experienced with financial matters. This indicated that he was likely to provide sound alternatives to her problems. This was the card which offered Lorna hope, as she was floundering financially, having always left financial matters to the men in the family.

As a final question Lorna asked, 'What does the future hold for me financially?' The outcome card was the upright Sun card, confirming that the current financial burdens will pass and that Lorna will feel content with life again in the future.

Recognising that Lorna had avoided tackling this financial issue because it seemed overwhelming, she was urged to speak with her brother as soon as possible, and she was given names and numbers of reliable, objective accountants.

Lorna was reminded as she left that the Sun card lay ahead of her and that her financial crisis would pass.

It was important to offer Lorna a few possible people to assist her, because the decisions she was about to make were likely to determine her quality of life for the rest of her life.

Clients usually consult tarot readers when life seems bleak, and it is the reader's task to remind the client that this is a personal winter. Although painful and exhausting, winters do not last and they can serve a useful purpose. A bleak time can offer the client a chance to reflect upon life and consider their current life direction. It also offers you the chance to consult those parts of you which know your long-term destinations in life. If you cannot reach those parts of yourself directly, consulting a tarot reader may offer you the insight you seek.

When you have explained to a client that their former partner is not returning and that the love relationship is over, they may not appreciate being told that someone else will arrive in two or three years' time. Later, when replaying the tape of the reading, that information may prove invaluable, offering them much-needed hope. This hope does not remove the pain they are experiencing, nor does it hasten the new relationship. It merely offers a reminder that a summer is ahead.

Without glossing over real issues in the client's life, every reading is an opportunity to offer hope. Before you can ascend a mountain, you must believe that it is possible to do so. Sometimes a tarot reading is a reminder that the mountain's summit awaits you and that the view is worth the effort.

Wands people look forward to the conquest, while Cups people hope that the summit offers insightful company. Swords people are curious as to what is at the top of the mountain, whereas Pentacles people are likely to take a camera so they can sell postcards of the views from the summit to those at the foot of the mountain. These postcards may inspire others to make the journey.

Your life journey is unique and the tarot can offer insightful reflections along the way. The tarot can mirror your challenges, highlight the obstacles you are facing and remind you of the innate strengths you possess to overcome these obstacles. Most importantly, the tarot offers a reminder of your spiritual purpose, often concealed beneath the events of everyday life. It is the spiritual wisdom gleaned from your life challenges which you will take with you when this journey has reached its conclusion. The tarot offers a map for this journey. Keep your map close at hand and you are less likely to lose sight of your true purpose along the way. May you go with courage when your path calls to you.

INDEX